The

Last Voyage

OF THE

SS Henry Bacon

by
Donald R. Foxvog
and
Robert I. Alotta

PARAGON HOUSE
St. Paul, Minnesota

First Edition, 2001

Published in the United States by
Paragon House
2700 University Avenue West
St. Paul, MN 55114

Manufactured in the United States of America.

Library of Congress Cataloging-in-Publishing data

Alotta, Robert I.
    The last voyage of the SS Henry Bacon / by Robert I. Alotta and Donald R. Foxvog.—1 st ed.
        p. cm.
    Includes bibliographical references and index.
    ISBN 1-55778-801-4 (cloth)
    1. Henry Bacon (Ship) 2. Liberty ships—United States—History. 3. Merchant marine—United States—History—20th century. 4. World War, 1939–1945—Naval operations, American. 5. Shipwrecks—Arctic Ocean. 1. Foxvog, Donald R. (Donald Rogers), 1922- II. Title.

D774.H43 A46 2001
940.54'5973–dc21
                                                                    2001033136

10 9 8 7 6 5 4 3 2 1

For current information about all releases from Paragon House,
visit the web site at http://www.paragonhouse.com

Dedication

To the *Bacon* Crew:

The Steamer was the *Henry Bacon*
The name we remember so well;
She was searching for the long lost convoy,
When down came the Angels of Hell.

The planes came quick and were many,
The number I believe was twenty-three;
But five were shot down by the Gunners,
And went plunging to death in the sea.

Walker, who was a Navy Gunner,
Was manning number seven, we know;
Saw a "Jerry" coming in from the starboard,
And sent her flaming to the waves below.

But the odds were still against them,
They were waging a losing fight;
And knew without help from the escorts,
That death might be riding that night.

Then came death and destruction,
She was hit just abaft the beam;
But the Gunners still manned their stations,
And abandoned were the rest of the crew.

Now the Chief Engineer was an old fellow,
Said, "Boys, I've lived my time;
There's no more room in the lifeboat,
So one of you young fellows take mine."

That was something we can never forget,
We would never survive it, he knew;
Still he gave his last chance for life,
For the sake of the rest of the crew.

There were also passengers aboard,
But they all got safely away;
Leaving officers and crew aboard her,
To go down with their ship that day.

The Captain was a fellow we all admire,
Stayed on the bridge to the end;
Would rather rest on the bottom forever,
Than to go back without all of his men.

Joe's the guy who sails bo's'n,
But was making this trip as an A.B.;
Saw the others away in the lifeboats;
Then plunged into the icy sea.

Then there were others who followed,
Not knowing if they would survive;
But knew that they were useless to their country,
Unless they made it back here alive.

For hours they stayed in the water,
Some died in that cold Arctic sea;
But they knew that the lives they were giving,
Would keep us all happy and free.

Some were rescued by English Destroyers,
Who heard their "S.O.S." from faraway;
And rushed there as quick as possible,
Lest they should go down that day.

Those brave men we will always remember,
They were shipmates to you and to me;
They gave their homes and their loved ones,
For an unknown grave in the sea.

Perhaps their names will never be heard of
Just sailors in the Merchant Marines;
But they've kept Old Glory waving,
Though we don't realize how much it means.

So gather close around the table,
Let's drink a toast to the *Bacon* and crew;
Let's give them a word of thanks, Boys
They gave up their lives for you.

Lloyd D. Carver
SS *Horace Gray*

Contents

Preface

News stories highlighting the last voyage of the Liberty ship SS *Henry Bacon* exploded across the pages of America's newspapers in 1945, the closing year of World War II. A headline in the *New York Times* in April 1945 read: "15 US SEAMEN DIE SAVING 19 REFUGEES; Skipper and All Senior Officers Lost as Germans Torpedo Liberty Ship Off Norway." A subhead noted that Crown Prince Olaf, later Norway's King Olaf, praised the heroism of the men involved.

Abbreviated accounts of the attack came out in various short stories in the years that followed. But there was no detailed account describing the rough waters, the separation from the convoy, the attacks by Nazi submarines and fighter planes, the abandoning of the SS *Henry Bacon*, the rescue of the refugees, and the heroism of the Navy gunners and crew, some of whom sacrificed their very lives. Each account, each version of the event was ensconced in the memories of the survivors.

Two decades later, in the early sixties, Don Foxvog, a Washington, DC, writer with a Norwegian heritage, began to take on the task of making lists of the names and "dry-land" addresses of the Navy gunners and the ship's crew. In part his interest grew out of his special admiration for the men who saved the Norwegian refugees, who were taken to the British Isles and eventually returned to Norway. His effort was extended to making contact with the men based on 20-year-old addresses. Some men could be located, some could not.

While survivors came from the Midwest, including Minnesota, and from the South, including Alabama, most came from the Northeast.

After initial contact was made by phone or by correspondence, Don made personal visits to a number of survivors. Many of his contacts resulted in one-on-one interviews. One special memory was a pleasant overnight visit with Joseph Pszybysz and his wife Mary in Smithtown, Long Island, New York.

Relatives occasionally became involved. They sometimes sat in with the survivors. When the gunner or crewman was among the missing, relatives would recount what they had heard or read. In many instances photographs were offered. Some families offered thick albums with snapshots of family and friends, plus newspaper clippings from the forties.

In only one instance was the contact not amiable. A woman, who was a magazine editor, declined to be cooperative because no survivor had recalled exactly what happened to her relative who was lost at sea.

In addition to one-on-one personal interviews, information was gathered through lengthy phone calls. Many letters were exchanged. Don dutifully kept carbons of his typewritten letters and clipped them to the responses he received, usually handwritten letters. All of these he filed away in cardboard boxes and old attaché cases.

When this vast amount of details was still being gathered, Don began the challenging task of blending the information. Since there were no tape recorders or stenographers aboard Liberty ships in World War II, of course, descriptions, conversations, and the like were reconstructed from the memories of the men involved. Another consideration was a reflection on the words of Napoleon, who said that "war was like a dance; you only see your partner's moves." This is true in our reconstruction of the events that were part of the life and death of the SS *Henry Bacon*. Men recalled only what they remembered, or what they read or had been told.

But the crucial details gathered in the early sixties were still not in the public domain. The first draft of *The Last Voyage of the SS* Henry Bacon, along with boxes of detailed information, photos and the like, remained stored in cardboard boxes in the attic of Foxvog's suburban Washington, DC, home for more than three decades.

In the closing years of the millennium, the original draft and boxes of additional material resurfaced and Don looked for some-one—less involved—to help him put the material into book form. Ironically, when Dr. Bob Alotta was brought in by Don to help finish *The Last Voyage of the SS* Henry Bacon, he went up to his attic and found his clippings that his mother and grandfather helped him accumulate as a young boy during the Second World War. There was something about the story of the SS *Henry Bacon* that triggered a more than fifty-year memory. He recalled a young man from a neighboring community who had some involvement with the sinking of the SS *Henry Bacon*. Bob found the clipping about Seaman First Class Mason Kirby Burr, from Lansdowne, Pennsylvania. Four and a half years after the ship sank, Kirby's body was found perfectly preserved in a floating block of ice. That little touch of history had made an impression on Bob at thirteen! Later, Don showed Bob a clipping about the recovery, and they proved to be the same clippings. The working relationship between the two was welded.

The timing for the publication of *The Last Voyage of the SS* Henry Bacon is fortuitous. The recent publicity over the sinking of the *Titanic* has aroused new widespread interest in historic sea disasters. When this preface was written, *Titanic*, "The greatest American musical in 15 years" in the eyes of a London reviewer, was playing at the Kennedy Center Opera House in the nation's capital.

The *Last Voyage of the SS* Henry Bacon is again underway, making a forgotten story of bravery and uncommon valor available to the American public.

Henry Bacon Drive that leads to Memorial Bridge in Washington, DC, is a much-traveled road, but its name is one of the untold stories of World War II.

Liberty ship SS *Henry Bacon* left the United States late in 1944 on a secret mission. The ship was carrying a railroad locomotive and other lend-lease supplies for Russia. The bloody run through the Nazi blockade to Murmansk was one of the most dangerous maritime assignments of all. Often convoys on the Murmansk run lost more than half their ships and men; sometimes only one ship in ten got through.

The first lap of the *Bacon's* trip, from the United States to England, was almost uneventful, except that a man was washed overboard. There was also the night when the aging first mate became confused and allowed the *Bacon* to become lost in the convoy. They turned up leading the commodore's flagship! Another time, the American master of the ship, highly-regarded Captain Alfred Carini, was a man who liked his food highly spiced. The cook, naturally enough, tried to please the top man. A near mutiny broke out.

Leaving Britain after the 1944 Christmas holidays, the SS *Henry Bacon* steamed northward, broke through the Nazi blockade, passed through the fjords on the western coast of Norway, crossed the Arctic Circle, rounded the bleak North Cape, and delivered its cargo safely to Murmansk. Its only contact with the enemy was when the ship scraped on something that passed beneath the engine room. It was then that a German U-boat surfaced within gun range. But, other ships in that convoy were lost.

Each man on the SS *Henry Bacon*, merchant seaman and US Navy gunner, had his own unique experiences in Murmansk. The young men, not too surprisingly, looked for female companionship. Even Soviet female winch operators who worked in the harbor and on the ships were tempting—despite their manlike appearance. In disregard to the strict "hands-off" policy and the language barrier, two merchant seamen worked out a plan to hide two pretty Russian sisters aboard the *Bacon* so they could escape to the free world. Their scheme backfired, though no one ever publicly identified the seamen...until now. "Bad luck. We'll have bad luck," one of the old-time crewmen muttered when he learned the women were aboard.

Just before the SS *Henry Bacon* pulled up anchor in Murmansk, two British destroyers steamed into the harbor, carrying some five hundred Norwegian refugees who were left to die when the Germans withdrew from northern Norway after a heartless scorched-earth program. All shelter had been destroyed, all food taken, and the inhabitants left to die.

Saved from the "white death," the refugees were distributed among the various ships in convoy RA64 for the trip to England. Nineteen women, children, and old men were assigned to the SS *Henry Bacon*. Many of the ship's officers gave up their quarters to these pitiful people. The simplest modern facilities created problems. Flush toilets, electric heaters, water from faucets were mysteries that had to be demonstrated to people who did not understand English. One woman bared her breast to indicate she needed milk for her infant. She was bewildered when the *Bacon*'s cook offered her cans of condensed milk.

Beyond the harbor, the menacing Nazi U-boat wolf pack awaited. British warships serving as escorts had an impossible task trying to hold them at bay. A destroyer sank one submarine and then had its prow blown off when it stopped to rescue German survivors. The British corvette *Bluebell* disappeared in a blinding flash. The Liberty ship that alternated with the *Henry Bacon* was torpedoed.

The sea, continually rough, suddenly went wild. The mighty storm—the worst ever experienced by the seasoned seamen who were there—temporarily dispersed the stalking submarines. At the same time, the storm scattered the convoy all over that section of the Arctic Ocean. The storm smashed the *Bacon*'s steering gear and one of her four lifeboats as well. Mechanical trouble developed. Only the skill of Captain Carini kept the ship from being swamped.

When the ship was back under its own power, the captain, still maintaining radio silence, did not know where to find the convoy. At one point the *Bacon* limped northward while the rest of RA64 steamed southward.

Shortly after lunch on February 23, 1945, the crew of the *Bacon* sighted what first appeared to be a flight of geese flying in formation from the Norwegian coast. The "geese" turned out to be a squadron of Luftwaffe torpedo bombers, Junkers Ju-88s—23 in all. The Navy gunners were determined that the *Bacon* wasn't going to be a sitting duck for these "geese." Five German pilots had their planes shot out of the sky; others were badly damaged.

The skillful hand of Captain Carini at the wheel of the *Henry Bacon* maneuvered the ship out of the way of one torpedo after another. The men were convinced the planes had used up all their torpedoes when a fanatical pilot dove in for the kill. At that moment the *Bacon's* damaged rudder gave way again and the ship could not respond to calls for evasive action. The torpedo exploded in number 5 hold. "That's where the Russian dames were hiding—I knew they'd jinx us!" a sailor shrugged.

The ship slowly began to sink. One sailor went berserk and chopped up some cork rafts and loosened others prematurely so they floated away. Other men displayed uncommon courage and presence of mind. The captain gallantly ordered the men assigned to the first lifeboat to give their seats to the nineteen Norwegian refugees.

Almost two dozen men crowded into the one boat that remained. The old chief engineer, who planned to retire and buy a gas station near Boston after this voyage, gave up his assigned seat and climbed back on the ship. "I've lived my life," he said. "One of you young fellows come and take my place." He walked to the bridge of the *Henry Bacon* and joined Captain Carini. An hour later, both men went down with the ship.

The heavy beams that moored the locomotive on the deck were fashioned into a raft by one seaman. He turned the raft over to the dedicated commander of the Navy Guard and half a dozen Navy gunners.

For a while the men on the *Bacon* hoped she would remain afloat until help arrived. Then it became obvious that the *Bacon* was going down. Most of the men jumped into the frigid Arctic Ocean wearing only their life jackets. Some were able to pull themselves out of the cold water by climbing on beams and debris; three shared the roof of the wheelhouse, but one of these men froze to death.

Several gunners volunteered to stay aboard the slowly sinking ship until the last moment to man the guns in case the German planes returned to strafe the helpless survivors in the water. They didn't jump ship until the *Bacon* began to slide under. As the bow of the *Henry Bacon* soared into the air before taking its final plunge, a huge ventilator slid off the tilting deck. Two men were hit. One was killed outright; the other suffered a broken arm.

The Arctic Ocean in winter is a killer. Men died of exposure and froze to death—in the water and on the crude rafts. Of the men who did survive, each had his own touching episode to relate. God received, and answered in various ways, a barrage of prayers from that tiny corner of the Arctic.

By the time the rescuing destroyers arrived it was starting to turn dark. Snow was beginning to fall. Had not the radioman arranged for a steady signal that provided a beam for searching destroyers, there might not have been any survivors. Sadly, the arrival of the rescue ships did not guarantee the survival of all the men. The gunner with the broken arm failed to pull himself aboard. The second mate was partway up the deck-moored rope when he lost his grip. The commander of the Navy Guard saw to it that all the men on his raft made it safely aboard the destroyer. By the time his turn came, the raft had drifted off and he had to dive into the water. He was never seen again. The Navy awarded him a Silver Star—posthumously.

When the rescuing destroyers approached Great Britain, Crown Prince [later King] Olaf, commander in chief of the Norwegian army-in-exile, came out to meet the ship carrying his countrymen. The gratitude of the Norwegians was expressed in both personal and official ways. The *Bacon's* first radio officer Spud Campbell and his wife were brought to Norway in 1999 and taken to Sørøya, along with Lieutenant Per Danielsen, then in his eighties. They were interviewed for hours at the point of the rescue of the Norwegians. Those interviews and others are included in a Norwegian television network production of the story of the Murmansk convoys. A Scottish production company is also at work on another documentary, interviewing Chuck Reed, Spud

Campbell, and Dick Burbine. Interest in the *Bacon* is so strong in that country that an attempt is being made to create a museum at Loch Ewe. While in Scotland, the Campbells spent some time in the Pool House Hotel where, they were told, the convoy conferences were held. Campbell attended one such meeting there with Captain Carini. Peter Harrison, the hotel owner, indicated he was planning to add an annex to the hotel, and was going to establish a museum commemorating the Russian convoys.

The Last Voyage of the SS Henry Bacon is filled with touching personal episodes, drawn from conversation and correspondence with the surviving merchant seamen and Navy gunners. Their accounts have been verified by declassified Navy and Maritime Commission records.

Acknowledgments

The authors would like to acknowledge all the survivors—and families—for their great cooperation. Especially thanks must go to Dick Burbine, Dave and Anne Goodrich—and their e-mailing daughter, [Dave didn't live to read the story. He died in August 2000, having only read excerpts.]—Spud Campbell, and the others who are acknowledged in the appendix. A special tip of the hat to Congressman Bob Goodlatte [6th-VA] and his energetic district representative, Charles Evans-Haywood, for freeing up the bureaucratic logjam. Because of Chaz' help, we can also thank Jay Gordon of the Maritime Administration's Office of Chief Counsel and his cohorts: Francis Mardula, Donald S. Post, and Jeannette S. Riddick, for making 338 pages of classified material on the *Bacon* available to us. We find great irony in the fact that these documents went unread for fifty-five years, only being declassified on August 3, 2000!

Thanks are also required for the manuscript readings by Col. Jack Humphrey, an Army "peacekeeper," Billy Walton, a veteran of Korea, and Commander Mark Danley, who commanded the USS *Laboon* on the United States' second attack on Iraq. All three offered thoughtful comments on the manuscript.

As usual, the wives of both authors gave of their time and energies to keep the book on track. Margie Foxvog survived more than thirty years' worth of Don's obsession. His daughter Sally Kalotra retyped the old manuscript onto computer disks and handled the numerous e-mails that Bob sent to Don. Margie's cousin, Arlene Spalding, helped out by interviewing Herbert McIsaac. Bob's wife Alice read and reread the manuscript more times than she should have. When they sat down for Saturday breakfast during the final writing phase, and Bob asked. "What's on the menu?" Her eyebrows would arch as she said "bacon and eggs," knowing that the conversation would veer toward the *Henry Bacon* very quickly. And, a final thanks to Costco, for having a reasonably-priced Hewlett

Packard Pavilion on sale when Bob's computer died during the final weeks of writing.

Don Foxvog; Chevy Chase, Maryland
Dr. Bob Alotta; Harrisonburg, Virginia

The Route of the Final Voyage of
the SS *Henry Bacon*

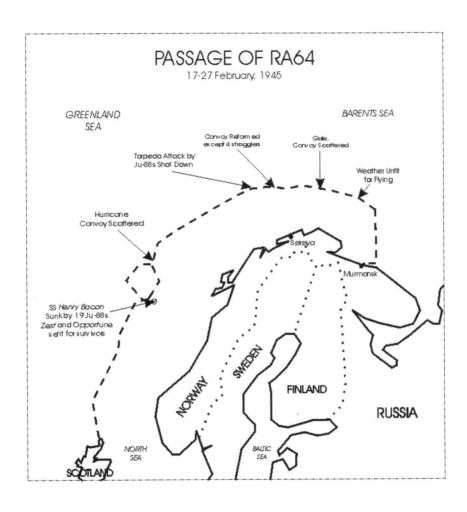

PASSAGE OF RA64

17-27 February, 1945

GREENLAND SEA

BARENTS SEA

Convoy Reformed except 4 stragglers

Gale, Convoy Scattered

Torpedo Attack by Ju-88s Shot Down

Weather Unfit for Flying

Hurricane Convoy Scattered

Sørøya

Murmansk

SS *Henry Bacon* Sunk by 19 Ju-88s Zest and Opportune sent for survivors

NORWAY

SWEDEN

FINLAND

RUSSIA

NORTH SEA

BALTIC SEA

SCOTLAND

Prologue

War brings out the worst in man. Evidence the inhumanity of the Third Reich against the "undesirables" of Europe, the Jews, the Poles, the Gypsies, the retarded, the homosexual populations. The atrocities of the Japanese concentration camps that followed the Death March of Bataan and Corregidor, where the bodies of dead Americans were thrown beyond the barbed wire fence to be consumed by watchdogs. Witness the incineration of civilian men, women, and children in Dresden, Hiroshima, and Nagasaki.

War also brings out the best in man, such as the uncommon valor that transformed a scrawny kid from Texas, Audie Murphy, into the most decorated soldier of World War II. Emergency medical care, including the use of sulfa, penicillin, and other "wonder" drugs, saw its first major tests on the battlefields of Europe, Africa, and the South Pacific. The development of jet-powered planes that reduced the time of travel between distant parts of the globe was also born of that war.

How men conduct war, and how they follow orders, tells more about the individual, the nation, and mankind. For many who recall the Nuremberg trials, the echoes of high-ranking Germans alibiing their crimes against humanity by saying they were just following orders can still be heard. Others have a more focused view, such as Captain J. H. Allison, who commanded the HMS *Zambesi* during the horrific ordeal of the SS *Henry Bacon*. Allison wrote: "I have always held to the view that war should be waged with whatever humanity as possible, however brutal or uninstructed are your opponents. In this matter [of the rescue] the standard is set by the principles dictated by Admiral Lord Nelson in his last prayer before the Battle of Trafalgar."

As the corps of journalists—and historians—becomes younger and younger each year, and as the younger people forget what didn't happen on their watch, it is important that the reader know certain things, items not often found in today's textbooks.

Lend-Lease

One development that has not received the attention it deserves is the development of the Liberty ships—a vital part of Franklin Delano Roosevelt's Lend-Lease program. Lend-Lease was a thinly-veiled attempt by the United States to retain its announced neutrality—but still provide war matériel for those nations bearing the brunt of the fighting, before the attack on Pearl Harbor on December 7, 1941, drew this nation into the conflict. In September 1940 the president negotiated the now-famous "destroyers-for-bases" agreement, which would provide Britain with fifty obsolete American World War I destroyers in exchange for 99-year leases of several British bases in the Western Hemisphere. Congress approved the Lend-Lease program, which gave Roosevelt almost unlimited authority to direct supplies, tanks, aircraft, ammunition, and other wartime necessities to our Allies in Europe—without sacrificing American neutrality, on March 11, 1941. During the length of its operation, Lend-Lease provided over $41 billion [some sources indicate the figure might be well over $50 billion] in aid to more than forty nations. The lion's share—roughly $30 billion—went to Great Britain; $11 billion to the Soviet Union; and $1 billion to China. Less than $10 billion was ever repaid by those nations. Lend-Lease, in reality, was more of a giveaway program.

Lend-Lease was the most evident sign of cooperation between the United States and Russia. The program started just three months after the Germans invaded the USSR in June 1941. About 70 percent of the aid reached Russia via the Persian Gulf through Iran; the remainder sailed across the Pacific to Vladivostok or across the North Atlantic to Murmansk. The program of aid ended officially in September 1945.

Russian leader Joseph Stalin never revealed to the Russian people the full contributions of Lend-Lease to the survival of their country. He did, however, refer to it at the 1945 Yalta Conference, saying, "Lend-Lease is one of Franklin Roosevelt's most remarkable and vital achievements in the formation of the anti-Hitler alliance."

Lend-Lease helped the Russians push the Nazis out of the Soviet Union and Eastern Europe, thereby hastening the end of the war. When Stalin took over Eastern Europe, the wartime alliance ended...and the Cold War began.

Liberty Ships

Roosevelt felt that the United States, because of its vast natural resources, should become the "Arsenal of Democracy," and to achieve this end he needed a way to supply American-made war goods to those nations that needed them most. The vessels needed for this transoceanic transportation were mass-produced merchant ships. The first ships to fulfill this need were constructed for the British on that nation's plan. The British Merchant Shipbuilding Mission approached the United States in 1940 and ordered sixty cargo ships with a capacity of some 633,000 tons. The cost for these vessels was in the vicinity of $96 million. The British paid in cash! Half of the ships were to be constructed at the New England Shipbuilding Corporation, Portland, Maine; the other half at the Kaiser-Permanente Yard No. 1, Richmond, California.

Each of these vessels carried the prefix *Ocean* before its name. The keel for the first West Coast vessel, the *Ocean Vanguard*, was laid April 14, 1941, and the ship was launched 156 days later– August 16, 1941. The Kaiser Corporation delivered the last of its thirty vessels five months ahead of schedule, in July 1942. The first East Coast vessel, the *Ocean Liberty*, had its keel laid on May 24, 1941, and delivered the last of its contracted vessels one month ahead of schedule in November 1942.

The basic model for the *Ocean* class ships was the SS *Dorington Court*, a British tramp steamer of the 1930s. It had a raked stem, cruiser stern, single screw, and balanced rudder. The ships of that class were propelled by a three-cylinder, triple-expansion, reciprocating steam engine. The patent for that engine, by the way, was dated 1896! Due to the fact that Great Britain had no domestic oil at the time, the ships of that class were powered by coal-fired scotch or fire-tube boilers. The ships had a length of 441 feet with a beam of 57 feet and displaced about 7,500 tons. In its five holds, a ship could carry 9,150 tons of cargo, with a cruising range of roughly eight thousand miles at a speed of 11 knots.

The United States Maritime Commission made a number of alterations to the design of ships of the *Ocean* class. Some were made to conform to American shipbuilding and manufacturing standards; others to adjust to the scarcity of certain materials; and still some others to meet the deadlines as quickly and as cheaply as possible. The end results of these alterations were ships designated EC Class, "emergency cargo, large capacity." When Admiral Emory S. Land, chairman of the US Maritime Commission, approached President Roosevelt for his approval of the Liberty ship plan, he noted that the president nodded his blessing, and then added, "a real ugly duckling." That name stayed with the ships throughout their existence.

Not everyone agreed with the president. Admiral Ernest J. King voiced his disapproval of the plan by writing Roosevelt: "The anti-submarine vessel program must be given the highest priority and must be maintained in that priority, even if it is necessary to reduce or postpone the construction of Liberty ships or similar vessels to accomplish this end." Roosevelt, of course, rejected King's priorities because of his strong belief in the future benefits of the Lend-Lease program.

In January 1941 the United States began a program of its own. At the launching of the first American "Ugly Duckling," September 27, 1941, Roosevelt said:

> This is a memorable day in the history of American shipbuilding—a memorable day in the emergency defense of the nation. Today, from dawn to dark, fourteen ships are being launched—on the Atlantic, on the Pacific and on the Gulf and among them is the first Liberty ship, the *Patrick Henry*....

> The shipworkers of America are doing a great job. They have made a commendable record for efficiency and speed. With every new ship,

they are striking a telling blow at the menace to our nation and the liberty of the free peoples of the world. They struck fourteen such blows today. They have caught the true spirit with which this nation must be imbued if Hitler and other aggressors of his ilk are to be prevented from crushing us.

We Americans as a whole cannot listen to those few Americans who preach the gospel of fear–who say in effect that they are still in favor of freedom of the seas but who would have the United States tie up our vessels in our ports. That attitude is neither truthful nor honest.

We propose that these ships sail the seas as they are intended to. We propose, to the best of our ability, to protect them from torpedo, from shell or from bomb.

The *Patrick Henry*, as one of the Liberty ships launched today, renews that great patriot's stirring demand: "Give me liberty or give me death."

There shall be no death for America, for democracy, for freedom! There must be liberty, world-wide and eternal. That is our prayer–our pledge to all mankind.

During the war, 2,710 Liberty ships were built in 13 states, by 15 companies in 18 shipyards.

Alabama Drydock & Shipbuilding	Mobile, Alabama
Bethlehem-Fairfield Shipyard	Baltimore, Maryland
California Shipbuilding Corp.	Los Angeles, California
Delta Shipbuilding Corp.	New Orleans, Louisiana
J. A. Jones	Brunswick, Georgia
J. A. Jones	Panama City, Florida
Kaiser Company	Vancouver, Washington
Marinship	Sausalito, California
New England Shipbuilding East Yard	Portland, Maine
New England Shipbuilding West Yard	Portland, Maine
North Carolina Shipbuilding	Wilmington, North Carolina
Oregon Shipbuilding	Portland, Oregon
Permanente Metals Corp., No. 1 Yard	Richmond, California
Permanente Metals Corp., No. 2 Yard	Richmond, California
St. John's River Shipbuilding	Jacksonville, Florida
Southeastern Shipbuilding	Savanna, Georgia
Todd Houston Shipbuilding	Houston, Texas
Walsh-Kaiser Company	Providence, Rhode Island

Of those 2,710 ships, only two survive: the SS *Jeremiah O'Brien* is berthed in San Francisco, California; the SS *John W. Brown*, named for the founder of the shipbuilders' union, is in Baltimore, Maryland. The *Jeremiah O'Brien*, outfitted as a troop transport, made the fiftieth anniversary pilgrimage to Normandy in June 1994.

Battle of the Atlantic

Because of the exigencies of war, quantity was more important than quality. During the Battle of the Atlantic [this was not a "battle" in the usual sense, it was more an issue of "control" over shipping in the Atlantic], during the early days of World War II, German U-boats [*Unterseeboot*] were sinking the Allies' merchant ships at an alarming rate. In fact, in May 1941 the Nazis were sinking merchant ships three times faster than the British shipyards could build them, and more than twice the speed of the combined British and American effort. Some sources suggest that 1942 was the most successful year for the German submarines, with 1,200 Allied ships sunk. Other sources believe the number of ships sunk was 1,664–1,097 of them in the North Atlantic. Between December 1941 and May 1942, however, the US Navy and Coast Guard sank only two U-boats!

If the Germans continued to destroy the merchant fleet at such an alarming rate, it would be necessary for the Allies to outproduce the destruction. As it was said at the time, the Liberty ships were "built by the mile and chopped off by the yard." The number of ships produced was of utmost importance. The more traditional methods of shipbuilding were discarded and new, innovative techniques were employed. Leading the way was Henry J. Kaiser, a 60-year-old California industrialist who had no experience in building ships. That didn't stop him, as he said on many occasions, "I always have to dream up there against the stars. If I don't dream I'll make it, I won't even get close."

Henry J. Kaiser, William Francis Gibbs, and the "Hog-Islanders"

Although Kaiser is given credit for the concept of the Liberty ships, the honor really rests with William Francis Gibbs [1886-1967], a naval architect and marine engineer, who directed the mass production of American cargo ships during World War II and actually designed the Liberty ships. In 1940, Gibbs began the design of a cargo ship suitable for mass production manufacture. He broke completely with the time-honored custom of shipbuilding by proving that different portions of a ship could be constructed in different places and brought together for assembly. The result was a reduced production time for a single ship from as long as four years to as little as four days! Yet, even before Gibbs conceived the idea, there were attempts to use prefabricated components.

During World War I the US government financed a large number of shipyards for the war production of freighters. The largest, Hog Island yard, was located in Philadelphia and operated by the American International Corporation. That yard had fifty ways, while the largest Liberty yard had only sixteen. The Hog Island yard, however, required 294 days from keel to launch. The time was later reduced to 178 days. The reasons for the slowness in production can probably be based on the fact that Hog Island was fully-established before the first keel was laid. The first "Hog Islander," the *Quistconck*, was constructed in a half-completed berth. Carpenters remained idle for weeks until construction workers completed the groundwork. Plant construction, it was said, interfered with ship assembly. Despite the innovation of prefabricated construction, the rest of the yard continued using traditional techniques.

An interesting side note to Hog Island is that it was the name donor to the world-famous Philadelphia "hoagie," originally called a "Hogie," after the shipyard. Italian housewives would prepare antipastos on the family's china for the men who worked at Hog Island. After the women discovered they were losing chinaware, they replaced the dishes with a roll of Italian bread, and thus began the tradition of antipasto-sandwiches, now known as hoagies. In Massachusetts, another area known for shipbuilding, the sandwiches were called "Submarines," perhaps for the ships built there. Elsewhere, the name "Hero" arises. Some seem to think that name arose because of the size of the sandwich and because it took an extraordinary person to eat the whole thing. But, it would seem more likely that the military—or naval—theme continued.

Henry J. Kaiser took advantage of the errors of the past and improved upon them.

As a younger man Kaiser had completed Boulder, Bonneville, and Grand Coulee dams...ahead of schedule. Henry J. was an engineering genius whose motto was, "A problem is an opportunity in work clothes." But he was more than an engineering genius. In 1938, while building the Grand Coulee Dam in eastern Washington state, he established a prepaid health care plan for the dam's builders. For the first time, the plan included workers' families. With the outbreak of World War II, Kaiser arranged with Dr. Sydney Garfield to arrange the same type of medical plan for the thousands of workers converging on the Kaiser shipyards of the West Coast. From an initial enrollment of six thousand members, the program grew to over thirty thousand people at the height of the war. This was the beginning of present-day Kaiser-Permanente.

Borrowing liberally from the experience of Henry Ford—and his manufacture of inexpensive automobiles, Kaiser had sections of the ships prefabricated in other locations across the country and transported by rail to his shipyards. There, the Liberty ships were welded together, not bolted. Once the production lines got up to full steam, construction time dropped to as little as 28 days. The Kaiser shipyard in Oakland, California, constructed the SS *Robert E. Peary* in 4 days, 15 hours, and 30 minutes.

On the average it took 529,000 man-hours to build one ship. Construction for one Liberty ship required 3,425 tons of hull steel, 2,725 tons of plate, and 700 tons of shapes, including 50,000 castings! The average cost of a ship was $1.8 million, and it was considered if such an "expendable" ship could complete just one trip, it would be a financial success. The Liberty ships were not things of beauty, but they never were intended for anything more than carrying the "Arsenal of Democracy" to those who needed it. The availability—or nonavailability—of merchant shipping determined what the Allies could or could not do militarily. The military direction of the war was affected when the sinking of Allied merchant vessels exceeded production; when convoys were delayed, destinations were reached by circuitous routes to avoid the "wolf packs" of Nazi submarines. In fact, the cross-Channel invasion, known as D-day, was planned for 1942, but postponed for many months for reasons that included insufficient shipping.

Two-thirds of all cargo that left the United States during World War II was transported on Liberty ships. Had these ships not been produced, in all likelihood the war would have been prolonged for many months—if not years. Some historians argue that the Allies would have lost the war since there would not have existed the means to carry the personnel, supplies, and equipment need by the combined Allies to defeat the Axis powers. It must be remembered that it required seven to fifteen tons of supplies to support one soldier for one year during World War II. Two hundred Liberty ships were sunk but, because there were so many, the Germans could not close off all sea-lanes and crucial supply lines.

War also provided the arena for men to show their mettle, to sacrifice their lives for a greater cause, for something in which they believed: Democracy.

The Merchant Marine

One of the unsung, heroic groups of the Second World War was the Merchant Marine. Before the war, the Merchant Marine numbered only 55,000 experienced seamen. During the war the number multiplied, through US Maritime Service training programs, to more than a quarter million.

Merchant ships faced the same dangers as Navy vessels—attacks by submarines, cruisers and destroyers, aircraft, mines, and any other element the enemy could present. The main difference between the merchant fleet and the regular Navy was that the merchant mariners were civilians, and paid less than their naval counterparts. They also paid their share as did the Navy. At least 8,651 mariners were killed at sea; 11,000 wounded, of whom at least 1,100 died from their wounds, some drowned, some froze, and some starved. Sixty died in prison camps. Of the 733 large ships of the US Merchant Marine sunk, 31 vanished without a trace.

The fatality rate for these men is frightening. One out of 29 mariners serving aboard a merchant ship died in the line of duty. Merchant mariners suffered a greater percentage of war-related deaths than all other US services. Despite the sacrifice they were making, the federal government denied them veterans' rights. In a 1988 court-ordered decision, the Department of Defense granted them the status of veterans. During the war, casualties were kept secret to keep information of their success from the enemy, and to attract more men to the sea. American newspapers carried the same story, week after week: "Two medium-sized Allied ships sunk in the Atlantic." In 1942, the average was 33 Allied ships sunk each week!

In a postwar report to President Harry S. Truman, the War Shipping Administration wrote:

> Our merchant ships ran innumerable gauntlets of air, surface and submarine attacks ranging from the early danger zones of the Red Sea and the Indian Ocean to mid-Atlantic and the Mediterranean, and the Kamikaze attacks off the islands of the Pacific. But none of these combined all the elements of danger from man and nature alike, such as did the Murmansk run....

> Through icy, fog-bound seas, their flanks exposed to the dive bombers, surface raiders, and submarines moving out from the Nazi-held fjords of Norway, the slow gray convoys moved—and kept on moving. Nor was there sanctuary at their destination, for every hour on the hour, it was said, the black-cross planes of the Luftwaffe blasted heartbreaking delays in the grim business of unloading the ships in the ice-cluttered harbor of Murmansk. Yet the cargoes were delivered.

Fleet Admiral King, by then commander in chief of the US Navy and chief of naval operations, changed his tune in 1945:

> During the past three and a half years, the Navy has been dependent upon the Merchant Marine to supply our far-flung fleet and bases. Without this support, the Navy could not have accomplished its mission. Consequently, it is fitting that the Merchant Marine share in our success as it shared in our trials.

> The Merchant Marine is a strong bulwark of national defense in peace

and war, and a buttress to a sound national economy. A large Merchant Marine is not only an important national resource; it is, in being, an integral part of the country's armed might during time of crisis. During World War II, this precept has been proven.

While the civilian Merchant Marine was carrying cargo to the allies of the United States, they were sailing on "slow rust buckets," with no protective armor or elaborate weaponry for defense. For some unknown reason the United States did not arm the ships. Neither did they provide escorts or air cover. Admiral King was responsible for this inaction. To add to the danger...the US government did not order a blackout of seacoast cities until June 1942, leaving the merchant ships silhouetted against the shoreline.

US Navy Armed Guard

The Germans through their network of spies, radio interceptions, and informants knew beforehand of many of the sailings of merchant vessels, leaving the ships and their crews vulnerable. To protect these civilians—and their vital cargoes, the government established the US Navy Armed Guard to protect merchant ships from enemy submarines, ships, and aircraft. During World War II, the Armed Guard totaled 144,970 men, who served on 6,236 merchant ships. The casualty rate for the Armed Guard was second only to the US Marine Corps. Many Armed Guards were killed outright or died from exposure in lifeboats, freezing water, or blistering sun. Members of the Armed Guard had to be in perfect physical condition and health, because few—if any—of the merchant ships carried a doctor aboard. These gun crews stood watch for four hours on and four hours off around the clock. Some of their off-time was spent maintaining weapons, painting, cleaning, and doing the other chores of a naval seaman.

In 1997, following his death, the remains of M. Larry Lawrence, the US ambassador to Switzerland, were buried in Arlington National Cemetery. This caused a political furor. Lawrence died in office as ambassador, and this was used to obtain a waiver, together with his prior service as a veteran of Merchant Marine service during World War II.

Patrick F. Kennedy, assistant secretary of state for administration, in requesting the waiver, wrote:

> Ambassador Lawrence served in the United States Merchant Marine during World War II. His ship [the Liberty ship S.S. *Horace Bushnell*] was torpedoed in the Arctic Ocean and he was severely injured....

> This service and his wartime injury in the line of duty should be considered equivalent to military service and the award of a Purple Heart in present terms, thus entitling Ambassador Lawrence to burial at Arlington either directly or through an exception.

The Department of the Army, custodian of the cemetery, disagreed. According to the superintendent of Arlington, John C. Metzler Jr., he was unable to confirm Lawrence's service in the Merchant Marine. Of the approximately 81 members of the Merchant Marine buried or inurned at Arlington, his was the only one without confirmation of service. Rather than sully his memory, his family had his remains removed and buried in a private cemetery...notwithstanding that the Russian government, in January 1993, presented him with the Russian Federation's Fortieth Anniversary Medal of Honor, "for his valiant service on the notoriously dangerous Murmansk Run..."

The debate was ignited by veterans' groups that did not consider Merchant Marine service reason enough for interment in the nation's most hallowed ground.

Though facing the same dangers as the regular Navy, Army and Marine Corps, the Merchant Marine contingent never received the respect due them...or the benefits as veterans of World War II. It has only been in the past few decades that attempts have been made to recognize them for their contribution, above and beyond the call of duty, to the cause of Democracy.

CHAPTER 1

Women on the *Henry Bacon*

"Women on the *Henry Bacon!*"

A grizzled merchant seaman with a stringy beard muttered the words with contempt as he carefully spat tobacco juice downwind over the rail. The brown spray was lost in the morning mist rising from the thin sheet of ice covering Murmansk harbor.

The mumbled words came through surprisingly sharp and clear to two clean-faced youngsters wearing the uniform of US Navy gunners.

"Women!" they shouted almost in unison as they hurried to the rail from a nearby passageway. Their eyes lit up, but quickly their excitement began to fade.

"Oh, you mean those women who are coming aboard with those Norwegian refugees, don't you?"

The old salt, who was not as ancient as he appeared behind his unkempt whiskers, shook his head, ignoring the tone of disappointment.

"Nah. That'll be bad enough, but I ain't countin' them—they'll be like passengers...kind of. I'm talkin' about those Russian gals they found livin' down in the hold."

The worry in his voice thickened. "You mark my words," he said with absolute certainty; "them dames will bring us bad luck."

"Bad luck?" smiled the shorter of the two gunners. "Dames on this ship sound like good luck to me. They're just what we've needed on this old tub." He absentmindedly dug a little black comb out of his tight pants and ran it through his greasy black hair.

"What the heck you talkin' about?" the other asked. "I never heard about no stowaways."

"If you kids didn't spend all your time playin' cards, you'd know what was goin' on. Fact is, them gals is down in the officers' mess right now."

"The officers always get everything," Shorty snapped, and disappeared hurriedly into the passageway.

His buddy only delayed long enough for a parting shot. "Thanks a lot, Grandpa. I'm glad I ain't so old that I got more superstition than romance in my soul."

He didn't quite hear the grunt that was meant for a reply.

"Stupid kids—always thinkin' of dames. Don't give a damn about what's ahead of 'em."

Peering through the thin mist, the merchant mariner ran his eyes over the murky shapes of the nearby ships in the deep harbor. Most of them, like the SS *Henry Bacon*, were United States Liberty ships performing yeoman service during the closing months of the war.

A sister ship, the SS *Thomas Scott*, was close enough for him to make out some of the crew leaning over the rail. He had a buddy aboard the *Scott*.

Portside, in the distance, he could see a Soviet submarine breaking the thin ice as it began to surface.

Several British warships lay to starboard. The closest was the corvette *Bluebell*. A little farther off were the crossed masts of several destroyers. A baby aircraft carrier, not discernible in the fog, would also be in the flotilla that would protect the convoy of Liberty ships from the Nazi U-boat and Luftwaffe patrols that operated off the coast of northern Norway.

The cold mist froze, turning to ice in his beard. He was brushing away the rime, when Donald F. Haviland walked up. Haviland was the *Bacon*'s chief engineer, a man respected by all aboard as a gentleman and a competent engineer, and by the younger members of the crew as a source for sound advice and short-term, no-interest loans. Haviland had first seen sea duty during World War I, but took a land job between wars. But when the urgent call came for experienced seamen, he dusted off his chief engineer's license and went back to sea.

His first World War II trip was to Trinidad. Later he made two trips to Persia and survived a torpedoing in the Mediterranean.

Back home in November 1944, he decided to make just this one last trip on the *Henry Bacon* before retiring from the Merchant Marine and buying a gas station near Boston. Though a bachelor, Haviland was a family man at heart and planned to earn money to help send his nephews through college. He kept their pictures in his office.

"You heard about those Russian gals they found down in the hold, Chief?"

"Yeah."

"Where'd you suppose they came from?"

"Well, I don't suppose anyone is going to ever really tell us that. Maybe they're some of the girls the young fellows met in the canteen. But probably they're a couple of the winch operators who managed to hide out somewhere when the Russians finished unloading."

"Women on a ship bring bad luck—you know that, Don!"

Haviland clapped him heartily on the shoulder.

"Snap out of it, mate. This is 1945! They even have WAVES in the Navy these days. Anyway, Captain Carini will have to get rid of them. You know, all the bad luck we can handle—maybe even more than we can handle—is right out there." He nodded in the direction where the Tuloma River left Murmansk and joined Kola Bay and the mouth of the Arctic Ocean. The observation did not noticeably brighten the seaman's outlook.

* * *

When the two young Navy gunners approached the officers' mess, their courage left them. They stopped at the hatchway and peered in.

Most of the ship's brass were gathered about the girls who were standing between the mess tables in the small room. The young gunners figured the stowaways to be about their own age and "cute chicks" in a pitiful way. Obviously frightened, the women were wearing shabby, bulky jackets and pants and heavy boots. Their dark hair gleamed in the bright light when they pushed the fur hoods of their heavy parkas back onto their shoulders. One girl was slightly taller, a little heavier, and perhaps a year or two older than the other.

The short captain of the *Henry Bacon*, Alfred Carini, stood in the center of the room flanked by First Mate Lynn Palmer and Second Mate Carl Fubel. Navy lieutenant John Sippola was nearby, and one of Sippola's gunners stood back against the gray steel bulkhead, guarding the girls.

The stowaways were talking in Russian and occasionally attempted to explain something in broken English, but it was obvious that the men did not understand what they were saying.

Fubel suggested to the captain that there was a man on board, Joseph Stanislav Pszybysz, a 32-year-old messman, who might be able to act as translator. While Pszybysz was born in Brooklyn, he had learned some Polish and even a little Russian at home. His father had been a postmaster in Poland and could speak several languages.

With Captain Carini's approval, the second mate went looking for Pszybysz and found him on the deck. Pszybysz had already heard about the stowaways from some of the Navy gunners.

Seaman First Class Charles Harlacher returned from the head and cracked, "Just like home; I couldn't get in the john because a couple of girls were in there sprucing up."

"Naturally we all went to have a look," added Normand Croteau, coxswain. "When we got there they were gone, so we opened the bulkhead door and we could see footprints in the snow going to the hatchway that led to the hold."

Gunner's Mate Third Class Frank Reid, who was on watch, had also seen the girls. "Right away I checked the gangway guards and asked if any boats were alongside. The answer was 'no.'

"Since I was the guy on watch I went to Lieutenant Sippola and told him, and we started to investigate. Finally we found the girls on the ballast in number 5 hold. They had a good supply of blankets and clothing and canned fish and other stuff."

"We brought them to the lieutenant's cabin first. They didn't exactly resist, but they began to cry when we took away some knives we found in their felt boots."

Captain Carini, who spoke with a heavy Italian accent, had been unable to understand the girls at all, and when Pszybysz joined the group in the officers' mess the captain instructed him to ask the girls how they got aboard ship and how they managed to live aboard without being found before then. Terrified, the young girls did not want to say anything. Finally they told Pszybysz:

"*My nas ubyut!*" (We'll be killed!)

"*Nas soshlyut v Siber!*" (We'll be sent to Siberia!)

"*Oni budut muchit nas!*" (They'll torture us!)

Pszybysz tried to get the information the captain asked for, "but they wouldn't say anything about that."

The girls told the Polish-American seaman that they wanted to get away from the conditions they were living under in Russia.

Captain Carini notified the Russian port authorities that he had stowaways aboard before he even met the girls and when he had Pszybysz explain this to them "they were as close as anyone could be to being scared to death."

"They cried silently and tears streamed down their cheeks."

When Pszybysz told Captain Carini about their fear of being tortured or even being put to death, he shook his head and clucked in a sympathetic manner. But he had already decided that he should not get the United States government "into trouble" with the USSR by helping smuggle out Soviet citizens.

"Even though he spoke with an accent, the skipper was strictly American," Pszybysz remembered.

Finally, when it was clear that Pszybysz could not get any information from the girls concerning how they had stayed undetected aboard the *Henry Bacon*, Carini concluded, "Guess that's all."

Messboy Chuck Reed, who worked in the officers' mess, had drifted in and stood quietly near the refrigerator. He and Pszybysz were close friends, and the two left together.

The girls were then taken to another section of the officers' quarters to await the arrival of the Russian port authorities.

Back in his own cabin, the ship's master discussed the situation with the Navy lieutenant and several other officers over a drink.

"I suppose the Russians were looking for these girls when they came aboard the other day," Sippola observed.

Carini stiffened to his full sixty-four inches but was still almost a foot shorter than the Navy officer. The incident that Sippola referred to had been an unpleasant one for both men. Soviet officials had boarded the *Bacon* in a belligerent manner and demanded through their female interpreter that they be allowed to search the gun crew's quarters.

Sippola asked the interpreter why the Russians wanted to search.

"I don't know."

"Ask him," Sippola replied bluntly, pointing to the Russian who obviously was in charge.

"He won't tell me."

At this, Captain Carini said they had no business searching the ship anyway, and a heated argument broke out. "This is my ship!" Carini roared. Merchant ship captains are generally a tough, independent, hardheaded breed and Carini was as hard as any of them.

At first he refused point-blank to allow the Russians to conduct a search. But finally, when he saw that the Soviets were determined enough to make trouble, he relented to avoid a possible international incident. He reasoned that his adopted country must have a serious purpose in trying to work with these people, if US ships and men were sent on the dangerous mission to haul Lend-Lease cargo to Murmansk in the first place. He had no particular reason to object to the Soviet's request, but it was the attitude of the hard-faced woman and the curt arrogance of the man in the business suit, possibly an NKVD agent, that had made him refuse.

"Okay, but the chief mate and the lieutenant go with you."

A slow, laborious search was made of the quarters of the Armed Guard, the engine room, and the shaft tunnel, but the Russians did not find whatever they were looking for at the time. When they left, their attitude was as brusque and unpleasant as when they had boarded.

As the captain looked out to sea, he thought the approaching vessel was the same harbor tug that had made the fruitless mission a few days before.

Carini ordered the women brought out on deck to be ready for the Soviet officials. He wanted the sad business completed as quickly and efficiently as possible.

The girls, who said they were sisters sent to Murmansk to work after their parents and brother were killed at Leningrad, sobbed quietly.

They seemed to be in a daze as the forty-foot tug approached and the Russian port authorities and soldiers, including a woman in a black uniform, drew alongside the *Henry Bacon*.

The strong arms of the *Bacon* guards held the girls firmly. The men did not release their grip until five stern Soviet officials came up the gangway, conferred very briefly with Captain Carini, and assumed jurisdiction over the stowaways.

Deceptively docile, the taller girl, who had started down the gangway first, suddenly gave the official in front of her a brutal shove and jumped past him into the icy water between the two vessels. The shock of the cold water numbed her body and she was helpless to fight off or cooperate with the Russian sailors trying to pull her from the harbor with a boat hook.

The younger sister was hurried aboard the tug. She too became hysterical and tried to jump overboard to join her sister in the water. A Russian soldier held her back and shouted, "*Molchi!*" (Be quiet!)

But the girl wailed, "*Ya pokonchila s zhiznyu, ya pokonchila s zhiznyu!*" (Finished with living, finished with living!) The soldier pushed her roughly into the cabin and slammed the door.

Within a few minutes the Russians had managed to rescue the other sister from the water. Limp and blue with cold, she had to be dragged into the cabin. The door closed again and the tug quickly headed back to shore.

The men on the *Henry Bacon* were stunned. They had all heard that the girls had expressed great fear about being turned back to the Russians and rumors that they had threatened suicide. "But I guess we didn't really believe them," one gunner recalled.

Most of the crew lingered at the rail until the tug was out of sight. They found their own role in the tragedy distasteful and were appalled by the hard "Russian way" they had witnessed. The younger girl's lament seemed to echo in their memories—"*Ya pokonchila s zhiznyu, ya pokonchila s zhiznyu.*" Had they sent the girls off to be executed, or worse?

Many of the men were genuinely superstitious and feared that having women on the ship would bring bad luck. "Something terrible will happen!" was repeated by many of the older crew members.

Lieutenant Sippola stood at the rail a long time, watching the craft until it was out of sight. He could not help but think of the brutal treatment his Finnish kinsmen had received at the hands of the Russians just five years before.

The crew generally agreed that the two girls had kept themselves hidden until they thought it safe to venture out when the *Bacon* moved from the dock out into the harbor. It was never determined whether the girls had stayed aboard after working on the ship, or whether some of the merchant seamen or Navy gunners had smuggled them on. Either way, it seemed likely that someone had brought them supplies. No one confessed. The mystery has only been answered in the year 2000, more than fifty-five years later. The details can be found in chapter 9.

Later in the Navy crew quarters, irrepressible Steve Allard observed, "Those dames would have been quite a sight walking down Fifth Avenue, the way they were dressed."

And, life went on aboard the *Henry Bacon*.

CHAPTER 2

The Birth of the *Henry Bacon*

The SS *Henry Bacon* was not the first of the "ugly ducklings," nor would it be the last. The *Henry Bacon* was only one of 126 Liberty ships built at the North Carolina Shipbuilding Corporation, a new $10 million shipyard in Wilmington, North Carolina. That firm was the largest single industry for any one city in that state.

It took only about six weeks from the time the keel was laid for Hull 862 on September 29, 1942, until the *Henry Bacon* was launched.

The United States Maritime Commission used broad guidelines in the adoption of names for these emergency vessels. Looking over the 2,710 Liberty ships built between September 27, 1941, and September 2, 1945, one can see that the ships were named initially for eminent Americans from every walk of life who had made noteworthy contributions to the history or the culture of the United States—some were famous, some forgotten; others were heroic...or even mystical. As the war progressed, 120 Liberty ships were named for heroes of the Merchant Marine. These included all ranks, from master to seaman; those who lost their lives by enemy action—or in other disasters at sea. More than a hundred ships were named for women, while another group honored war correspondents killed in the line of duty. Only one Liberty ship was named for a living person—in error. The *Francis J. O'Gara* was named for the purser of the SS *Jean Nicolet*, which had been sunk by a Japanese submarine. He was thought to have died. In reality, he returned from a Japanese prisoner of war camp after the war. There were also complaints about names. The US Maritime Commission's public relations office reported that one prominent politician complained: "...I understand my name has been given to a Liberty ship. I am not dead, not in dry dock and do not need my bottom scraped. Please cancel the name." The politician was advised that the ship had actually been named for another person of the same name who had been dead for many years.

James McKoy, a grandson of Henry Bacon Sr., thought it appropriate that one of the Liberty ships being built on the Cape Fear River should be named in his grandfather's honor, since he had worked as a civil engineer on the river. In June 1942, Carroll Perry Jr., of the Committee on Launchings for the US Maritime Commission, agreed.

Thus, the fortieth Liberty ship launched at Wilmington was named for Henry Bacon Sr., a prominent engineering authority on rivers and harbors in the last half of the nineteenth century. He was born at the family farmhouse on the outskirts of Natick, Massachusetts, August 17, 1822, the son of John and his wife Lucy Sawin. His ancestors included men who had fought at the first battlefield of the Revolution, Lexington.

The family's farm was a large one, and the land—according to family records—was orginally deeded to the Bacon family by the Indians. Henry was one of a large family of brothers and sisters: John William, Jonathan, Moses, Lizzie, Katherine, Lucy, and Hattie. Of the brothers, John William was jolly; Henry, serious; Jonathan, jolly; Moses, musical; Hattie, the youngest, was artistic; Lizzie and Katherine were homemakers. Henry attended Leichester Academy. After a year of schooling—Henry wanted to be a civil engineer—he dropped out of school and spent a year teaching at a country school to earn enough money for another year of engineering education. He spent another year as a teacher before he earned enough to finish his own training. While he was teaching, Henry Bacon's patience was tried by a student, bigger than he and a bully to boot. After several days of torment, the teacher called the boy outside and gave him a licking. The pages describing this incident were ripped out of Henry's diary by his wife, when she realized her grandchildren were reading the diary.

After he married a friend of his sisters, Elizabeth Kelton, he began the nomadic life of an engineer. As a young man he worked for the Boston & Maine Railroad; years later he was chief engineer of that line. Between those two positions Bacon was in charge of improvements to the harbor of Ontonagon on Lake Superior in Michigan. Then he became chief engineer on the Illinois Central, based in Terre Haute, Indiana. In 1876 he was sent to North Carolina, through an appointment by his personal friend, Colonel William P. Craighill, chief of the US Engineers in charge of improvements on the Cape Fear River.

Bacon was headquartered at Smithville [now Southport], near the New Inlet and the mouth of the river. Later, he, his wife, and children: Francis Henry, James, Henry Jr. [known as Harry to the family], Katherine, Alice, and Carl, would move to Wilmington. The main thrust of the work on the river at the time of his arrival—and for years later—was to increase the depth of the water on the bar at the mouth of the river. It was thought at the time, that this could be accomplished by closing the New Inlet, a gap formed by a 1761 storm. This "new" inlet had been used by the blockade runners of the Confederacy during the Civil War and was defended by Fort Fisher. Via this inlet, Wilmington was the last port open to the South.

Before his arrival, little work had been accomplished on the New Inlet project. Bacon decided to build a dam. Small stones were first placed on the bottom of the gap, and then larger ones with gravel and sand. Later a wharf was built out in the middle, and tugboats with scows brought brush and other materials to make "mattresses" which, when finished, were dropped directly on top of the stones and gravel already in place. These mattresses were crisscrossed frameworks of wood packed tight with twisted brush and tied together. Rocks were piled on top to make the whole thing sink. Larger stones were place on that mass until the surface was reached. Finally, very large, hewn stones were laid on top and secured with cement. When complete, the dam was about one and a quarter miles across. The dam permanently closed the inlet.

To supervise his work, Bacon used the steamer *James T. Easton*. He used the craft to go back and forth from home to work site.

One night he arrived home looking ill. "What is the matter?" he was asked. "The *Easton* is burnt." Bacon had made it a family ritual on his children to take trips down the river but, as the family history writes, "he was very careful not to impose on the government in any way. They must carry their own lunches or provisions for the day, though the cook was allowed to cook the meat for the party and even to furnish the bread."

After the demise of the *Easton*, Bacon ferried himself back and forth to work in an open rowboat. He was out in a storm and contracted a cold that finally resulted in his death from pneumonia in April 1891…a further twist of fate in the life of the *Henry Bacon*.

Berthed next to the *Easton* was a dredge. Much later—in 1940—and after Henry Bacon's death, a large pipe-line dredge was named in his honor. The man behind this naming was Robert Merritt, who began his career with Henry Bacon as a young man. He grew up and grew old in the service by the time the dredge with his mentor's name on it was put into service. Another dredge, carrying Merritt's name, was launched in 1963. Even though his Cape Fear work capped his career, the naming of a Liberty ship after him carried with it more honor, more prestige.

Bacon died in Wilmington at the age of 69. One of his four sons, Henry Bacon Jr. [1866–1924], was an architect whose more important works include the Danforth Memorial Library, Paterson, New Jersey (1908); the train station in Naugatuck, Connecticut, built as an Italian villa; the observatory and other buildings at Wesleyan University; and the Union Square Savings Bank, New York City. He collaborated with sculptors Augustus Saint-Gaudens and Daniel Chester French. It was the latter who carved the huge statue of Abraham Lincoln that sits within Bacon's last and most famous work, the Lincoln Memorial (dedicated May 30, 1922).

An 84-year-old daughter, Mrs. Katherine Bacon McKoy of Wilmington, was selected by the federal government to christen the ship the SS *Henry Bacon*. Mrs. McKoy was the only daughter the shipyard ever selected to christen a ship named for a father. Shipyard officials, however, doubted she was strong enough to break the traditional jacket-clad bottle of champagne.

"My suggestion," Roger Williams, head of the shipyard, wrote her son, "is that in case she does not feel up to it herself to select some young lady to act for her." Though a member of the first women's crew at Wellesley College in 1880, this was now 1942, however, and she was tiny, frail, and delicate.

Mrs. McKoy was visiting her brother Carl at his home, "Green Pastures" near Scituate, Massachusetts, when she learned she was to christen the *Bacon*. During that visit it was her habit, as with many other older individuals, to rise before anyone else. She often wandered the estate and strolled in the orchard.

One morning Carl Bacon's chauffeur, who had been with the family more than forty years, happened to rise early himself and was astounded to find Mrs. McKoy in the orchard throwing apples. Quite upset, the chauffeur first consulted with the maid and later with his employer when he came down for breakfast. Joined by his wife, Carl Bacon hurried to the orchard. There, they were greeted by a barrage of apples—Mrs. McKoy was still hurling "as if she was a Christy Mathewson," as one relative put it. Mathewson, a Baseball Hall of Fame inductee, pitched his way to 373 wins in a career that went from 1900 to 1916 with both the New York Giants and the Cincinnati Reds.

"Kate," her brother called, "what are you up to?"

"Oh, I'm working up some muscle in my arm. I've got to have it in good shape so I can really smash that bottle on father's ship!" The Bacon family had grit, and so would the ship that bore the family scion's name.

High tide arrived at Wilmington at 11:56 A.M. that Armistice Day—the eleventh hour of the eleventh day of the eleventh month, the day set aside by the federal government to remember the end of "The War to End All Wars." The weather, for North Carolina, was chilly. While the temperature had reached 80 degrees the day before, it was only in the upper forties when the family, guests, company officials, and workers gathered to launch the fortieth Liberty ship built in Wilmington.

The company announced to the crowd that it had just been

notified it would receive its second award for outstanding Liberty ship construction — they could now sew a gold star on the shipmaker's Maritime Commission "M" pennant.

When the time came for Mrs. McKoy to break the champagne bottle, the fragile woman momentarily held it aloft and said, "In honor of my father, I christen this ship the *Henry Bacon*." With that she smashed the bottle down so hard on the hull of the ship that champagne and bits of glass splattered over her, her maids of honor and those standing nearby. Christy Mathewson would have been proud!

The SS *Henry Bacon* slipped down the waterway into Cape Fear River to the cheers of the crowd. The time was 1:15 P.M.

As the whistles in the shipyard shrieked, Mrs. McKoy's 11-year-old grandson, James H. McKoy Jr., who stood by his grandmother on the launching stand, got his first taste of champagne. He wiped the champagne off the launching stand rail and licked his fingers. He finished cleaning the rail with the tail of his new suit. The launching party was invited to attend a "small luncheon" following the ceremony, to which little Jimmy retorted, "Who wants to go to a small luncheon!"

The permanent plaque that was to be installed in the captain's cabin didn't arrive before the ship was launched. The *Bacon* went to sea with a temporary plate. The shipyard planned to install the permanent item when the *Bacon* returned from a voyage. It stayed at the Wilmington shipyard until it closed. The plaque was given then to grandson James H. McKoy, who placed it on his office wall in Wilmington.

The *Henry Bacon* was born, lived, and died in war; born November 11, 1942; died February 23, 1945.

CHAPTER 3

The Shakedown

Less than two weeks later, November 24, 1942, the 7,177-ton *Bacon* was delivered to the United States Maritime Commission. Shortly before it was accepted by the Maritime Commission [November 2, 1942], 115 dozen white pillowcases and 8-1/2 dozen white coats were delivered to the ship. Whichard Brothers Company of Norfolk, Virginia, never received payment [$580.49] for these items. As they wrote in June 1943: "Our merchandise is sold to retail merchants and for the past year it has been impossible to get enough cotton goods to supply our regular customers. Regardless of this fact, about seven months ago, we delivered to [the Norfolk office of the US Maritime Commission's Procurement Division] every pillow case we had. Our reason for doing this was that we felt that our Government should come first although our retail customers felt that we should have let them have these goods." Dick Burbine later remembered the pillowcases. "When the ship would send ashore the dirty laundry in Italy, several of the men hid the brand-new pillowcases in the dirty wash. Once ashore, they'd sell the brand-new pillowcases for spending money."

In December 1942, just a year after the Japanese attack on Pearl Harbor brought the United States into World War II, the *Henry Bacon* was registered in the Port of Wilmington. She measured out at 442 feet; her beam 57 feet, and her depth 37 feet.

Since the US government did not consider Liberty ships as part of the fighting Navy, the *Bacon* was operated for the War Shipping Administration by the South Atlantic Steamship Line of Savannah, Georgia. The *Bacon* set sail from Philadelphia with cargo aboard for "Russian aid" and destined for Karachi, India. The first skipper was William Preston Lawton. His chief engineer was Glen

Wilson. Captain Lawton experienced a number of problems with the *Bacon*. The *Bacon* was afloat on January 15, 1943, at Crisobal, Canal Zone, and subsequently at Balboa, Canal Zone. Problems, however, began to appear. When the *Bacon* was ready to sail, the flywheel on the starboard generator, installed January 18, was "carried away," causing considerable damage to the center and starboard generators. The chief engineer, Charles C. Stokes, and his assistant, George Marston, were injured. Stokes had a broken leg; Marston, both arms broken. Both individuals had to be replaced before the ship set sail. Stokes recalled that he "had been up with the refrigerating man and the machinist all night.... At the time I started to leave my room the current breakers kicked out a second time. I started down to help out and when I got halfway from my room to the engine room I heard the generator running away..." He was between the outboard generator and the ship's side "just as she turned loose. I got knocked down, leg broken, bruised in several places and a flesh wound to the back of the head." The oiler and the fireman tried to drag him out of the engine room so he could give orders, but "the escaping steam being so great they couldn't make it so I crawled down two flights of stairs to the bottom engine room. Then I got them to understand that I wanted a pencil and paper so that I could give orders as the noise of the steam was so great you couldn't hear...." Marston said he was "warming up the main engine at the time and I turned around and discovered that the outboard generator was going, instead of 400 revolutions, all of 600 or 800 revolutions. And then I went up and started to close the throttle valve on the same generator and the accident happened. And I don't know what happened after that." Forty minutes after the accident a Navy doctor from the USS *Trenton* arrived to assist the men. They were taken by launch to the Gorgas Hospital for extensive treatment.

Repairs were completed and, on February 12, 1943, the *Bacon* was certified as seaworthy. The matter did not end with the repairs. A suit was brought by the government against Whitin Machine Works, of Whitin, Massachusetts, regarding the fracture of the generator. The government contended that Whitin did not have a resident inspector on site and that neither tests nor inspections were made of the machinery. A trial date was set for May 21, 1946—and again, February 6, 1948. Records from the Maritime Commission indicate that the case was tried in early 1950 by the District Court of Massachusetts. The district court rendered a judgment in the amount of $96,650.43. The case was carried to and tried before the First Circuit Court of Appeals and the judgment reversed. Lawyers representing the *Bacon*'s insurance underwriters received payment of $8,996.34.

In March 1943 the federal government was notified in a secret communique that the *Henry Bacon* was torpedoed and sunk en route to the Persian Gulf—with all hands lost, but the report turned out to be a mistake caused by a garbled message "and call sign probably garbled." The *Bacon*'s crew was unaware of their demise and continued serving the nation by transporting matériel where needed, arriving in Bushire [Bushehr, in Iran on the Persian Gulf] on April 20, 1943.

Lawton's problems were not all mechanical. According to his official log, beginning in January 1943 the captain wrote that when he boarded the ship at Balboa, Canal Zone, on the afternoon of January 19, he found George F. Leak, messman, drunk and using abusive language to the second officer: "Yes, I am drunk, and you can't prove it." It wasn't the first offense, the captain recorded. Leak had been warned several times. His pay for one day—$3.92— was deducted from his wages. The next day he was again absent from his station. For this, two days' wages—$5.83—were deducted. When the log entries were read to him, he replied, "I am sorry and I will try not to let it happen again."

Two months later, in Fremantle, Australia, the captain wrote that the vessel was ready to sail, "except for the shortage of the following crew members: William Renta, F.W.T.; Thomas Brennan, F.W.T.; Charles Thompson, steward; George Leak, messman; Joe Camblor, messman; Charles [or Chalmers] Anderson, messman; Marshall Greleck, A.B. and Walter H. Griffiths, A.B." The crew, the captain added, "had been sufficiently notified the evening before of the vessel sailing time." Later the captain learned that Rentz, Camblor, Anderson, and Griffiths were in the local jail at Perth, "awaiting deportation as aliens." The ship finally proceeded to the anchorage in Gage Roads, after 1:30 P.M. Two hours later the third officer and custom officials arrived, by launch, on the *Bacon*. Four men did not return: Rentz, Griffiths, Anderson, and Camblor. Though Leak returned, he was in no shape for duty. Again the captain deducted one day's pay—$6.25. On May 3, 1943, the captain was called to the cook's quarters to inspect a fire caused by Leak, who was smoking in bed while drunk. The captain deducted the cost of the mattress—$5.00—from his wages. That next morning the native checkers complained they could get no sleep because of Leak manhandling them and demanding his liquor.

On May 8, Leak served the gun crew while drunk and refused to serve the checkers. Two days later he was again unable to function and lost another day's pay—$6.25. This pattern continued throughout the month of May, with Leak docked four more days' pay for being drunk and disorderly. When the *Bacon* finally reached Durban, South Africa, in June, Captain Lawton requested the US consul there to remove Leak and have him detained ashore until the ship was ready to sail, as his "record shows that his presence aboard is definitely detrimental to the ship when in port."

The day, June 25, Leak was removed, steward Charles Thompson and assistant cook Sam Barclift prepared, what the captain called, "a very unsatisfactory supper a half hour late. I informed both these men that if they could not do their work…I would reduce them to messmen's ratings next day."

Able-bodied Seaman Marshall J. Greleck also proved to be a problem. Greleck was absent from his station and duty in Fremantle, Australia; Bushire, Iran; Durban, South Africa—for a total of twelve days between March 20 and June 26.

The steward, Charles P. Thompson, was also plagued by drunkenness. June 24, in Durban, he was found "in his room dead drunk lying across his desk." According to Lawton's log: "He has never been able to do his job due to ignorance but has only been tolerated as there was no one available to take his place."

Thompson's drunken behavior continued throughout the month of June. On June 25, Captain Lawton recorded finding him in his room and found him "dead drunk and his wash basin full of drunken spew.... I left orders with the Officer on deck to take his pass and inform him that his shore liberty was stopped and that he would be reduced to a utility man's rating as of June 26." The next day the captain reduced him to utility messman. From June 24 until June 27, Thompson was docked eight days' pay! Thompson did not return to the *Bacon*. He was declared a deserter by the ship's master, and immigration officials were alerted to detain him if he were found. His pay—or what little was left of it—was stopped as of June 28, 1943. Thompson's desertion and subsequent capture and return posed a problem to the government and the South Atlantic Steamship Line. Thompson, according to communication between the owners and agents and the War Shipping Administration, "was repatriated as a passenger on the USAT *George W. Goethals* from Capetown, South Africa, to New York. He joined this vessel on June 28, 1943 and arrived in New York August 15, 1943." The question arose over who was responsible for Thompson's travel as a first-class passenger on the *Goethals*. E. H. Wilson for the South Atlantic Steamship Line wrote: "We have never been able to have a seaman returned to the States at the expense of the State Department, therefore, where we cannot obtain reimbursement from P. & I. Underwriters or from seaman's wages, will you kindly advise if it is in order to charge such expenses to the War Shipping Administration vessel's account." According to recently [August 3, 2000] declassified files, the matter was never resolved.

Assistant Cook Sam L. Barclift joined Leak and Thompson by continuing the tradition of drunkenness in the galley. On June 27 he was reduced to a messman's ration.

On March 18, 1944, the *Bacon*'s propeller was damaged by ice. Temporary repairs were made by the ship's crew, but more lasting work would have to be done in dry dock. While in the port of Karachi, India, during April 1943, he found it necessary to have the Karachi Engineering Works & Foundry weld around leaking flanges and on various pipes. Two months later, while in Durban, South Africa, the Union Whaling Company, Ltd., welded one steam elbow. A problem with leaky plates surfaced in July 1943. At the same time, Lawton requested windlass drum gear replacements upon the arrival of the *Bacon* in the United States.

After a series of short voyages, the *Bacon* returned in the summer of 1943 from a trip around the world full of dirt and dust after carrying a load of bauxite, that important aluminum ore needed for war production. But the *Bacon* was plagued with troubles. "Between Durban and Capetown," Captain Lawton wrote August 2 to the South Atlantic Steamship Line that "the #1 L/H was accidentally filled with water while filling #2 D/T with ballast and all efforts to pump this water out failed. Upon arrival in Bahia, this water was bailed out with deck machinery and the following damage resulted from the water being there:—Fore and aft bulkhead midships and aft, 50 percent carried away. Ladder in after end of hatch carried away. Steam smothering line #2 D/T port and starboard carried away. Extension rod to #2 D/T Equalization and #1 D/T starboard filling and discharging valves, carried away." In his estimation, Lawton attributed the damage to faulty welding. Necessary repairs were made to the ship April 8, 1943, in Karachi, India, and on June 23, 1943, at Durban, South Africa, with the bills to be turned over later by the master.

The ship was turned over to 27-year-old Ben Kuta, from British Guiana, who had just been hired as the youngest master employed by the South Atlantic Steamship Line.

Eager to do a good job, Kuta had the *Bacon* and her records shipshape before he embarked on his first voyage to Plymouth, England, September 28, 1943 [a former crewman, Donald F. Davis, gave different dates, indicating the trip was from September 17 to November 19, 1943]. Leaky plates again affected the *Bacon* and were noted in a letter, dated September 10, 1943. That was not the only problem Kuta faced. Steward Charles P. Thompson Sr. was suspended one month for "misconduct—intoxication, inattention to duty, fraud." His suspension lasted one month, beginning August 28, 1943—at New York.

A devoted mariner, Kuta stayed awake and on duty for seven straight days and nights while the ship was lost in a heavy fog. The *Bacon* was the first wartime American ship to enter Plymouth through the enemy-infested English Channel. A tourist attraction to the military community, the *Henry Bacon* was toured by British naval officers who were amazed that a ship of the *Bacon's* quality could be turned out in such a short time.

When Kuta and the *Bacon* returned to the United States and Philadelphia, the South Atlantic Steamship Line made arrangements with Glen Wilson to employ him as chief engineer. The company advanced him fifty dollars "to complete some personal business," before he left Mobile, Alabama, for Philadelphia. In addition, they provided him with thirteen dollars for subsistence during the trip. Wilson subsequently declined the assignment and refused to return the money to the company, saying he felt the company owed him wages for the time he had spent. Frank J. Zito, assistant general counsel for the War Shipping Administration, noted that "it was 'in accordance with the customary practices of commercial operators' to advance funds in reasonable amounts to seamen after they have agreed to sail on a vessel but before they have signed on, to enable them to report to work...." In other words, the South Atlantic Steamship Line would have to eat the money it advanced to Wilson. Yet, on February 4, 1944, the matter resurfaced and it was decided that "Wilson has taken the wrong position on this matter and should return the funds advanced."

The *Bacon's* next voyage was to take it from the Persian Gulf to Cochin, India, in an order made June 29, 1944. That assignment was canceled and the ship was directed to proceed directly to a North Atlantic port.

Kuta's second trip in command of the SS *Henry Bacon* was to Molotovsk, an uncharted Russian port and naval base on the White Sea, via Murmansk. He arrived February 28, 1944 [again Davis's dates differ: December 10, 1943, to April 3, 1944], experiencing "boisterous weather, Force 8...." Documents from the American Foreign Service indicate Kuta was in Molotovsk on February 3. While at the shipyard in December, Davis wrote that "they blew insulation into all the bulkheads and doubled the size of the radiators in every room on board. We knew we were headed for a cold climate."

As part of the ship's deck cargo, Davis remembered, "we had two narrow-gauge locomotives on the forward deck. One on starboard and other on the port. During a storm, the one on the port side broke loose and slammed into the midship structure; however, our deck crew managed to get it secure during the storm." On March 18, 1944, the *Bacon*'s propeller was damaged by ice. Temporary repairs were made by the ship's crew, but more extensive repairs were completed later in dry dock. The bow of the ship was also strengthened at this time, to make it better able to cut through the ice. Davis reported that "it was a four-bladed prop and on the return trip to Murmansk, the Russians put some tanks under our stern and raised it until the center of the shaft was exposed. Then, they measured the broken blade, rotated the shaft around to the opposite blade and cut off an equal amount. Also they made a shaft for a water pump for us."

Captain Kuta's last trip on the *Bacon* began in Philadelphia in April 1944 and, after spending the previous winter in northern Russia, it seemed only logical to spend the summer visiting the Persian Gulf, one of the hottest parts of the globe. While there, the *Bacon* loaded one thousand tons of sand ballast at Port Sudan. On the voyage from Port Sudan to Suez, the *Bacon* carried a Greek national as a passenger. The War Shipping Administration was concerned with who had authorized the transport. They were under the impression that the man, George P. Trisis, had made "private arrangements between him and the Captain of the vessel." This was proven false by the presentation of a letter of authority from the British Ministry of War Transport. Written authorization was promised Captain Kuta but did not reach the ship prior to sailing. The ship returned to port August 9, 1944. As late as 1948, the Isthmian Steamship Company had not received payment of $30 for his passage.

Though he had frequent trouble with the steering, Ben Kuta

regarded the *Bacon* as a good ship. Henry Bacon Jr.'s wife received a phone call from a Navy captain, wondering if the SS *Bacon* was named for her husband. She told him, "No, it was named for his father." The reason for the captain's interest was he believed the *Bacon* had acted as a "shield" for his ship during the D-day invasion of Normandy, June 6, 1944. Unfortunately that sailor was mistaken, since the ship was a little farther south at the time.

Kuta returned to New York City in mid-August 1944 and relinquished command of the *Bacon* to its new skipper, Captain Alfred Carini.

CHAPTER 4

The Skipper

A lfred [he was born Alfredo, but Americanized his name for his chosen land] Carini was born in Palermo, Sicily, June 16, 1882, and had about a half-century of experience before he guided the *Bacon* on her final voyage. Short—about five feet four inches—and weighing less than 130 pounds, Carini had thin hair and a prominent Sicilian accent. Courtly in manner and bearing, he was regarded as an outstanding seaman even if he tended to get excited in an Italian manner.

The son and grandson of Italian naval officers, Alfred Carini had gone to sea as a boy, sailing out of various Italian ports, including Palermo.

At 18 he attended the Royal Nautical Institute in his birthplace before serving as a sailor in the Royal Italian Navy from 1903 to 1907. Later, after serving seven years as third officer on Italian steamers, Carini returned to the Royal Nautical Institute and was graduated with an Italian Master's License in 1915, the year Italy declared war on Germany in World War I. He continued to serve aboard Italian steamers. He emigrated to the United States in 1918, a seasoned mariner.

Carini entered the Port of New York, and became a naturalized US citizen in New Orleans on his thirty-ninth birthday, June 16, 1921. After spending a year in Mexico as an agent of the Weinberger Fruit Company of New Orleans, he returned to New York. Though his official address was 44-15 34th Street, Long Island City, he was rarely at home, usually traveling the sea-lanes of the world as a second or third mate on American steamers.

Carini's attractive wife Josephine was a commanding personality in her own right—"energetic, persuasive, talkative," as one person remembered. Captain Kuta told the story about the time the South Atlantic Steamship Company, for whom Carini was working, was approached by Mrs. Carini, who wanted a certain piece of equipment for her husband's ship. To get rid of her, company officials referred Mrs. Carini to the War Shipping Administration. To the amazement of all, Josephine Carini went to the nation's capital and triumphed over the bureaucracy by securing the equipment she wanted for her husband's ship.

In April 1933, Carini received a license to serve as master of any steamer in any ocean. Although he held a reserve commission in the United States Navy—as an ensign—a few years before the United States entered the Second World War, Carini devoted himself to the civilian arm of the American fleet.

When World War II broke out, Carini was entering his third year on the tanker *Pan Massachusetts*, having served as second mate beginning November 18, 1939, and later being promoted to chief. On February 19, 1942, the *Pan Massachusetts*, loaded with gasoline, was torpedoed, repeatedly shelled, and sent to the bottom off the coast of Florida by a U-boat. Twenty of his shipmates died, and Carini and the rest of the crew were rescued by an English steamer and taken to Jacksonville, Florida. Carini received the Combat Bar for that engagement. Soon he was back to sea as chief mate of the *Pan Delaware*—March 30–August 16, 1942. For this service, he was authorized to wear the Atlantic War Zone bar.

On August 23, 1942, Carini took over as master of the *Pan Virginia*—the first of four ships that he was to command in World War II. He signed on as master of the SS *Robert Toombs* on May 1, 1943, and his initial assignment was to take the *Toombs* on its first voyage around the world—May 1 to October 29, 1943, via the Panama Canal. Again, his chest carried more service bars: the Pacific Zone and Middle East Zone bars.

Later that year Carini applied to the US Maritime Service for a suitable rating and he became a US Maritime Commission Commander in November 1943. No formal training was required for a man of his experience.

Early in 1944, Carini captained the *John Gorrie* for a few weeks—April 19–May 30, 1944—before he signed on to take over the SS *Henry Bacon*.

Carini was anxious to make his first voyage aboard the *Henry Bacon* because she was going to Italy, where he could visit relatives he had not seen for many years. But the trip to the Soviet Union that was scheduled to follow was not appealing to Carini. He was apprehensive, perhaps he had a foreboding of his fate. By chance he met the *Bacon*'s former captain, Ben Kuta, in the New York office of the South Atlantic Steamship Line late in November 1944, and expressed his apprehension. Kuta sought to reassure him, saying he got along fine when he took the *Bacon* to Russia. In fact, Kuta said, "I wouldn't mind being in your shoes." "Okay," Carini said, "then you and I can change command."

"If it weren't for all the paperwork," Kuta replied, "I would."

CHAPTER 5

The Crew

U nlike the "fighting" Navy, merchant ship commanders had to interview and hire their own crews. Captain Carini proceeded to gather a crew for the ship's next trip and he filled his top spot with a 62-year-old first mate of the old school. His second mate was Lynn Palmer, 37, of New York, and Carl Fubel of East Boston, only 22 years old, became third mate. David Goodrich recalls the crew being "invited to attend [Fubel's] wedding in Chelsea. It was a great time, and lasted all night." When asked if he went to the wedding, Dick Burbine said, "No, those members of the crew didn't associate with the officers. It was not something we did."

While most of the merchant crew signed on when the ship was in Boston, many, like Fubel, were from other parts of New England. The heart of the ship, the engine room, was under the command of Chief Engineer Don Haviland of Weymouth, Massachusetts. While only 50 years old, Haviland was older than anyone else aboard with three exceptions—the captain, the first mate, and fireman Fergus White of Boston. Haviland carried the rank of commander in the Merchant Marine.

Michael Norris, a young utility man from Chelsea, Massachusetts, who took care of Haviland's room, said, "The chief was the finest man I ever met. He sure was good to me. When I got on the ship I didn't have any money. He had never seen me before, but lent me some. I paid him back. He was good to all the fellows. Everyone liked him."

Like the chief, eight of the eleven men in the "black gang" were from New England, including two of his top three men. While First Assistant Engineer Edgar Snyder, 37, was from Robinson,

Illinois, Second Assistant Engineer Joseph E. Provencal, 41, was from Danielson, Connecticut, and Third Assistant Engineer Lawrence E. Champlin, 40, from Worcester, Massachusetts. It was Champlin who reported that the *Henry Bacon* was a simple ship, and "did not have elaborate equipment in the engine room."

The chief radio officer was a young Alabaman, Earnal (Spud) Campbell, 22. Campbell remembered that day in November "when I first saw the battle-weary SS *Henry Bacon* in the shipyard of Boston Harbor." It was the fourth ship he served on following graduation from Gallups Island Radio School.

"As I walked up the gangway of the *Bacon*, I was also battle-weary for a 22-year-old from a farm in Arley, Alabama, who had seen almost three years of service at sea." He had just returned from leave in Birmingham, Alabama, and an engagement to his sweetheart, Bea McCullar. "My thoughts at that time," he recalled, "ranged from wishing for that war to end to curiosity about what my next adventure would be.

"Captain Carini gave me a quizzical look when I walked into his office for my interview. He was small and wiry with a rather intense and stern-looking face. His first questions were how old are you and what is your past shipboard experience. He seemed relieved when he looked over my documentation which included a first-class radio telegraph license with endorsements of satisfactory service on three previous ships and seemed to be impressed that I graduated from Gallups Island in 1942. I told him I was 22, and he commented that I looked about 17! We had a 15-minute conversation, in the process of which we bonded and established trust and respect which was to serve us well over the next months. The captain expected every officer and crewman to do a job which would support his idea of old-fashioned discipline and teamwork."

Campbell noticed that welded steel reinforcement plates were being added along the sides of the ship and mentioned it to Captain Carini. "He looked at me," Campbell said, and told me that they were "also installing heating radiators and insulation and that I could figure it out [our destination] for myself. I did. All I could think of was cold weather and rough water and that could only mean the dreaded Murmansk run. Every merchant mariner had heard the horrible tales of those convoys that, of necessity, traveled near Norway where the Nazis had established many bases for their submarines, aircraft, and even some larger surface ships. Since this was the only practical route for getting supplies to the Russians, who were giving the Germans a tough battle, the Germans didn't intend for these supplies to get through if they could possibly prevent it. My instincts told me to get off this ship now while I still could. However, I was young enough so there was still a flickering desire for great adventure. The latter emotion won the day, and I stayed on board."

William A. Herrmann, 32, was the second radio officer. Herrmann, on his first voyage, was a professional arranger and musician who had played in the Ben Bernie orchestra, a big-name dance band in prewar days, and appeared in musical shows, including "Best Foot Forward" and "By Jupiter." This was his first assignment after graduating from the US Maritime Service Radio Training Station, Sheepshead Bay, New York. "I had never worked with a second operator," Campbell said, "although on one ship we had a couple of Navy radiomen who were assigned along with the Armed Guard.... Bill was about ten years older than I.... He was a very personable and entertaining guy and I always enjoyed having him around.

"Unfortunately, the three months' training Bill received at Sheepshead was not adequate to give a person with no previous training in Morse code and radio operations the competence to stand a watch alone," Campbell continued. "So, anytime we were in a war zone with communications traffic coming in, I had to cover for him. Usually I would go to the radio room at four-hour intervals to copy the traffic list then back to get a couple hours of sleep before the next schedule. Captain Carini never trusted Bill's competence, based on his lack of experience, and many times I was awakened by the captain asking me to go make sure Bill wasn't missing some of our traffic. Combining this with my regular all-day shift made for some tiring times. In reality, my workload with a second operator was about the same as it would have been when

I served as sole radio operator."

"While we were in Boston Harbor," Campbell remembered, "Captain Carini ordered us to put a lifeboat in the water for a test of the emergency transmitter system. Normal procedure would be for the second operator to be in the boat with the chief standing by to receive signals in the radio room. The technical chore of assembling the mast and antenna and operating the transmitter was too much for Bill, so the captain asked me to do it. I, of course, didn't realize how important this drill would be in the future. I have always wondered if Carini had some premonition since this was the only time in my years at sea that the drill had been ordered."

All Liberty ships in wartime service carried guns manned by specially-trained gunners from the United States Navy. Known as the Armed Guard, the gun crew was a separate Navy unit of young men under the command of a Navy gunnery officer who also served as morale officer, chaplain, and doctor for his men. The commanding officer of the gun crew aboard the SS *Henry Bacon* was Lieutenant (JG) John Sippola, a soft-spoken, sandy-haired Finn from Hibbing, Minnesota.

Most of the twenty-seven-man Armed Guard crew had already completed a voyage aboard the *Bacon* by the fall of 1944 and Lieutenant Sippola, popular with his men, was prominent in snapshots taken by the crew during a stop at Bari, Italy, on the Adriatic Sea. While in Bari the *Bacon* loaded its cargo—for discharge at an American Atlantic port. The load included 15-3/4 tons of various equipment, 453 tons of 500-pound incendiary bombs and 99-3/4 tons of 100-pound incendiary bombs. A court-martial was also held in the Mediterranean zone for Chief Steward Ernest B. Womack. He was tried and convicted for the larceny of a watch.

During combat the commanding officer of the Armed Guard shared authority with the ship's captain, but at other times he and his men took no part in the operation of the vessel. Aboard the *Bacon*, however, Captain Carini included Sippola as a senior officer of his crew. The Armed Guard lived in quarters apart from the merchant seamen, cared for their own weapons, and stood lookout duty—two hours on, four hours off.

The Navy gunners received intensive training—they learned to swim under burning oil, to identify enemy ships and aircraft, and, of greatest importance, to handle guns and shoot holes through anything that flew or floated. Unlike the gunners on a warship, they are never the hunters, always the hunted. This meant that they and others on the freighter were attacked only when the enemy was convinced the odds were in their favor. Then, and only then, could they respond.

On many merchant ships in World War II there was a certain amount of friction and ill-feeling between the Navy Armed Guard and the merchant seamen; basically the Navy envied the higher wages, the freedom, and the better quarters of the Merchant Marine while the merchantmen resented the fact that the Navy received "all the glory" while they took the same risks. However, there was a high degree of mutual respect and cooperation aboard the *Henry Bacon*, and the two groups were on excellent terms. Only once, the survivors recall, was there any friction, and that was when the messmen refused to serve up dinner to the gunners after they had cleaned up the mess. "We were one big family aboard ship," Joe Scott of Maine reported. "We were all ready to help one another as long as we were afloat." And, as it turned out, even after.

The armament on the *Bacon* was similar to that on most Liberty ships—eight 20mm machine guns and "big" guns on her prow and stern. Three gunners mates third class were the ranking enlisted men under Lieutenant Sippola. The ranking petty officer, Jerome (Jerry) Gerold, a rawboned lad from Minneapolis, was in command of the 3.5-inch gun tub in the prow. William M. Moore, a dark-haired, dark-complected North Carolinian, had charge of the ship's biggest gun—5.38 inches—located in the stern.

The eight 20mm machine guns—four on the gun deck and four on the bridge—were under the command of Frank Reid. A brawny heavyweight, Reid had joined the Navy from Kentucky, but he was reared on the shores of the Atlantic and knew the ways of the sea. He "caught the S.S. *Henry Bacon* August 23, 1944," then accompanied it to Bari, Italy. The ship returned to New York, then underwent her annual inspection by the United States Coast Guard at the Bethlehem Shipyard in Boston. It was decided at that point [October 23, 1944] to put steel bands around her "to keep her from buckling up in the heavy seas." A conscientious taskmaster, Reid insisted that all eight guns be kept in top condition and cleaned every day, no matter what the weather.

When repairs were completed at the Bethlehem Shipyard and the *Bacon* was judged to be in A-1 seaworthy condition, she left Boston on November 17, 1944, heading for New York to pick up the rest of her crew, her cargo, and her next assignment. For safety purposes she was equipped with one motorized lifeboat, three rowing lifeboats, four large rafts, two medium-sized rafts, and a few small rafts as well.

The trip to New York via the Cape Cod Canal, Long Island Sound, and the East River, without ballast, took two days in windy weather. On November 19 the *Bacon* docked in New York where additional minor repairs were completed. Shipping articles were signed on November 21, 1944. Boatswain [bos'n] Holcomb Lammon Jr. signed on the *Bacon* that same day. Lammon previously had served on two other ships, the SS *Azalea City* [December 18, 1943–March 3, 1944] and the SS *Jerome K. Jones* [April 3, 1944–June 12, 1944]. On June 12 the *Jones* came under air raids and attacks by U-boats five or six times. He was an experienced hand.

Spud Campbell recalls the loading of war supplies for the Russians in New York, "then I went ashore to meet my sweetheart Bea, who had traveled by train from Birmingham to New York. We were very much in love," Campbell said, "and as we walked the busy streets, craning out necks to see the tops of the tall buildings, I wanted to confide in her about the ship and our probable destination. But I just kissed her good-bye without mentioning the possible dangers because we had been trained to not talk about such things to anyone. But we did talk about setting the date of our marriage upon my return in several months."

Wartime security was supposed to prevent the men from knowing and telling the ship's destination, but this was more fiction than fact in the case of the *Henry Bacon*. Gunner Gerold said, "We loaded at Pier 60 and as soon as I saw the cargo I knew we were going to North Russia." As the 16-year-old David Goodrich remembered: "When the crates came aboard marked 'Destination Murmansk, USSR,' we lost many of the crew." One of the few men who had made such a trip, Gerold said he "hated to go again. It was such a dreary trip, snow, sleet, darkness almost all the time, plus knowing what the Germans can do to you. I told Gene (his bride of a few weeks), because I thought it best that she did know." When Gerold visited the ship he heard the familiar taunt, "You'll be sorry," coupled with "You'll be cold."

One of the young members of the Navy Armed Guard, Mason Kirby Burr, told his father, "Dad, I'm going on a very dangerous mission…pray for me." Second Radio Officer Herrmann of Cincinnati remembered seeing Russian lettering on the locomotives on deck. "We're undoubtedly going to Murmansk," Purser-pharmacist mate Bob Hunt of Greensboro, North Carolina, told Herrmann. Hunt, it was recalled, had served on the SS *James Oglethorpe*, a ship that had been torpedoed and sunk on March 16, 1944.

In the shipping hall in New York City, where members of the Seafarers International Union (SIU) gathered to await assignments, many stories were told about the Murmansk run. A booklet, *The SIU at War*, put out the previous summer by the union, carried both a photograph and a personal account of one Murmansk run sinking.

It began:

"Many stories have been told of the run to Russia, a trip that no man who made it will ever forget."

This particular tale involved George Bomareto and Floyd Reed, whose convoy was hit hard by Nazi U-boats and the Luftwaffe. They managed to get into a lifeboat when their freighter started to go down and, after five hours, a West Coast ship came alongside to rescue them.

"We'll stay in the water," a man in the lifeboat shouted. "You'll only get hit after a while anyway." Shortly thereafter the vessel was torpedoed.

The last paragraph reported that Bomareto and Reed left hundreds of their shipmates "at a final rest under Arctic waters." Sobering literature for men preparing to sail.

One of the young men talking to the old SIU seadogs was 18-year-old Robert (Chuck) Reed of Michigan. Reed had joined the Merchant Marine as a utility and messman after receiving his seaman's papers in the Great Lakes area, having worked on the Ann Arbor car ferries to earn money for college. "While waiting in the shipping hall," he said, "I heard many tales of the 'suicide' run to Murmansk. I was elated to be returned to the shipping hall after a mistaken assignment to a ship being loaded with goods labeled 'USSR,' only to find an assignment to a Liberty ship called the *Henry Bacon* taking on cargo at the North River pier." This cargo was also labeled "USSR." The 7,500 tons of cargo included heating equipment, farm machinery, construction equipment, and, on deck, a number of locomotives.

Finally, on December 5, after a stay of more than two weeks in New York, the SS *Henry Bacon* had a full crew and was prepared to ship out.

Even in peacetime, the event would have passed unnoticed from a port where more than 90,000 tons of domestic and foreign cargo moves in and out in a typical year. More than half of the foreign trade of the United States normally moves through the port of New York. And under wartime regulations, any mention of the departure would be a severe breach of security. There were, however, always spies and informants who parlayed such information into personal gain…and the loss of Allied lives.

Those aboard the *Bacon* who managed to pick up a copy of the *New York Times* that Tuesday morning found the paper, as usual, full of war news:

• More than 4,000 Allied planes dropped nearly 12,000 tons of bombs on German rail centers in a concentrated twelve-hour assault.

• The United States Navy sank an enemy destroyer at Ormoc Harbor on Leyte, but General Douglas MacArthur announced that the US also lost a destroyer.

- US war bonds sales had reached a total of nearly $9 billion.
- Norwegian patriots destroyed a ball bearing plant in German-held Oslo.
- The Russian embassy in Washington DC, advocated "absolute mercilessness" in dealing with the fascists.
- Nelson Rockefeller was named assistant secretary of state by President Franklin D. Roosevelt.
- Arthur Krock's column carried the headline, "Unsatisfactory Status of Pearl Harbor Case."
- Six American industrialists completed a tour of the western front in Europe and found the war was "far from won." They said reconversion to civilian goods must be put aside and sorely needed supplies rushed to Europe.

Probably there was a bit more interest on the *Bacon* in the racehorse Block Buster winning the eighth race over fast track at Gulfstream Park in Miami than the fact that rail stock reached a seven-year peak. The men were more concerned that they were on a "very satisfactory ship" in a well-guarded convoy, and that the weather was clear and mild, ranging from a low of 27 at night to a high of 49. The winds were moderate. Gulls swooped low over the ship and many men took their last glimpse of the Statue of Liberty as the *Henry Bacon* maneuvered into her position in the convoy and began the first day at sea on the initial leg of her final voyage.

Meanwhile, back in New York, Mayor Fiorello LaGuardia announced that each person should set aside one minute on Pearl Harbor Day "in solemn tribute of the men and women of our armed forces who are giving their lives for their country." The *Times* ran a three-column picture of employees of Hearn's Store forming the words "Remember Pearl Harbor."

Equally unknown to the men was the fact that on that day Congress passed a pension bill to provide aid for the families of deceased veterans of the First World War—a boy in Maplewood, New Jersey, shot himself to death because he was rejected for military service—and civilians at Camp Kilmer were limited to two packages of cigarettes a day. Without these conversational tidbits, talk aboard ship centered largely on women and the nasty quirk of fate that was sending them all on the dreaded run to Murmansk.

Captain Carini and Chief Radio Operator Campbell attended a convoy conference to set communications routines and codes on the day prior to departure. "I remember," Campbell said, "that we talked of our family matters as we spent the day together. Then it was off to Scotland."

Navy lieutenant Sippola conferred with Captain Carini and made known how many tenders, shell-passers, and the like would be needed from the merchant crew to assist the Armed Guard. Assignments were made and drills were held to acquaint the merchant seamen with their duties on the guns. One night during the Atlantic crossing, when the elderly first mate was on watch, the weather became foggy and it was difficult for the ships to maintain their position. "This particular evening we were in the rear of the convoy and by daylight we had gone through the whole convoy and were leading the commodore's ship," one merchant mariner reported. "This shook up the crew so much that the union delegates approached Captain Carini and requested the chief mate's removal due to old age.... This was done on arrival at Clyde (Scotland) on Christmas Day," he said.

Second Mate Lynn Palmer moved up to first mate and young Carl Daniel Henry Fubel became second mate. Fubel's new wife, the former Nellie Vaccarro, was proud to learn of his promotion. Forty-three-year-old veteran Joseph L. Scott, of Norway, Maine, who signed on as an able-bodied seaman, was selected as acting third mate by Captain Carini. He had patriotically returned to maritime service after more than two decades ashore following World War I; he had let his third mate's license lapse in 1923. Scotty enjoyed talking over "the good old days" with Chief Engineer Don Haviland. "We used to sing some of the old songs that came out at that time," and talked about the changes that had occurred between wars.

Radioman Herrmann recalled "an added event" during the Atlantic crossing when the union representative of the crew protested the frequent use of spicy Italian dishes on the daily menu.

"They were evidently to the captain's liking and caused a minor mutiny. The hot sauces, almost needless to say, were discontinued in greater part for the balance of the voyage."

Except for scattered reports of U-boats, with the escort vessels dropping depth charges, there was no known enemy action against the convoy during the trip across the Atlantic Ocean. The weather continued fair and the seas moderate. The lifeboats were rigged outboard and fire and boat drills were conducted weekly.

The *Bacon* entered the Irish Sea from the south through St. George's Channel two weeks after it left New York. As the convoy moved northward, considerable German U-boat activity was encountered. Escort ships protecting the convoy dashed about dropping many salvos of depth charges. "On that day, 19 December," Third Engineer Champlin recalled, "on the 8 to 12 evening watch, it got pretty hot with many ash cans dropping close by. One time the ship's bottom seemed to scrape something and it gave us a peculiar sensation in the engine room.... At that time the fireman, Fergus White, gave me a glance and he said he thought he would go back to hacking. He had been a cab driver and also drove hansom cabs in Boston in the old days.... White was 57 years old and so short (five feet, two inches) he had to stand on a box to reach the feed valves on the boilers.

"At this time the oiler was not in the engine room. He had gone aft to oil the steering engine. He did not come back for some time and I wondered if he had an accident as it was dangerous at night making your way aft. We had a deckload of locomotives, so in order to make traveling easier a catwalk was built above the deck between the locomotives. This was wet and slippery, and some of the men had near accidents which could be serious if they fell to the deck below.... However, my worrying was for naught as Woodie Pozen came back and brought with him our life jackets which he hung up on the generator deck. After that day we always brought our life jackets below when we went on watch."

Later on the night of the nineteenth the *Henry Bacon* anchored in the Firth of Clyde at Gourock, Scotland, and stayed there about a week. The men made some light repairs but did not dare undertake any heavy work because they did not know at what moment the *Bacon* would receive orders to up anchor.

Two men joined the *Henry Bacon* in Scotland. One was James Martin who signed on as an ordinary seaman. A redheaded boy of 18, Martin, formerly lived in the United States, but returned to Ireland to live with relatives. Now he was trying to get back to the United States so he could join the Army. His mother was Mrs. Millicent Martin of Belfast. The other man to join the ship in Scotland was a Navy gunner, Louis Walker. A heavyset man, Walker was about 30, much older than the other gunners. Married, he was the father of five children.

Both the youngest and oldest members of Captain Carini's crew were paid off and left at Gourock. The old chief mate, Cecil P. Colchester, left "by mutual consent" and a 16-year-old seaman, John F. Rogers, was hospitalized for a stomach ailment. Colchester, in fact, was found to be incompetent and, after inquiry by the Coast Guard, paid off. He was repatriated to the United States, where he arrived January 24, 1945. He was not entitled to bonus or wages during repatriation. Some of the men received shore leave the week before Christmas and almost all sent letters home.

Chief Haviland wrote his sister in Massachusetts on December 20:

Dear Flora,

Arrived safe somewhere in Scotland, but this is only half the distance. It will be well after the New Year before we arrive at our destination. The War Department gave us some warm clothing. Here are some of the items: One sheeplined coat, a fur hat, two suits of heavy underwear, two pairs of woolen stockings, and a pair of felt boots with rubber bottoms.

While I was at New York I sent several Christmas cards to your friends. I hope they don't think we've gone nuts. This is all I can think of to write about until I start that gas station.

So goodby,

D. F. Haviland

Military life, whether on land, on the seas, or in the air, is fueled by rumor and gossip. Until the heavy clothing was issued, Joe Pszybysz reported, some of the men lived with the hope that the cargo would be transferred to other ships for the final leg of the journey to the USSR. Many of the crewmen fortunate enough to have shore leave made the ten-mile bus trip to Glasgow on Christmas Eve. Engineer Champlin visited the Seamen's Club in Glasgow and talked with other mariners who were assigned to northbound ships. Goodrich remembers it well. "I remember when I was conned by a Scotsman. He sold me a bottle of Scotch for a few packs of cigarettes. When I got back to the ship and tried to impress the men, we found out it was tea! Was I embarrassed, but all in all it was a good time." It was also the first time he "heard of mistletoe. The Scottish lassies would hold it over our heads and give us a kiss. I thought that was great!"

One fellow told Champlin that the "homeward bounders" said that "things were popping off Norway.... He said in addition to subs...planes came at you.... The people operating the club tried to soft-pedal the stories of the North."

All shore leave stopped on Christmas Day and the *Henry Bacon* moved out of the Clyde to Loch Ewe between the fog-swept hills the next day. Loch Ewe was the protected harbor in Northwest Scotland where convoys for Murmarsk were assembled. As Spud Campbell recalls, "Some three dozen ships were at anchor here, and no shore leave was allowed for the crew. Captain Carini and I were taken by motor launch to a convoy conference in the little village of Poolewe." Campbell remembers that the captain was quite worried about the journey into what he described as "the most dangerous waters in the world." He told the young radio officer that he "was getting old and tired," and was anxious to retire to be with his wife Josephine and their one daughter. "Captain Carini," as Campbell remembers it, "always said he wanted a son, but was not to have one. I sort of felt he looked on me as that son he never had, and I must admit he was somewhat of a father figure to me."

Two days later, on December 30, 1944, the *Bacon* sailed with some thirty vessels of all types, sizes, and nationalities under the protection of a heavy Naval escort which included two aircraft carriers, a cruiser, and several destroyers and corvettes.

Leaving Scotland, the convoy was soon in U-boat territory again. When passing the Hebrides, Orkney, and Shetland Islands the warships guarding the convoy frequently dropped depth charges. Much of the time the convoy received the added protection afforded by gloomy weather. With sleet and snow squalls making visibility poor and with heavy seas running, it was almost impossible for subs to operate.

The *Bacon* made emergency turns several times but there was no actual combat except when a German U-boat suddenly surfaced among the ships of the convoy. The *Bacon's* gun crew together with gun crews from other ships fired anxiously and the submarine promptly submerged. The rumor was that she was sunk by the escorts. At dinner that evening Captain Carini remarked that it was a bad practice to fire with ships at such close quarters and added that the Navy Armed Guard on the merchant ship should leave that action to the escort ships. However, Navy gunnery officer Sippola said his orders were to fire on sight.

"One day on the morning watch," Engineer Champlin said, "I smelled smoke and told Woodie, the oiler, that I thought the blackout curtains on the engine room skylights were afire.... The fire was caused by sparks from the galley range, which burned coal or coke." Captain Carini and other officers rushed to the galley where they found a huge kettle of soup cooking on top of the stove. When all other efforts failed, they ordered the disgruntled cook to pour the soup into the range to stop the sparks. Champlin reported that the fire "was quickly extinguished but not before the commodore of the convoy knew about it, for which the ship got a blast from said commodore."

"That fire in the engine room skylight threw out great amounts of black smoke and sparks," Bill Herrmann explained, "and could have revealed our position to an observing enemy." The Ohio radioman also retained wonderful memories of the spectacular northern lights he saw during this leg of the voyage: "The sky was a massive color organ covering the complete spectrum of colors and was shimmering and constantly changing colors, blending in and out. This covered the whole sky from horizon to horizon—the most impressively beautiful sight I have ever seen."

Champlin said there were no emergency alarms on the way up north. "Except for drills, we had no alerts, as they were called on merchant ships."

The long voyage was completed under fair weather conditions and the SS *Henry Bacon* arrived at Kola Bay off Murmansk, Russia, on January 8, 1945.

The Murmansk run was an incredibly dangerous route. Liberty ships and their older counterparts not only battled the Barents and White Seas but also the relentless Nazi enemy. This supply route was vital to the Russians if they were to hold out against German aggression. Without the Allied ships supplying them with vital materials, the Russian war effort would have been lost. The only other deepwater route available to Russia ended in the Persian Gulf ports. The rail lines and roadways from the Gulf to the interior of Russia, because of their length and limited capacity, would have been unable to carry the vast tonnage of munitions and food needed by the Russian people. The other supply routes were all under German control. Convoys were subject not only to storms, arctic ice, and submarine attack but also attack from the air.

The route for the Murmansk run brought the ships within easy striking distance of German air bases located strategically along the coast of Norway from Bodo, just above the Arctic Circle, to Banak, a short distance from North Cape.

It was here that the *Bacon* and her crew docked.

Chapter 6

Sørøya: Hidden Behind the Pages of History

During the first half of the twentieth century, the world was thrown into the most cataclysmic war in its history. All the major nations and scores of smaller countries were drawn into the conflict—by choice or by chance.

The largest land, sea, and air forces ever assembled raged against each other in colossal military engagements. Some of the engagements are permanently recorded in the pages of history—the Battle of Britain, the Battle of Midway, the Siege of Stalingrad, the D-day invasion, and the Battle of the Bulge. At the other end of the scale were thousands of encounters that went almost unnoticed. Yet many of the smaller conflicts were just as dramatic and horrific. For those who paid the full price, it didn't matter if it was a major encounter or a minor skirmish. They still were dead.

After months of diplomatic haggling, the Soviet Union declared war on Finland on November 30, 1939. Seeing the success of Hitler's *blitzkrieg*, or lightening attack, on weaker nations, Stalin wanted one of his own. His plan faltered. The Finns, under the command of Marshal Carl G. Mannerheim, were experts at winter warfare. The Soviet troops, however, were often poorly led. This deficiency in command was due to earlier political purges that had claimed many of the Red Army's more senior, experienced officers.

The attack on Finland drew negative world opinion against the Russians and provided an opening for the British and French. Both nations had long coveted a mine at Kiruna in northern Sweden that was the Germans' main source of iron ore. During the summer the ore was shipped through the Baltic Sea; in winter through the ice-free Norwegian port of Narvik—then through neutral Norwegian waters to Germany. The Narvik-Kiruna railroad connected on the east with Finnish railroads. An English-French force sent to help the Finns, however, would be in a position to occupy both Narvik and Kiruna. If only the Allied forces could get Norway and Sweden to cooperate.... Both countries refused.

Stalin, fearful of outside intervention, ended his war on March 8, 1949 on terms that cost Finland territory—but still let it retain its independence. With the Russians out of the picture, the British and French had to find another way to cover their proposed actions in Narvik and Kiruna. The joint decision was to place mines outside Narvik's harbor. It was the British and French commanders' opinions that this should provoke some violent German action, and allow them to rush to Norway's assistance...and into Narvik.

Norway, like many of its neighbors, began World War II by proclaiming neutrality. When the Allies mined the Norwegian coast to put a stop to German naval activity there, Hitler's Germany invaded Norway—April 9, 1940. For months, Germany's naval chief, Admiral Erich Raeder, urged Hitler to occupy Norway for its valued open-water ports on the Atlantic. Hitler was not interested until late January 1940. He changed his mind when the weather and the discovery of invasion plans by Belgium forced him to delay the attack on the Low Countries and France indefinitely. Studies he ordered showed that Norway could best be captured by simultaneous landings at eight port cities, from Narvik to Oslo. Hitler realized the troops would have to be transported on warships, and these would be easy game for the British Navy. As a result, the decision was reached for an invasion—when the nights were long. Denmark, which posed no military problem, would be included in the stroke because of its airfields near to Norway. The invasion was successful, though not without its problems.

The Germans, facing almost twenty-five thousand British, French, and Norwegian soldiers backed by the guns of the British Navy, held the advantage because of the rugged terrain and still a greater one, in the Allied units' slow and methodical moves. The Germans held Narvik until May 28, but by the first week of June they forced the Allied coalition against the Swedish border—with a choice of surrender or imprisonment or death.

Though they set up a puppet regime, the Germans met with strong resistance. A government-in-exile was established in London by members of the former Norwegian government. Together with resistance movements, they worked to prepare to return to power when Norway was finally liberated. Liberation was a long way off; it did not occur until May 8, 1945.

The German attempt to reduce Arctic Norway to a deserted polar wilderness is a little-known story, almost unrecorded in American history books. This tragic example of man's inhumanity to man was shaped by larger events. Despite Norwegian sympathy for Finland during the Russo-Finnish conflict, the strange fortunes of war made Germany an ally of Finland and cast Russia as an ally of Norway as well of Great Britain and the United States.

After Germany overran trusting Norway in early 1940, the Nazis eventually brought in perhaps a half million troops—the number is debatable. Arctic Norway, a territory the size of Scotland and half of England, was occupied early. Despite the low temperatures and barren shores, northern Norway with its stark beauty offered significant military advantages to the German armed forces. The incredibly irregular coastlines, indented with thousands of islands and bays and deep fjords, provided the German Navy with safe havens for its U-boat fleet and warships. The Germans also took over Norwegian airfields in Bardufoss and other places, which were used as bases for Luftwaffe fighters and bombers. New airstrips were constructed at various other locations.

Working out of their northern outposts in Norway, the German Navy and the Luftwaffe could protect shipments of Swedish iron ore down the long Norwegian coast and at the same time could, at least in the early years of the war, wreak havoc on Allied convoys to Murmansk almost at will. The bases were too remote to be attacked by Allied bombers.

Early in 1943 the nucleus of the German Navy moved to Altafjord, an inlet on top of the world just south of the Norwegian island of Sørøya. The largest German military base in the Arctic was Kirkenes, a little town in the northeast corner of Norway, just a few miles from the Russian border. In addition to port facilities and airfields, there was a huge military dump in Kirkenes and an ironworks nearby.

In these remote northern areas, German and Finnish troops held back the Soviets for years. However, following the signing of the Russo-Finnish armistice in September 1944, Finland ordered German troops out of the country. They poured over the border into eastern Finnmark, the most northern province of Norway.

Finnmark covered more than 18,500 square miles and was thinly inhabited by some fifty thousand simple — but brave — souls, scattered in small communities along the long, twisting coast. These Norwegians, with a strain of Lapp, were patient, sturdy people who for centuries had eked out an existence in the Arctic area mainly from the sea about them. Hammerfest, the capital, was the northernmost town in the world; the most important town in the province of Finnmark. It had a population of about 3,500.

The treaty ending the Russo-Finnish conflict freed up Soviet troops tied down in the Finnish campaign. With newfound freedom they began to step up their activity in northern Norway by bombing small German-held towns, including Kirkenes. After sloughing across Finland, the Red Army fought a small but decisive engagement with the Germans on the Norwegian frontier in, as one Russian journalist put it, "an eminence festooned with ice-covered dwarf birch."

Without warning the Soviets crossed into Norway in October 1944 from nearby Jakobselv, Russia, and stormed into Kirkenes. Dressed adequately for Arctic combat with warm, stuffed uniforms, fur jackets, and thick felt boots, the Soviets traveled light and fired at any moving target.

There was outright panic among the Germans when the Russian offensive began sooner than expected. By the time the second wave of Russians moved into Kirkenes, all German resistance had ended and the Nazis engaged in a broad-scale pull-back to Lyngenfjord in northwest Norway — some 250 miles by air and twice the distance by sea. The Russians, however, did not press their advantage, but were content to camp in Sor Varanger, west of Kirkenes. On October 28, Moscow Radio broadcast an order of the day from Marshal Stalin indicating that troops on the Karelian Front had crossed the Norwegian frontier and entered Kirkenes on October 25.

The Germans began their retreat the same day, and October 25, 1944, marked a historic day for Norway and a new phase to the long war. The German yoke was finally pried from the backs of the northern Norwegians. In the process, however, beloved Norge suffered her greatest catastrophe.

Devoid of normal human concern for the people whose land they had appropriated for almost five years, the Nazis thought only in terms of slowing down the expected Soviet advance. To accomplish this, the Nazis issued an order stating that the Norwegians were to be "deprived of the basis for their existence...."

The humble Norwegians read the official order carefully, almost unbelievingly:

TO THE POPULATION:

The evacuation of a part of North Norway has been rendered a military necessity as a result of the treachery of a Finnish Government clique.

This evacuation necessitates the removal of the civilian population, as the enemy proved that, in those territories occupied by him, he ruthlessly and brutally forced the civilian population to give him active assistance in achieving his aims.

This means that no shelter or means of existence of any kind can be left to the Bolshevik enemy.... All such installations as housing accommodations, transport facilities and food stocks must be destroyed or removed.

The population in these districts will therefore be deprived of the basis for their existence so that in order to be able to survive they must evacuate to those Norwegian territories which are still protected by the German Wehrmacht.

For this reason, the German occupation authorities have declared themselves prepared to support, by all means at their disposal, the civil evacuation which the Norwegian authorities are carrying out.

In the interests of the people themselves all means by which they can effect their own evacuation are to be used to the greatest possible extent.

It is above all essential for a successful evacuation that all fishing smacks and other craft which are available in this area shall be fully employed. Owners of craft who try to evade evacuation must be prepared for severe counter-measures such as the shooting and sinking of craft and crew.

He who does not comply with these unequivocal instructions exposes himself and his family to possible death in the Arctic winter without house or food.

> (signed) RENDULIC
> Colonel-General
> (signed) TERBOVEN
> Reichskommisar for the Occupied Norwegian Territories

In short, the Nazi strategy was to prevent or delay any sustained Russian advance by leaving only a frozen, barren wilderness—without shelter, without people. Norwegians in the area were to be evacuated from their homes and shipped to a concentration camp in German-held territory. If individuals refused to leave willingly, they were to be taken forcibly or shot. Every home and shelter was to be leveled. Nothing, not even a fireplace, was to be left standing. All possible communications were destroyed as well as all bridges that provided vital connecting links between the islands and the mainland. According to the Allied International Military Tribunal that heard the case of Germany's crimes against Norway, "The grossest case of compulsory transfer of civilians was the evacuation of most of the population of Finnmark county, as a part of the German 'scorched earth' policy in Finnmark, during the advance of the Russians in November 1944." It further was reported that, "As a result of this, about 30,000 houses were damaged, apart from 12,000 items of damage to chattels, amounting to a total of about 176 million kroner."

The Norwegian answer was clear. Echoing the "Give me liberty or give me death" sentiments of America's Patrick Henry, they preferred to take the German alternative and expose themselves "to possible death in the Arctic winter without house or food," rather than submit. Taking with them only those possessions they could carry, thousands fled to retreats in the rugged mountainsides. They left their homes, shops, and all they owned to the ravages of the merciless Germans, who promptly moved in and took or destroyed everything. In many instances the Norwegians were forced to watch their homes being set afire or blown apart by dynamite, and their livestock shot and the carcasses left to rot. In some cases animals were sprayed with gasoline and set on fire—alive.

There was a military rationale for the German tactics. Following an attack by the US Army's Eighth Air Force in November 1943, the Nazis decided to dismantle their installations at Vermork and send the machinery to Germany. As soon as this intelligence reached London, February 1944, the Norwegian foreign minister approved plans to attack the rolling stock en route, despite the danger of reprisals against the local inhabitants.

The Germans had drafted special SS troops into the Rjukan Valley. Aircraft patrolled the area daily, and new guards were stationed on the railroad line from Vermork, in the province of Telemark, to the ferry quay on Lake Tinnsjoe. By some freak twist of fate, not one guard was posted on the ferryboat *Hydro*. At about 1 A.M., on February 20, 1944, three Norwegians boarded the boat undetected and laid time bombs constructed from alarm clocks in the bow. Ten hours later the *Hydro* sank after a "mysterious explosion," taking down with her 3,600 gallons of "heavy water" [deuterium oxide]. The explosion of the *Hydro* marked the end of heavy water manufacture in Norway. All stocks available to German scientists from that source were lost. Such a setback to German atomic energy research could not go unpunished.

Because of the sudden advance of the Soviets into eastern Finnmark, however, the Germans did not have time to round up more Norwegians than they already had under their control in slave work battalions. In Kirkenes, a town of about five thousand, the Germans were in such a rush they left standing more than a dozen little homes. The unfortunates who were captured often were forced to walk with Nazi soldiers on the way to the evacuation ships to protect the Wehrmacht from possible bombing attacks. They were allowed to carry only a small bag as they were herded like cattle into overcrowded troopships and sent to Nazi concentration camps. Some were so crowded in the holds that they could neither sit nor lie down. Hatch doors were kept shut and the air was stifling. There was little or no food other than the meager supplies the refugees had brought with them.

Before the Germans could organize the evacuation completely, however, some twenty thousand of the twenty-three thousand residents of eastern Finnmark managed to escape to the mountain wilderness. But westward the story was different.

Since the Soviets halted their advance at Sor Varanger, the Germans were able to leave rearguard troops to enforce their inhumane scorched-earth policy more completely throughout the rest of Finnmark. The horrible thoroughness of the German policy was intensified as the Nazis moved farther west. At Alta, for example, down the line from Kirkenes, the Nazis carried away 350 horses, and slaughtered 1,500 cattle and 200 sheep. Only 10 percent—150 of 1,500—people were able to get away. Opportunities for escape varied from place to place. Whenever the Norwegians were not within sight of German guns, they fled. Some managed to escape into Sweden, but most simply suffered from cold, hunger, and exposure in the mountains. After the home folks were uprooted and gone, the German Wehmarcht completed its looting, ravaging, and destruction and slowly moved westward to stay well beyond the range of the Red Army.

The Arctic province of Finnmark, where life was hard even during good times, became almost a dead country. Almost a dead country, but not quite. When the Norwegians who fled were sure the Germans were gone, they began to steal out of their hillside caves and return to survey the ruins of what had been their homes and towns. The Nazis had taken or destroyed virtually everything— except the will of the people to live and to rebuild. It turned out that some of the prudent had buried foodstuff and firearms which they could dig up later and use. Some fishermen were able to refloat fishing boats they had sunk. Norwegians in east Finnmark slowly began to rebuild—almost with nothing, even while the German Army was still carefully leveling communities some miles to the west.

In the few areas where the Russians moved in, the grateful Norwegians flocked to greet their liberators—at first. When the Soviets sought to pursue the Germans, the Norwegians gladly guided them over fjords and through the ruins to speed the rout of the despised Nazis. However, minor difficulties developed with the Russians, intensified by the language barrier. In Kirkenes, for example, the Norwegians returned from the hills and restored the telephone line that the Germans had ripped away between Kirkenes and Bjornevatn, a mining community a few miles away, only to have the Russians tear it out again.

Nevertheless, the deteriorating relationship between the Norwegians and Russians gradually eased and by November 10, 1944, Norwegian soldiers entered Finnmark at Bjornevatn, marking the first time a unit of the Norwegian Army set foot on Norwegian soil since shortly after the German invasion of Norway in April 1940.

While the situation began to improve in the Kirkenes area, two hundred miles to the west the Germans were just moving in on the island of Sørøya, across the fjord from Hammerfest. As in other places, the Germans came in and destroyed everything. With communities smashed by the Nazis, Terboven's evacuation bulletin had not been received by the people on Sørøya until five days after the burning had started in the towns of eastern Finnmark. As in the areas to the east, the people, almost two thousand from various communities, fled to the mountains. Alfred Jensen of Sorvoer relates his experiences in a Norwegian book titled *Finnmark I Flammer (Finnmark in Flames)*.

On November 12, the Germans came and laid waste to Sorvoer, the homestead of one of this book's coauthors. Settlements in Breivikbotn and Hasvik went the same day. Many freeholders from Sorvoer and nearby places had escaped the day before to a large mountain cave in Sandfjord where, by the end of the day, there were 160 people. But four or five days later the German ships came and took them away. It is certain that someone had given away where the evacuees were hidden.

"Two of my sons and I escaped from Sorvoer in my motorboat *Solbris* to Bolefjorden," Jensen wrote. "Here from Bolefjorden on the other side of the island we observed German boaters on a mission to burn half the houses in Donnesfjorden. Otherwise it was rather still as we lay in Bole. Four other boats lay there also."

As the weeks went by, the Norwegians hiding in the caves of Sørøya began to grow increasingly uneasy. They had been able to take only a small amount of food and clothing. Now the food was beginning to run out and the weather was getting colder. The full intensity of the Arctic winter would soon be upon them in the wilderness.

Unlike in the east, the German armed forces did not entirely abandon Sørøya. A small contingent continued to camp on one side of the island. Patrols occasionally invaded the rugged mountain area to hunt down the Norwegians who preferred to face the Arctic winter without shelter than submit to the Germans.

Richard Severin Pedersen of Hasvik remembered the hopelessness of those who had been captured as well as the bleak prospects of those who were living in the mountain wilderness:

> Both the deportation of the population and the total waste-laying of the island were carried out with the most decisiveness and rigidity one could imagine.
>
> Nobody who saw the endless line of helpless people, most with only a little package in their hands, could ever forget it. Man and wife, hand in hand and with a flock of children, just like an eider duck family, a strange, unreal sight in the midst of the noise from heavy panzer cars, transport columns, uniforms and commando cries.
>
> Day after day they kept passing. They settled and waited like excited birds...reports on fires, camps which were lighted red, injured animals running about, forgotten sick people and helpless ones left behind kept coming to our ears continuously.... Fleeing people had tried to settle in the wilderness during the cold polar nights. Off and on the Germans succeeded also in capturing some of these, but that so many managed to stay alive in Finnmark without houses shows something of the people's ability to do with little.

One cave dweller built a cottage; the Germans came and found it and burned it down. Most of the cave dwellers found shelter in caves and turf huts. During the last six weeks there were up to ten and twenty people in some huts and the possibilities for sanitation were slim. Many had gotten lice and many families scabies.

Births and deaths took place under open sky or in the turf huts. However, nobody complained or cried because now the first difficulties had been conquered and soon help would come from...England.

There was great concern for the children and older folks as the limited food supplies continued to dwindle and the temperature continued to plummet. As time passed it became increasingly clear that they could not survive the long Arctic winter living in the wilderness. Unless the Germans should pull out of the area, and it seemed that was not their intention, something had to be done.

Word was received of the token force of the Norwegian Army that had joined the Russians near Kirkenes and a desperate plan was worked out. Several Sørøyans had managed to hide their boats from the Germans and it was decided that four motorboats would attempt the trip to east Finnmark to appeal for assistance. German ships patrolled the shores regularly and the risks were great, but, with careful planning, the little boats managed to get away from Sørøya undetected. "Several weeks passed," Pedersen wrote, "and one started to fear that the Germans had caught the boats. And now we could expect a catastrophe with starvation if the help did not come soon." Days and weeks passed before the people on Sørøya learned if the boats had gotten through. As it turned out, the Germans caught one boat, *Sjoglimt*, and killed the two Norwegians aboard. But, three boats got through and made contact with Norwegian Lieutenant Per Danielsen. The survivors told him that some seven hundred Norwegians were starving to death in the Sørøya mountains.

Lieutenant Danielsen immediately arranged for two boats to carry in food and supplies. On January 26 he sent an urgent message that a group of Sørøyans should be gathered in one spot, Reppan, so that they could be evacuated by the small craft bringing in supplies.

On Sørøya, the men scurried about under the cover of darkness, anxious to gather a capacity load of cave dwellers for the trip to east Finnmark. Within a few days the little ships sneaked in undetected by the Germans, unloaded their supply of food, and departed with about 180 people from various places in Sørøya. "But soon we got more and even more exciting orders from the military," Pedersen reported. Word of the doomed people of Sørøya had reached London. In particular, the plight of the Sørøyans reached the ears of one of the most remarkable men in the Norwegian-army-in-exile, Dr. Gunnar Johnson.

Head of surgery in an Oslo hospital when Norway fell under the Nazi heel, Dr. Johnson, a powerful, determined, and outspoken person, left his wife and four children, escaped across the North Sea in a fishing boat, and joined the Free Norwegian forces in England. Dissatisfied with the handling of the Free Norwegian Medical Service, he characteristically joined the Army. Dr. Johnson always had a fascination for Finnmark and had spent many years in the area. He was the father of the medical service plan in the Arctic islands and the ambulance boats used in Finnmark were designed by him. When he learned in late January that large numbers of Sørøyans had been trapped in the Arctic wilderness, he approached Norwegian Crown Prince Olaf, commander in chief of the Norwegian-armed-forces-in-exile, and later king of Norway. Johnson persuaded the prince to accept his plan: to have British warships detached from a convoy en route to Murmansk evacuate the cave dwellers.

To organize the evacuation, Johnson personally made a daring flight to Sørøya in a PBY Catalina flying boat which set him down with only a rubber dinghy and a radio set—and strong determination. He made contact with the cave dwellers and explained that he had arranged for all of them to be taken to safety in Scotland. He immediately and energetically took charge. The man who became known as the "Tito of Finnmark" (when Marshal Tito [Josef Broz] was still a hero in the West) directed that the Sørøyans hidden in the rough hills all over the island should be brought to a central gathering point.

"During the days or, more correctly, the nights that followed we worked feverishly to gather all those from the most remote caves and turf huts wherever they were hidden," Pedersen wrote. "We went through a period of great excitement." The great danger, of course, was that the Germans would learn of the plan and move in with an overwhelming air, sea and/or land force and wipe them out.

Doctor—now Colonel—Johnson received a radio message saying everything should be made ready for the mass evacuation on St. Valentine's Day, February 14. With only a few hours of winter light per day in the Land of the Midnight Sun, the men had many hours of darkness to contact the scattered cave dwellers and make preparations. The gathering place was swarming with activity. Rumors were flying: "Can you really believe...we shall be evacuated to Scotland?" The waiting time was used for work. Many of the men repaired huts and boats.

A number of younger, physically able men decided that rather than flee, they would stay behind and carry on a resistance effort to harass the Germans. Ski patrols, meanwhile, were stationed at strategic points in the mountains to watch for any unusual activity by the Germans. Even the children caught the excitement. They began to play Englishmen and banged away at the Germans from behind snow forts. The women knitted frantically for the young men who had signed up to remain behind. Tension, however, remained in the air.

Colonel Johnson was still a doctor first and foremost, and provided medical treatment as best he could during those busy days, and with few medical supplies. The Sørøyans had not had proper medical attention for more than half a year, but Johnson found the same problems everywhere.

Many of the people were bothered severely by the vermin that infested the caves of Sørøya and brought misery to those who had to live in overcrowded quarters without a change of clothing or even a bar of soap. An attempt was made at the gathering place to delouse everyone. Soap and new clothes were issued to families with infants and young children.

Finally, February 14 arrived. All was in readiness. Colonel

Johnson and Lieutenant Danielsen, who had joined the group, were to meet the warships in the fjord. Both were to join the cave dwellers on the British ships, and when they reached England they hoped to have the British radio signal strengthened for the men remaining behind. With preparations completed, Colonel Johnson breathed more freely. Orders were given. Everything was at the ready. One of the men was waiting in Storelv where, according to the plan, he would lead the transporting of the folk to the destroyers. He would follow along on board. In Nordfjord, Johnson would follow the destroyers. Danielsen would take one of the boats into Borfjord and go along on the trip to the West. Johnson breathed a sigh of relief.

Then suddenly everything was off. The radio operator, John Lorentsen, stormed out of the radio room with a message for Johnson. It read:

> INASMUCH AS EVACUATION HAS ALREADY TAKEN PLACE, DESTROYER WILL NOT—REPEAT NOT—CALL AT SØRØYA.

Johnson and those with him sat stunned. What happened? Could there have been a misunderstanding? Was there treachery? Perhaps London had received a belated, inaccurate, or incomplete report about the evacuation of the smaller band some days earlier and did not realize the large group was still waiting.

Colonel Johnson tore into a rage. Here he was on the shore of the Arctic Sea, where he was risking the lives of more than five hundred people by bringing them to a single collection point—a concentration that the Germans might discover at any time—and now he was abandoned. What should he do? Should he send the disappointed people back to their caves—perhaps to their doom now that food was again in short supply? Or should he break radio silence and risk an attack by alerting Germans who might—and could—intercept the message? He waited only until that evening before instructing radioman Lorentsen to break radio silence and send the following message to London:

> 500 CIVILIANS DESPERATELY WAITING FOR EVACUATION.

There was no answer that night. There was nothing to do but wait. Finally, early the next morning, the following message came through:

DESTROYERS ARRIVING TODAY 15TH AT NOON.

After the night of bottomless despair and fury over the confusing first message, the flame of excitement was rekindled. But Johnson and others could not shake a lingering doubt. Would the destroyers really arrive today, or were the cave dwellers in for a fresh disappointment?

Word went out to the other villages. The weather remained clear. By midday, February 15, the refugees understood what was expected of them. Two men rowed out into Galtenfjord with Johnson and Danielsen on board. Each would board his own destroyer. Near noon, a signal from Borfjord indicated that destroyers were in sight far out in Galtenfjord. The convoy divided, with two in Sandfjord to Storelv, and the other two took Nordfjord and Borfjord. It was a miraculously clear and sparkling winter day. The sun flamed red on the top of Borra. On Borfjord Point, a watch was set up to present arms when the destroyers passed.

When about one hundred meters from shore, the *Zambesi* backed up. The refugees looked at the ship, and saw, for the first time on Borfjord, the White Ensign, the British Marine flag.

"It is self-evident," Richard Pedersen wrote, "that all this gives material for historians. Even though one would prefer to forget what happened that fall and winter, it is both right and necessary that some of this is recorded for the future. Not that it is necessary for those living up here to be reminded of it, but that a crime against a whole district of a country should be kept on record. However, it is not the details of what happened we are concerned with. It is something else, something that tells about a healthy people's soul under struggle and suffering. While the tragedy unfolds in all its breadth, the people's thoughts are filled with a remarkable strength. We all saw our homes burn. One must say and must record that tragedy for all...."

CHAPTER 7

Operation "Open Door"

The Admiralty in London received word from the Norwegian high command, and a decision was made to rescue the Sørøya refugees—if possible. Ships from Convoy JW64, heading for Murmansk, were selected to do the job.

Commanded by Rear Admiral Roderick R. McGrigor, a short, robust man of 52 with a huge, impressive head—he later became Britain's First Sea Lord—the convoy consisted of 26 merchant vessels when it sailed from the Clyde on February 3, 1945. The main body of the escort, consisting of two light aircraft carriers, a cruiser, and 17 destroyers and other escort vessels, joined the convoy from Scapa Flow.

Captain J. H. "Teak" Allison, a determined 43-year-old veteran who had served at sea on destroyers for years, was captain of the HMS *Zambesi* and in charge of the convoy's important outer screen defenses. He was present at the evacuation of Dunkirk and Crete. He also served in the North Sea, in both the eastern and western Mediterranean, in the Indian Ocean, and at Malta. Captain H. W. S. Browning led the close escort inner screen.

Captain Allison was operating under something of a handicap when he joined the convoy. His specially-equipped leader ship, HMS *Zephyr*, had been mined and severely damaged a short time before, and he was transferred to the *Zambesi* just two days before the convoy sailed. This dislocation meant he had to operate with a greatly reduced staff and with less special radio and radar equipment than was normal to handle the control and operation of the numerous units involved.

Before sailing from Scapa Flow, the commander in chief of the British Navy, Admiral Sir Henry Moore, brought the plight of the Norwegians on Sørøya to the attention of Admiral McGrigor and Captains Allison and Browning.

The British had learned that in spite of the severity of the Arctic winter, hundreds of these determined Sørøyans had chosen to risk their lives in caves, snow-huts, and other makeshift quarters rather than submit to the Germans, who had destroyed their homes and ravished their land. The British knew that German forces, still quartered in Sørøya, continued to send frequent expeditions into the mountains to hunt down the people. The patriots were nearing the end of their endurance; their food supply, dwindling.

An initial decision was made to attempt the rescue if it could be carried out without unduly endangering the convoy. If the scale of enemy attack during the trip was so weak that the convoy could detach four destroyers for the rescue and not jeopardize the merchant fleet, the rescue plan was to be implemented.

The rescue was fraught with danger, as entries from the log of HMCS *Sioux* indicate:

"The first direct contacts were obtained," the log entry read, "at 0759 7th February, one enemy aircraft being shot down during the day. We lost one fighter, from then until the end of the trip the convoy was frequently shadowed."

On February 17 a German submarine was sunk by HMS *Alnwick Castle* in the approach to Kola Inlet. By mid-morning, the *Lark* was torpedoed near Kilden Island, as was the merchant ship SS *Thomas Scott*. HMS *Bluebell* was torpedoed and sunk in the early afternoon. "The trip was uneventful," the *Sioux*'s commander, Lieutenant Commander E. E. G. Boak, wrote in the log, "once the submarines had been shaken off, until 0635 20th February when the first shadowing aircraft were reported. At 1000 enemy aircraft attacked. Many torpedo explosions were seen, but with no results.... This attack having been weathered, although frequent shadowers were present, no further attacks were experienced until 1430 23rd February" when the *Bacon* was sunk.

It was emphasized that the safe arrival of convoy JW64 was to take priority over the rescue operation, but this fact was not publicized by Admiral McGrigor or his two captains. The final decision was left in the hands of Admiral McGrigor. Other officers aboard the British destroyers were given the word of the impending rescue no more than 24 hours before they were to sail from Scapa Flow. They had no idea how many refugees there might be, nor did they have information about local ice conditions, boats, or land facilities in Sørøya. Lieutenant Gavin Hamilton, second in command on the *Zambesi*, arranged with a depot shipyard for the construction of a ladder that would be long enough to reach the ice from the forecastle of the *Zambesi*—a considerable feat in the time available, and on a Sunday at that. Large quantities of clothing and food were also taken along for the Sørøyans.

As a gesture of cooperation, officers of the Norwegian armed-forces-in-exile were taken aboard the British destroyers in the convoy. The *Zambesi* had two interpreters; one was a Tromsö trawler skipper named Thor Johnson who was serving as a Navy lieutenant, and the other was a quiet flight lieutenant in the Norwegian Air Force. Some of the British officers felt this man was Thor Heyerdahl, author of *Kon-Tiki*, but as Heyerdahl wrote, "There seems to be a definite confusion of me with some other Norwegian…. True enough, I fought for the Allies in Northern Norway, but although I had been in the Norwegian Air Force for my training, I was a parachutist lieutenant in a special branch of the army…. The confusion seems to originate in the fact that I was really on board *Zambesi* during the war when it had a very rough crossing from Murmansk back to Great Britain." Captain Rudolph Amundsen was on the *Zealous* as liaison officer and interpreter, and Lieutenant Olaf Johannsen of the Royal Norwegian Navy was on the *Zest*.

As it turned out, the enemy maintained almost constant contact with the convoy both by air and by submarine. While destroyers in 1945 were able to give a good account of themselves in battles with U-boats, they were still at some disadvantage as far as aircraft were concerned. The Germans had taken over all the Norwegian airfields and based their Luftwaffe squadrons of Ju-88 torpedo bombers along the west coast. These planes were able to outfly the Allies' outdated Grumman Wildcat fighters, the only type that could be spared for carrier service in this theater of war. Yet the antiaircraft fire from the escorts managed to beat off all major attacks. No torpedo bomber penetrated Captain Allison's outer screen although in one attack his own ship, the *Zambesi*, came within a few feet of being hit by a torpedo.

The commanding officer of the destroyer *Zest*, R. B. Hicks, recorded the following in his log for February 10:

> A real torpedo bomber attack developed about 1030 (A.M.) by about two dozen JU 88s. Visibility was very patchy and seldom more than 4000R so we only fixed a dozen sounds. Convoy suffered no damage in spite of (Lord) Haw-Haw's later claim, and cs (chief of staff) decided that fighters had shot down two and gunfire four more. Only good opportunity was about 1140 after we'd gone back to defense stations when a solitary retiring a/c (aircraft) flew quite close across the bow.

On the way to Murmansk, the *Bacon's* convoy [JW64]consisted of thirty-five ships but, as Goodrich wrote, "the enemy knew where we were going and had planes checking our progress.

"One day, while at General Quarters, the German recon planes were on the outskirts of the convoy. Our Navy gunner on the 5-inch 38 cannon kept tracking. He fired and the plane was shot from the sky. I was on the 20 mm gun next to him and couldn't believe it. The commodore of the convoy signaled 'Well Done.'"

Just before the destroyers alerted for the rescue effort were scheduled to peel off and rescue the Norwegians in Sørøya, the operation was called off and the Norwegians and lower ranking officers in the convoy were left to wonder what went wrong. There was, in fact, considerable misunderstanding. One British officer said that "on the day before we were due to detach we were told that a message had been received to say the whole thing was off and we continued with the convoy." But Captain "Teak" Allison concluded the expedition was called off because the destroyers were needed to protect the convoy from the frequent enemy attacks.

Regardless of the success of British defenses against the frequent Nazi attacks, the Germans managed to torpedo a frigate near Kola Inlet. As the convoy entered into Kola on February 13 it was dark and the fog was dense. Visibility was down to fifty yards. While normal procedure on arrival was for merchant ships like the SS *Henry Bacon* to go to wharves lying towards Murmansk and unload their cargoes, destroyers and frigate escorts anchored off in areas similar to nearby Venga Bay.

The food and clothing brought along from Britain for the Norwegian refugees they had expected to pick up was now transferred to a Norwegian trawler also anchored in Venga Bay. The two ranking officers from the *Zambesi*—Captain Allison and Lieutenant Hamilton—took advantage of their day ashore in Murmansk to go skiing. "He was no better on skis than I," the captain confided. The men were totally unaware that, while they were skiing in Murmansk, more than five hundred refugees were waiting desperately for them on Sørøya.

That night Allison invited the commanding officers of some of the other destroyers aboard the *Zambesi* as his dinner guests. Among others, the guests included Lieutenant Commander R. B. N. Hicks of *Zest* and Commander R. F. Jessel of the *Zealous*, both experienced destroyer officers, though Hicks was only 35 and Jessel, 41. Allison, Hicks, and Jessel ended the war wearing the Distinguished Service Order. That medal ranks just behind the Victoria Cross in stature.

During the third course, between 8:30 and 9 P.M., an officer from the admiral's flagship arrived bearing important sealed orders for Captain Allison from Admiral McGrigor. Word had come from London and the message ordered the immediate rescue of the Norwegian refugees on Sørøya. The project was called "Open Door." Four destroyers, the *Zambesi* along with the *Zealous*, the *Zest*, and the *Sioux*, a Canadian destroyer under Lieutenant Commander Boak, were assigned to the mission. The operation was to be carried out according to the earlier plan with Captain Allison in command.

The ships, however, could not be ready for sea in less than an hour or two inasmuch as they were operating on orders to cut back steam to give a rest to the engine room crews and to allow time to replenish the stores. Under the circumstances, Captain Allison followed the example of Sir Francis Drake in an earlier operation. Just previous to his encounter with the Spanish Armada, Sir Francis Drake and his second-in-command, a Mr. Howard, were playing a game of bowls on Friday afternoon, July 19, 1588. As the story goes, Captain Fleming of the *Golden Hind* rushed up to say that the Spanish fleet was sighted only sixty miles away. All eyes turned to Drake. Not wanting to alarm his men, he whispered an order to begin preparations, and then said aloud, "There's time to end our game, and beat the Spaniards too." After issuing appropriate instructions, Allison and his guests completed their dinner in leisurely style before returning to their command positions on their respective ships.

Lieutenant Hamilton and others were spending the evening in the wardroom watching the movie, *How Green Was My Valley*. Halfway through the film the men were interrupted by the order to raise steam. They wondered what had happened to call for the sudden change in plans that required such swift action. It was not yet known that Norwegian Colonel Johnson had dared to break radio silence to inform London of the plight of the refugees and, according to standing practice, British intelligence assumed that Johnson had given his position away to the Germans. The British Admiralty therefore ordered that the rescue attempt be made before the Nazis had time to prepare and execute an attack on the area. To deny the Germans any possible further assistance, the Admiralty, while issuing orders to the destroyers on the night of the 14th, delayed notifying the people on Sørøya until the morning of the 15th, a few hours before the convoy was due to arrive. This lessened the time any intelligence could be obtained by the Germans. Without this information, however, many British officers were in considerable doubt. As some of them had understood the situation, the first message from the underground said that the refugees had already left Sørøya. Now came a message to rush to the rescue. Was one message false? Which one? "I was well aware that there was a possibility of a trap," Captain Allison said later.

The small flotilla of four destroyers was at sea before 11 P.M.— less than three hours after the message was received. Sailing under a clear, starlit sky, they moved along at high speed, about 30 knots. There was little or no wind, the temperature was 5 degrees below zero celsius (about twenty degrees Faherenheit). Captain Allison set a course some forty miles off the northern coast of Norway and the ships passed within thirty miles of North Cape in order to avoid possible minefields and hostile inshore patrols. The route chosen from Kola Inlet near Murmansk to the Island of Sørøya was about 350 nautical miles and the destroyers arrived at first light.

In mid-February, this close to the North Pole — 72 degrees latitude, dawn came about 10 A.M. The sun made only brief, usually hazy, daily visits low over the horizon. This day, however, was notably clear and bright when the ships neared Galtenfjord.

The plan was for *Zambesi* to evacuate the refugees from the southern inlet and *Zealous* to penetrate from the northern inlet. *Zest* was to support *Zambesi*, and the *Sioux* was to support the *Zealous* by patrolling seaward. The strategy was to anticipate the possibility of a surprise attack by German warships and to have at least two ships in a ready position to provide immediate antiaircraft fire in case the Luftwaffe should make a sudden appearance. The odds of a possible enemy attack were great. In addition to the strong probability that the Nazis had picked up Dr. Johnson's radio message and might turn up momentarily with an overwhelming force, it was known that German armed trawlers and patrol craft actually were in neighboring Eastern Bay on Sørøya at that very moment. Also, German planes carried on almost daily reconnaissance between North Cape and Spitsbergen. But, by good fortune, they neglected to cover the Sørøya area that morning.

All guns were manned when the ships swept down the eight-mile-long Galtenfjord. Captain Allison in *Zambesi* pushed into the southern inlet between high cliffs which gradually narrowed to less than one hundred feet across before opening out into a roughly circular harbor. At the entrance to the bay, a Norwegian partisan, who had boarded *Zambesi* in Murmansk to assist Captain Allison, announced that there was a sandbar across the entrance which would not permit the passage of a vessel the size of a destroyer. The captain, however, was already committed to his course in the extremely narrow channel and he decided to take the chance. In fact, he reported, he had just one foot to spare.

As the *Zambesi* entered the harbor it was approached by a small Norwegian fishing boat; there was no other sign of a living human being. Where were the hundreds of refugees? Was a German trap unfolding? The fishing boat moved in close to the *Zambesi* and the destroyer's guns swung over to take dead aim on the small craft.

A tough, gray-haired, middle-aged man directed the little boat to the side of the HMS *Zambesi*. Powerfully built, he briskly swung himself up on the deck of the destroyer where he was greeted by Lieutenant Hamilton, who jammed a revolver into his stomach. Captain Allison took over the questioning. The captain was soon convinced that the rough-looking man was Dr. Gunnar Johnson himself, the man who had parachuted into Sørøya to arrange the evacuation. Following this strange meeting near the top of the world, Hamilton and Johnson became friends and visited each other's homes after the war. "It was a sad day in 1957 when I attended his funeral in Oslo," Hamilton wrote.

When both sides were satisfied, a signal was given and the impoverished Sørøyan people began to emerge from caves and holes in the ground near the shore. Delighted to see the White Ensign—the flag of the ships of the Royal Navy—flying in their harbor, they waved happily as they moved down to the water's edge.

There was no need to use the ladder that Lieutenant Hamilton had brought from Britain; the harbor was free of ice. The *Zambesi* crew lowered the ship's lifeboats into the water to set up a shuttle service from the icebound shore. The boats were able to carry about thirty refugees a trip, and on the *Zambesi* strong hands lifted the women and children aboard. The men preferred to manage for themselves. "The English," one survivor wrote, thought "it amusing." As the children were passed from man to man along the deck, many of the British sailors popped chocolate or other treats into the mouths of the delighted youngsters.

Doctor Johnson directed the evacuation, and the *Zambesi* and the *Zest*, which had moved in to help, together took aboard some

250 refugees ranging in age from an 85-year-old man to a new-born infant. The refugees were settled in the troop quarters, over-joyed to be in a warm, clean room for the first time in many months. Tables were set in the mess and the white bread, coffee, and choco-late served to them provided more of a feast than the cave dwellers had seen or tasted for more than a year. While at the table the Sørøyans shouted *Skøal!* and drank toasts to the king of England in the traditional Norwegian fashion. The British officers were interested in the islands and asked many questions through inter-preters. "Where are the Huns?" many British sailors wanted to know, and Per Danielsen explained there were two Nazi guard boats lying nearby in Breivikbotn. A telephone message arrived that the boats had just come in. "I should like to see them here," Danielsen chortled.

Meanwhile, the Sørøyan drama was reenacted over in the northern inlet. The men on the *Zealous* and *Sioux* marveled at the sun gleaming off the snow-covered mountains whose sides de-scended to the water's edge on each side of the fjord. "As we steamed farther up the fjord everything was very quiet," Commander R. F. Jessel reported. "There was not a sign of life."

After the two destroyers proceeded about a half-dozen miles, a small boat carrying two men rowed out into the center of the fjord. The crewmen on the destroyer were uneasy. "Things looked very suspicious," said Commander Jessel, "until a man jumped up in the boat and fired a Very (signal) light. It was a prearranged signal, and then followed one of the most impressive sights I have ever seen. Down the snowy slopes on skis came the Norwegians, men and women carrying babies and their few humble belongings, and even the youngsters were on miniature skis. They were obviously very glad to see us."

The *Sioux* first remained back on guard while the *Zealous* moved in close and sent her boats to the pier to pick up the refu-gees. Later the *Sioux* also entered and took aboard the rest of the refugees—about 250 in both ships. Like those taken on the *Zambesi* and *Zest*, they ranged in age from the very young to elderly grand-parents. Lieutenant Commander Boak of the *Sioux* was intrigued with Sørøya and proposed futilely that they stay "for a couple of days to study the situation."

One of the cave dwellers had shot a pair of grouse and brought them to the captain on the bridge. Others brought reindeer steak aboard the *Zest*. The ship's doctor received a pair of skis. The *Zealous* and *Sioux* also furnished the Norwegian underground fighters remaining behind with grenades, explosives, guns, ammunition, food, tobacco, and a keg of rum. The British allowed the men who would remain to serve in the resistance effort to come aboard and inspect the destroyers. They were permitted to look at the artillery and the torpedoes. "I'd like to see the Germans come now," one impressed Norwegian commented. After being oppressed by Nazis for five years—five long years of nothing but the German flag and German symbols, they had learned to hate the German uniform—it was an emotional experience for the men to mingle pleasantly with the uniformed British Navy and tramp confidently over the decks at will. The Englishmen were impressed to see the women carrying Russian pistols. The *Sioux*'s captain requested permission to stay a few days to study the situation. But there was a blank refusal. All ships, the convoy commander ordered, must come back to the convoy. When it was time to leave, the men who remained behind went down to the lower deck to say good-bye to their loved ones—wives, children, sweethearts, and parents.

After a couple of blasts of the whistle the ship's loudspeaker made the final announcement: "Hallo, hallo. All who shall not evacuate must get off the ship." Danielsen was the announcer.

After the men were finally back on the island, the *Zambesi* began to glide off and the water churned as the engine picked up power. As the *Zambesi* slowly moved away, the men who were staying behind waved awkwardly to their loved ones on the deck of the destroyer. Suddenly the women began to sing, "*Ja, vi alsker dette landet*"—"Yes, we love this land." Their thin voices sounded strangely clear in the cold winter air, and the men ashore quickly joined in singing the Norwegian national anthem. Men and women alike cried openly. Most families had never been separated before, and for some it was their final as well as their first parting. Within a few days some of the brave men were killed in combat against the Germans.

When the *Zambesi* and the other three destroyers churned out to sea leaving behind what one survivor called a "street of water" on the surface behind them, Norwegian guards onshore presented arms in tribute and the destroyers hailed in return with their White Ensigns. "Those left behind," Richard Pedersen wrote, "were military and about twenty civilians who joined the military in the struggle against the Germans.... Only a few days later, the Germans came to fight with the Norwegian military units left behind at Sørøya and suffered great losses in both matériel and people."

Traveling at high speed, about thirty knots, the return journey was made without making contact with the Germans, although this did not particularly please the Norwegian leader, Gunnar Johnson. Deadly earnest in his desire to wipe out the Nazis, Dr. Johnson sought to persuade Captain Allison to delay the trip to Murmansk and attack one of the German patrol boats known to be lying in the southwest anchorage off Sørøya.

The request was turned down, Captain Allison said, "because to my view, although the destruction of the patrol boat would have been certain, the operation would then have become known to the German headquarters in northern Norway. In such an event the rescue group would have been put to considerable hazard during return to Kola Inlet. The first priority," he added, "was clearly the safety of the refugees."

"The weather was nice," Pedersen remembered, "and quiet with frost smoke over the polar ocean. Nobody was seasick, neither children nor women. All was well with good humor aboard the cruiser *Zambesi*."

Aboard the four destroyers the British sailors did their best to care for and feed the suffering refugees. About 150 refugees were billeted on each ship. There were amazing scenes on the crowded mess decks of the warships—bewildered old women in shawls, young mothers nursing their babies, and weary old men asleep wherever they could find a place to rest their tired bodies. Children swarmed about the decks. As the result of the long weeks crowded together in the unsanitary Sørøya caves, with no opportunity to bathe, one of the most annoying and persistent problems with these refugees was body lice. Despite the valiant efforts of Colonel Johnson, many refugees still had to be deloused.

Supplies of every type were short. Inasmuch as the stores that had been prepared specially for the Norwegians had been left on a Norwegian trawler now waiting in Kola Inlet, the destroyers supplied the refugees with clothing as well as food. The ship's stores issued trousers to men and women alike. Destroyer crews gave up their bunks and many sailors of the British Royal Navy went without sleep that night so the children could have a place to lie down on the voyage to Murmansk. The sailors also used their own personal money to buy chocolate and cigarettes from the ship's canteen which they distributed to the impoverished people. The actual count was 502 refugees—196 children, 136 women, and 170 older men or fathers of young children. That first night the refugees did not have to hunt for conversation topics. The job was done, they felt. Their people had been rescued from the Germans. As one survivor put it: "All had something to speak about, their impressions had been so overwhelming. The unique floating boat, bread, coffee, tobacco, and guns."

"Their one fear," Commander R. E. O. Ryder said of the Norwegians, "was falling into the hands of the Russians." Another British officer disagreed, saying "The people of northern Norway have always regarded the Russians as their friends." Captain Allison sided with Ryder. "It may well be that some Norwegians regarded the Russians as friends," he said, "but this was not a general view. I had [served on liaison duty] with the Norwegian staff on another operation; they were unanimous in saying that the Russians were not to be trusted.

"Indeed, if the Russians were in reality so friendly," he continued, "why was it necessary to ship the refugees fifteen hundred miles, at some hazard, rather than leave them with the Russians?"

The entire trip from Sørøya to Murmansk took about sixteen hours, as Pedersen recalled. It was, he said, "a fairy tale-like and dangerous voyage."

There was no thought of landing the refugees in Murmansk, but Captain Allison, before arriving at Kola Bay, radioed ahead and asked if the Russians would provide facilities to carry the refugees from the warships to the waiting American merchant ships. The Soviets, however, refused to cooperate—with a firm *nyet*—and Captain Allison's four destroyers, after the wearying high-speed dash to Sørøya and back, had to move tediously from ship to ship to ferry the refugees in groups of fifteen or twenty to each of the merchantmen. The *Zambesi*, for example, visited fourteen ships in succession between Vega Bay and Murmansk.

The *Zest* spent all the afternoon and evening of February 16 going alongside various merchant ships—a dozen in all—to transfer small parties of Norwegians. The *Zealous* and *Sioux* went through the same procedure. "I was very tired by the end of it, as so many transfers involved a lot of concentration and ship-handling," reported the captain of the *Zealous*, Commander Jessel. But the transferring was not without its lighter moments. As the *Zambesi* was preparing to leave the side of one ship which had taken aboard a party of some twenty refugees, there was a howl of anguish from one man who was left behind on the deck of the destroyer. While the language of the far north is very different from the Norwegian spoken in Oslo, the desperate man finally made it clear to the sharp, city-bred Norwegian Air Force lieutenant in charge of arranging the groups that he had been separated from his wife and seven children. The young lieutenant carefully pointed out to the man that he had a different name from the woman and children. The anxious refugee had just enough time to explain before the *Zambesi* moved on that it was ten years since a priest had made a visit to his remote area, but he fully intended to get married formally at the first opportunity.

CHAPTER 8

Refugees to the *Bacon*

A board the SS *Henry Bacon*, the crew watched with great curiosity as the *Zambesi* moved from one merchantman to another and finally came abreast of the *Bacon* and transferred to her decks nineteen of the pitiful, homeless cave dwellers. They were placed in the custody of Bob Hunt, the ship's purser. The group included three families with a total of eight children, a lone teenage boy, and four women—three in their sixties or seventies. Of the nineteen people, eleven were named Pedersen and six Mortensen. Their condition did not go unnoticed by the crew. David Goodrich recalled that he "saw some of the bayonet wounds in the legs of the men."

Henrik and Ellen Pedersen were the parents of Inger, 2, and Sophie, 4, while Johan and Emilie Pedersen were the parents of Elbjorg, 6, and Modrat, 7. The two Pedersen families were not related to each other, nor to the other Pedersens—Ragna, 40, or two of the older women, Aasel Pedersen and Karen Pedersen. However, the third older woman, Ane Jakobsen, 67, was Henrik's aunt. The others were August Larsen, 16, and Simon and Berit Mortensen and their four children, Morten, 2; Bjarne, 4; Eldor, 6, and Nils, 8. Henrik Pedersen's brother, Richard Severin Pedersen, 32, was originally on the list to go aboard the *Bacon* but was transferred to another ship instead, the *Lebaron Russell Briggs*.

Communication was difficult since no American knew the Norwegian language and no Norwegian knew any English. But somehow problems were solved. US Liberty ships like the *Henry Bacon*, with full crews plus Navy gunners, were not equipped to accommodate additional passengers with any comfort. Various crew members had to double up to house the Norwegians. At first, Captain Carini sought to have the three men from Sørøya sleep in the same compartment, but the men wanted to be with their families. Consequently about half of the nineteen ended up in the hospital room meant for four patients. The grateful Norwegians, however, having spent long winter months in crowded Arctic caves, did not regard this as a hardship. "We had a nice and roomy stateroom right under the bridge amidship," Henrik Pedersen said later. "It looked like it might have been a sickroom."

A small crisis developed when none of the refugees wanted to share quarters with one of the women. It took some time, because of the language barrier, for the men on the *Henry Bacon* to find out that the poor female outcast was not disliked by all. The problem was simple: she was still infested with lice from the primitive cave in which she had sought refuge after her home was destroyed by the Nazis. The problem was finally solved by having two of the other women give her a bath—of kerosene.

At the request of Captain Carini, Second Radio Officer Bill Herrmann gave up his room, marked for "Four Cadets," to Simon Mortensen and his wife and four children. Chief Engineer Don Haviland gave up his room to another family and he retired to the office that adjoined his sleeping quarters and slept at his desk.

Soon one mother needed milk for her young child and when this need was finally conveyed to the steward, he went to the ship's pantry and returned with two cans of Carnation evaporated milk. The mother shook her head in disappointment. The steward was baffled and when he returned to the saloon he told the story to the men who were present. One sailor suggested that maybe the mother did not know what was in the containers. When the steward went back and opened the cans, the mother was delighted.

Messman Joe Pszybysz had the job of serving the refugees at mealtime and when he first set out pitchers of milk, made from powdered milk and water, everyone helped himself. But since the powdered milk was in short supply he indicated by sign language that the milk was for the children and the coffee was for the adults. Those residents from the northernmost communities in the world had to be shown how to regulate radiator valves and how to operate showers and flush toilets. The three Norwegian fathers were anxious to be helpful and offered to help the gun crews, but their offer was not accepted.

The crew of the *Henry Bacon* developed a sincere admiration for the nineteen refugees whom they praised for their forbearance. For their part, the Norwegians kept to themselves as much as possible and were anxious to do everything the Americans suggested in the exact way the Americans wanted it done. Eager to be shown what to do, they were pleasant, mild mannered, and grateful for the treatment they received.

"On board the *Henry Bacon* we were treated fine," Henrik Pedersen recalled. "The officers and crew all were nice and entertained us with singing and music." He recalled that the ship's second mate, Carl Fubel, told him that the crew would arrange a party for the Norwegian refugees when they all reached Scotland. A feeling of mutual respect and regard developed between the Americans and the Norwegians. They realized that they would likely share whatever fate had in store for them.

CHAPTER 9

Rest and Recreation in Murmansk

While the thought of dangers ahead were latent in the hearts and minds of those aboard the SS *Henry Bacon*, when the convoy began to form up there was no sadness at the thought of leaving Murmansk. The Norwegian refugees, on the other hand, never set foot in the city.

The refusal by the Russians to Captain Allison's request for assistance in transferring the Norwegian refugees from the destroyers to the merchant ships was, to the British, symbolic of the generally uncooperative attitude of the Soviet officials. The Americans and British could not help but wonder when they saw signs in Murmansk reading, "Welcome to Our Gallant Allies, Heroes with Their Gallant Russian Comrades in the Gallant Fight and Gallant Common Effort to Kill the Foul Nazi Vipers." The Russian approach was indeed different from British understatement and American casualness.

Not wanting foreign money to circulate in Murmansk, the Soviets gave 600 rubles to each officer—Spud Campbell remembers only getting 500 as an officer—and 300 rubles to each seaman upon arrival. Members of the Navy Armed Guard, because United States Navy policy did not allow naval personnel to accept money from a foreign power, had to satisfy themselves with vodka chits. Any goodwill over the rubles and vodka chits was promptly neutralized by the surly attitude of the Soviet officials with whom the Americans and British had to deal. This attitude coupled with severe restrictions caused the visitors to bristle, and sailors hooted in derision when the official Soviet greeting of welcome was read to them.

When Soviet officials boarded the arriving merchant ships, they

91

immediately ordered the Americans to remove all the transmitting tubes from their radios. As Chief Radio Officer Spud Campbell recalled: "This was not a problem, because it was universal procedure not to operate transmitting equipment in port. It did, however, demonstrate the mistrust the Russians had for allies who were giving them material aid and delivering it under the most dangerous conditions." The list of further restrictions was then read—no cameras, printed matter, or weapons were to be taken ashore. Each man was told he could bring into Murmansk only the amount of tobacco, cigarettes, or cigars he would consume personally within a twenty-four hour period. Men found on the street after midnight would be subject to arrest. "My friend Mike Harris and I stayed out after the...curfew," Goodrich recalled. "Two girls—about 16 or 17—with machine guns arrested us and marched us to jail. We stayed the night. The captain had to sign us out; he was not a happy man." Anyone who did not heed the orders of Soviet police was liable to be shot on the spot. Soviet restrictions required each man to show his pass three times if he went ashore. So much for the "Welcome to Our Gallant Allies...."

While Murmansk was on the bottom of the list of ports that sailors were anxious to visit, the men still wanted to get off their ship, feel solid ground under their feet, and roam about a strange city. There was no reason to keep many men aboard ship while she was idling at anchor; even the Navy let half its men ashore at a time. But the Americans found the city grim. During the six-week period the *Bacon* was in Murmansk the weather was bitterly cold—below freezing every day. Living was hard during the winter, even in peacetime.

A city of about one hundred thousand people before the war, Murmansk had taken a terrific battering by Nazi bombers for many months. Thousands of people died and hundreds of buildings were destroyed. The only large building still standing at this time was the post office. It, like so much of Murmansk, had the pervading aroma of molding, slightly wet plaster. Adding to the miasma was the vague suggestion of urine in the air due to a lack of public facilities. "We had to urinate down the cellar stairs" David Goodrich said. "It was at least a foot thick of frozen urine in shades of yellow and green. I wonder what it was like in the spring when it thawed."

The trains were odd, at least to the *Bacon's* crew. They, like medieval relics, had high, old-style funnels. These funnels were required because the trains were fired by wood. The need for cordwood for the trains caused the demise of many square miles of forest, cut down by prisoners of war, mostly Rumanians and others from the Southern Front, conscripts, and those from the ranks of the politically undesirable.

For a long time Murmansk had been a soft milk run for Luftwaffe bombers. The Russians had no fighter planes in the area that they could send up to drive off the bombers, and they were forced to rely on antiaircraft guns and barrage balloons tethered to long cables. Later, after Americans brought in P-38s and other fighter planes, the Russians were able to turn back the Nazi bombers and, by February 1945, German raids on Russia's only ice-free port came to nearly a halt. Now, every morning the lone German surveillance plane would be the only German aircraft seen from the city. Men from the *Bacon* said they could set their watches by its appearance at 4 A.M. Goodrich recalled the plane in a different way. "Many nights," he wrote, "the Germans would fly over, sometimes dropping leaflets stating they knew we were there and would take care of us when we left."

Life was difficult. Normal home life, as well as public life, was gone in Murmansk; it was virtually a military camp. Most families not killed in the raids had been evacuated, and the present inhabitants were generally Soviet officials and members of the work battalions. Most of them lived in big barracks, log huts, or underground. Though they worked a twelve-hour day, many received only two meals daily, and those were served in centrally-located mess halls. Russians who worked aboard the American ships would frequently raid the garbage cans to supplement their meager fare. The air was filled with martial music from loudspeakers scattered throughout the city. The music was interrupted occasionally for official government announcements. "Big Brother" needed to constantly reinforce the beliefs of his followers. "The Russians had one hotel in Murmansk," Goodrich remembered. "Out front was a huge stuffed Kodiak bear. In his mouth was a loudspeaker, playing the same song morning and night. It was enough to make you crazy. I can hear it now [more than fifty years later] as I write these words."

In addition to the Russian civilians stationed in Murmansk, the city was a temporary rest camp for Russian soldiers back from the front lines. R&R [rest and relaxation] meant something different to the Russian commanders than it did to the Americans. Red Army soldiers were ordered to spend twelve full hours a day on guard duty near the railroad switches, antiaircraft batteries, and other military installations, at the checkpoints leading into and onto the docks, and near the huge stacks of American canned goods. These canned goods filled mammoth sheds and were piled on the docks as high as a three-story building. "There's enough there to feed the Russians for the next twenty or thirty years," the Americans told each other.

Many Red soldiers standing guard duty in the bitter cold covered themselves with huge bearskins. From a distance they looked more like tents than sentinels. They were served only soup and bread before and after they went on duty, yet would often refuse coffee offered to them by American sailors. "They were afraid they'd be shot," Navy gunner Frank Reid suggested. "However, some did take a chance and accept cigarettes which they hid in their gloves." Radioman Bill Herrmann recalled that while the Soviet guards were under order not to fraternize with Americans, there were, nevertheless, many conversations through the use of sign language, pidgin English, and Russian-English phonetic dictionaries. Herrmann did bring his clarinet ashore to introduce the Russians to American jazz.

The Russian troops, dressed in their warm, heavy, winter uniforms, contrasted strangely with the pitiful men in the numerous work battalions who wore ragged clothing that was completely inadequate for the cold weather. Mainly composed of prisoners of war with a scattering of political prisoners, the work battalions included many Rumanians and others from the southern fronts who were not accustomed to the severe winter weather common in Murmansk. As they worked they frequently sang poignant melodies, made more meaningful because of their high mortality rate. There was little for the visiting sailors to do in Murmansk and, after a short while, time hung heavy on their hands. With little to entertain them, the men turned to mischief. At least one Navy boy got into trouble with the Soviet authorities who later came aboard the *Henry Bacon* to take him away on some minor charge. "You cannot take anybody off my ship—this is my ship!—and under the American flag!" Carini shouted, forcing the Russians to beat a speedy retreat. Another sailor told of visiting the open-air barter market where Russian peasants would come to trade. "They were willing to trade anything—such as a single shoe—or possibly some grain, or just anything imaginable," one sailor said. In the stores themselves necessities were scarce and luxuries were very expensive. A typical Russian doll was priced at 700-800 rubles.

Gangs of little children roamed the streets and the dock area. Their usual cry was "Cigarette?... *Chunga-ga* (chewing gum)?" Many of them had been orphaned during the bombing raids and survived by their wits and ingenuity. They were too young to be pressed into military service or work battalions and had not yet been rounded up for enrollment in Soviet reconstruction schools. Scavengers of the worst sort, these children pilfered the bodies of the dead, bartered with the visitors, served as procurers of women, and occasionally rolled a drunk or attacked a lone sailor to take his watch, money, cigarettes, shoes, and clothing.

The possibility of attack by gangs of hardened youngsters was just one reason why American sailors were ordered not to go to shore alone. Because of the war's manpower drain, males of the ripe, old age of thirteen were considered adults and expected to assume a productive role in society. In addition to the protection it offered the men, the group plan helped keep individuals out of other kinds of trouble as well. Coxswain Normand Croteau also explained that if an American sailor was arrested by the Soviets he would have his mates as witnesses—"This the Russians did not like."

While the temptation to barter with the youngsters was general, the Navy men, who lacked rubles and were not allowed to spend dollars, were especially pressed for ready funds. Despite the efforts of their officers, members of the Armed Guard from the Liberty ships brought ashore such contraband as cigarettes, soap, coffee, butter, toilet paper and, for very special occasions, nylon hose. For some Americans trading was a form of entertainment. Gunner's Mate Frank Reid was among those who reported bartering with the youngsters for skis and sleds.

"We'd give them soap for the skis and then when we were through skiing, the kids would get them back again," Reid said. Jerry Gerold, Croteau, and others also tried to ski. "I almost broke my leg and was carried part of the way back to the ship," Croteau reported. "Lieutenant Sippola and Steve (Allard) were excellent skiers and had a good time." Lieutenant Sippola also tried—unsuccessfully—to teach Spud Campbell how to ski. Campbell took the skis back to the *Bacon*, intending to bring them back home. "They're now resting," he said, "at the bottom of the Arctic Ocean."

Another sailor on the *Henry Bacon* reported that the crew "found the Russian kids sharp businessmen." He told of youngsters offering twenty rubles for a carton of cigarettes in a transaction conducted on a dimly-lit street corner. After the boys had vanished with their loot, the sailors discovered that they had received a one ruble note doctored up by having the seal colored orange with crayons so it would look like the seal on a twenty ruble note. Of course this trick could succeed only once with a crew. Word got around fast.

Messman Joe Pszybysz and 18-year-old Chuck Reed of the *Bacon* went ashore together and Joe's knowledge of Polish was helpful in communicating with the Russians. "Our favorite sport was trading soap, cigarettes and candy to them in return for homemade knives, the handles of which were formed of plastics from downed German planes," Reed reported. "I also acquired a pair of skis from a youngster." The knives became something of a fad with the crewmen on the *Bacon*. Everyone wanted one.

Pszybysz remembered that he was robbed by men in uniform,

one of whom pushed a revolver into his back. They forced him down a quiet side street where they cleaned out his pockets and billfold. They kept his change, cigarettes, and candy bars, and returned his passport, ship's papers, US paper money, and all Russian money, before directing him how to get back to the main street. Pszybysz reasoned that they returned his Russian money because they could not buy anything with it anyway unless they had a work card showing how many hours they had worked. While no other shady practices were reported by the crew of the *Bacon*, sailors from other ships told of having their pockets cut away so skillfully that they did not know what had happened.

But members of the *Henry Bacon* were involved in various other experiences. Herrmann purchased sheets of postage stamps to add to his collection. Chief Engineer Haviland, his thoughts ever of home, used part of his rubles to buy some Russian phonograph records so he could play them for his family back in Massachusetts. Spud Campbell remembered visiting the Murmansk post office and mailing a letter to his fiancée, Bea McCullar in Birmingham, Alabama. The letter traveled, he said, "through Moscow and God knows where else. It was delivered to her more than six months later with all sorts of Cyrillic stamping on it."

Two of Haviland's assistant engineers, Ed Snyder and Lawrence Champlin, had a drink on one occasion with a Russian Army lieutenant and reported, "The official policy seemed to be aloofness." While the atmosphere was not quite unfriendly, Champlin explained, "I would not say it was cordial." The 300 rubles given to the Merchant Marine crew "would buy," David Goodrich said, "about three glasses of vodka," and there was "only one seamen's bar in town."

Reed reported that he "found the Russian citizens very friendly, but immediately became distant when the members of the military or the NKVD (Russian secret police) were present." Assistant Engineer Joseph Provencal sent a telegram to his wife Marie stating he was "safe and well." On another occasion, Champlin and a buddy sought to enter a Murmansk hotel and were stopped by a Soviet infantryman who held his rifle at port arms against their chests. Apparently they had the wrong door. Armed Russian guards were on hand everywhere to preserve order, break up fights, and handle boisterous drunks. The Russians appeared to tolerate drunks and disorderly persons as long as they did not damage any property.

The main interest of many American sailors in Murmansk was that of sailors around the world—drinking and entertaining themselves, which often meant female companionship. Americans seldom ate ashore, taking their meals in the mess aboard ship. The menu choices in Murmansk were quite limited, and not amenable to an American palate...tea, small squares of caviar-covered black bread, watery cabbage soup, and a fish course.

There were two places for the crew of the *Henry Bacon* to buy drinks; one was the Seamen's Club and the other was the Officers' Club. Herrmann recalled the exotic aromas coming from a restaurant on a floor below the Officers' Club. However, "no admittance"; the restaurant was reserved for elite Communist Party members only. At the club where Americans were allowed, they could buy caviar, salami or cheese sandwiches, and vodka, wine, tea, or coffee. The Seamen's Club had a rule that limited each person to one generous drink of vodka—about a double-shot, with a large glass of green tea for a chaser. While this was plenty for some, the Officers' Club, which did not have a limit and was open to all seamen regardless of rank, received the biggest play, except once a week when the Seamen's Club had a dance. On one occasion Gunner's Mate Frank Reid visited the Russian Officers' Club with his buddy Steve Allard. "It was really a wild place. Gunshots were fired into the ceiling." Goodrich remembered drinking "with a Russian officer. After a few drinks I was on the floor. I was only 17 at the time." Dick Burbine remembered the two hot spots as the Intourist Hotel and the Arctic Club.

The unmarried women in bomb-torn Murmansk were quartered in a barracks colony inside a high stockade; obviously to keep them in, not keep others out. Many of these girls and women had formerly lived in other parts of Russia and were brought to Murmansk to work as waitresses in the Seamen's and Officers' Clubs, as well as do other chores. Women, for example, helped unload the ships as they came in to dock. Goodrich recalled that they were "mostly large women."

Inasmuch as Murmansk lacked facilities to unload large stockpiles, British crane ships were used to unload the heavy deck cargo such as the railroad locomotives carried on the *Henry Bacon*. Russian dockside cranes helped the cargo winches on the merchant ships lift the payloads out of the holds. Women came aboard the *Henry Bacon* to operate the ship's gear, but there was little to titillate the imagination of the men. In their bulky, padded jackets and thick, hip-length boots, the stocky Russian women and men were almost indistinguishable. Also, the official policy of the Soviets was to discourage friendships between the visiting Americans and the Russian women. Members of the *Henry Bacon* recall seeing men evicted from the clubs just for engaging waitresses in conversation.

Even the dances were closely chaperoned and the women were all herded back into the trucks for the return trip to the barracks after the last dance. Some men had a limited opportunity for romancing Russian girls during the showing of Soviet motion pictures to American sailors. The movies, with some exceptions, were of a poor quality, and the usual plot involved a Russian boy and girl who met and then parted so each could contribute to the work quota established by the Soviet government. The love interest, as in western movies of the time, was often between a man and his tractor, though the cowboy's love interest was usually a living, breathing animal: his horse. The pictures were shown with the Russian soundtrack turned off as determined Soviet women would translate the dialogue into English, ignoring gratuitous comments by American sailors. There usually was more affection displayed in the audience than on the screen. Despite the general lack of allure and the Soviet restrictions, American men did occasionally break the social barrier and meet Russian women beyond the confines of the dance floor or the movie auditorium.

There are stories about female Russian winch operators who were lured below deck to the crew's quarters while working aboard Liberty ships. One tale recounts how the Russian shortage of soap and hot water caused one such budding romance to end prematurely. Likely the incident was not an isolated one. No matter how hungry an American may be for carnal pleasure, the assault on the sensory glands can be a strong deterrent. In addition to brief encounters arranged by enterprising youngsters, more lasting attachments also developed. Russian girls could be seen occasionally in Murmansk proudly displaying non-Russian nylons, eating British candy, and smoking American cigarettes. Russian tobacco was coarse by American standards and smelled foul, perhaps to dull the senses to the fetid odors that permeated the area.

There were no reports of personal experiences with Russian women by members of the *Henry Bacon* during their cold, bleak stay in Murmansk, except for the two young stowaways. Nor did members of the crew report using the Murmansk library which stocked some English translations of Russian authors and even a few American books, like westerns, that were politically pure.

Spud Campbell remembered Murmansk as "an icy cold, dirty and uninteresting town." He was, however, very interested in learning about the people since they seemed so unhappy. He believed this was because of the frigid climate and dark winter days. "We were there during the midwinter months of late December, all of January, and half of February. During that time we saw very little sunshine. I spent many hours talking and playing chess with the old Latvian interpreter who was aboard the *Bacon* for the many days of unloading.

"After we got to know each other well, he confided that he was violently anticommunist and had been forced to serve in this Siberia-like place because of his excellent English and that fact that he was, in reality, a political prisoner.

"I was able to learn a lot about the aggressive tactics of chess which their people have always had. The first and cardinal rule was to never go on the defensive, but to find an offensive move which will surprise your opponent. He said a defensive move was a wasted move. And, a wasted move in chess usually leads to a loss.

"He said," Campbell continued, "that his small country [Latvia] had been overrun by the Soviets and his people were being held captive. He also told me that the Communist Party consisted of a very small percentage of members, even among the Russian citizens. This small minority held power and had cushy lives with good perks while most of the others barely survived.

"One thing he told me that impressed my young and somewhat naive mind was that the first thing the officials would do to the war machines and food items we delivered was to remove all labels or other indications from where these items came. He said the government and the system could only survive by keeping the people in the dark as to what the outside world was doing to help them."

Regardless of where they may find themselves, Americans almost always find a place to play baseball and Murmansk was no exception. The *Henry Bacon* Armed Guard crew, which six months earlier had played baseball in sunny Italy, now used hard snow for a diamond adjacent to the Murmansk Palace of Culture. The frozen surface made a surprisingly good playing field.

The Navy gunners aboard ship in the harbor had little to do other than "exercise the guns every hour so they wouldn't freeze in place. Generally we played cards all night and slept most of the day," one gunner reported. "We fished over the rail just to have something to do and we caught little whitefish. Occasionally we could use a shotgun to shoot seagulls that lined up on a rail. The point was to see how many we could kill with one shot." Bill Herrmann, formerly with Ben Bernie's band, would occasionally entertain his mates with clarinet and flute selections. And, there was always the radio.

Lawrence Champlin remembered that "every day we heard radio propaganda from German-operated radio stations and at this time [right before the *Bacon* sailed] they were saying they were stepping up the spring preparations for the U-boat campaign and even now in February the number of subs operating in the Arctic have been increased and they report a few sinkings that week." The crew wondered if the broadcasts were true and "if any were the ships we waited for."

Official duties brought Soviet officials to the American ships on a regular basis, but instead of these contacts leading to friendship and understanding, the visits frequently intensified the ill will that existed. There were arguments over the strict Soviet requirement—resisted by many informal, strong-willed captains of the American freighters—to account for shortages and overages in writing. These negotiations with the ship's masters were handled by businesslike woman interpreters who worked with the Russian commissars. Often a United States naval attaché would intervene. Many of the problems related to unloading the ships, and there were hot arguments over the rigging of booms and related ship gear. Yet there were some harmonious relationships. Frequently the Soviet captain of port and the ship chandler who furnished supplies would visit the officers' mess aboard the *Bacon* and pick up loaves of white bread, unavailable in Murmansk. On one occasion the chandler showed his appreciation by giving Bill Herrmann a papier-mâche image of Lenin.

The old harbormaster, like many Russians, had something of a reputation as a chess player and he regularly defeated Herrmann in a series of matches. Finally Herrmann arranged for him to play one of the *Bacon's* crew who had learned to play chess while serving time in prison. American prestige was reestablished when the seaman decisively defeated the Russian harbormaster. That checkmate did not engender amicable relations.

The soft-spoken Navy gunnery officer, John Sippola, had frequent bull sessions in the ship saloon with Soviet Captain Ivan Arloff, who was in charge of expediting the unloading operation. Sippola stressed the American traditions of freedom of speech, freedom of the press, freedom of assembly, and freedom of worship. The essence of Arloff's argument—the Communist Party line—was that the Russians were doing all the heavy fighting in the war, while the United States merely supplied the material. While this contention was incredible when faced with the fact that Americans were fighting in North Africa, Italy, and throughout the Pacific, it was particularly unfair in February 1945, eight months after the D-day invasion at Normandy and the establishment of a solid second front in northern Europe.

At one point Sippola asked Arloff what the Russians thought about the United States. "If I told you, you would get wild," Arloff blurted out as he stomped out on deck. "These 'fireside chats' did not make for better relations between us," according to Engineer Lawrence Champlin, who sat in on the conversations.

The biggest rhubarb with the Russians emerged over the ballast necessary to ensure proper stability of empty ships during their return trip to Britain. The year before when the *Bacon* was in Russia, she carried 2,400 tons of ballast on her return trip. Now, officially, the officers said they would settle for 2,000 tons, but when the Russians completed the job, few members of the *Henry Bacon* thought there was that much. First Mate Palmer estimated it to be hardly more than 1,600 tons; estimates by other crew members were even lower.

Some of the ballast was sand and fine gravel; however, chunks of frozen sand were included in the ballast. These tended to slide around once the ship was under steam. Also, a few times the Russians dropped large sections of concrete from bombed-out buildings into the hold. Third Mate Joe Scott protested that this was dangerous. He pointed out that the big chunks of concrete might shift with the roll of the ship and carry along tons of sand. Such a shift could cause the ship to list.

Engineer Champlin recalled that time passed slowly for all of them. It seemed that the six weeks would never end. He reported that the engine room crew did the usual keying up of the main engine and packed the pumps and auxiliary engines. The unusually long stay in port also gave the men time to take care of more extensive work, but often they did not have much to work with. "There was not a decent set of wrenches," Champlin complained. "Often we had to struggle with a clumsy monkey wrench. Many of the things we needed had been ordered by the chief, but we never received them."

Engineers had to cover the night watch in five-day stretches, which meant that each man was forced to stay aboard for five days at a time. That was not regarded as much of a hardship in Murmansk, however, since there was so little to do. The ship lay in the stream for the first three weeks or so before she was put into dock to unload. When the time finally came for the *Henry Bacon* to move to the water dock to get the tanks filled, the water from one of the hoses was hardly more than a trickle. In addition, the hose was taken away periodically to fill the tanks of the steam cranes operating on the next dock.

The *Henry Bacon* lay at the water dock for two days and finally was ordered away so another ship could be accommodated. She never did get enough water in the forepeak tank, although Chief Haviland had been told the ship was to be allowed back at the dock for more water. Finally, shore leave came to an end when the *Bacon* was instructed to move out into the stream to await the formation of the convoy. Despite the known dangers ahead, there were no expressions of regret.

Soviet officials, including a female interpreter, came aboard to collect the passes the Russians had issued and any rubles that had not been spent. Inasmuch as there was so little to buy with the rubles, a few men had money to turn back, but others kept some for souvenirs. The Soviets checked closely to see that all Americans were accounted for. Several men on the *Henry Bacon* could not produce their Russian-issued passes and the interpreter became very disturbed.

"Where is your pass?" she would keep asking in her shrill demanding voice. "That is not good to lose your pass; that is bad to lose your pass. Why did you not lose your American documents?"

The men shrugged their shoulders as the woman sputtered away.

It was while this checking was going on that a squad of Soviet officials approached in a patrol boat and boarded the *Bacon*. They asked through the female interpreter to be allowed to search the crew's quarters. But the careful search produced nothing. Later, after the ship was out in the stream and presumably free of further Soviet contacts, the two Russian girls came out of their hiding place. Spotted by Navy gunner Reid, who wrote that "I immediately check[ed] the gangway watch and ask[ed] if any boats were alongside. The answer was no. So I went to Lieutenant Sippola" and reported their presence. The lieutenant began an investigation "and they were found in number 5 hold...well stocked with blankets and provisions, supplied by Merchant mess boys." They were taken to Sippola's cabin, where they were questioned. They didn't provide much resistance, even though they knew they would be sent to the salt mines. Lieutenant Sippola had taken away the knives the women had secreted in their long felt boots. They remained under guard until they were reluctantly turned back to the Soviets. No one at the time said they knew how the women got aboard. Some theorized that they worked as checkers—comparing the cargo being unloaded with their clipboard lists—during the day. "The last day of unloading," Normand Croteau suggested, "they never got off.... The only thing the crew had to go on about who brought them aboard was by identifying the provisions and blankets. Knowing that whoever brought them aboard wouldn't use his own blankets—but someone else's—we didn't prejudge anyone."

The true story of the Russian women was not told until David Goodrich decided to come clean—years later:

Mike Norris and I met two sisters—about 17–18. They lived in a boxcar; blankets and straw for a bed. They wanted to get to England, [so] we dressed them up in overcoats and wool hats we got from fellow crew members.

It was snowing hard, and we got past the Russian guards at shipside; got up the ladder and crawled along the deck to the chain lockers. No one saw us.

We went to the steward and told him what we had done.

He gave us food for them. We got them out of the locker and put them in number 5 hold. It was warm next to the shaft alley.

The next morning we heard a commotion on deck. The girls climbed down the ladder out of the hold and were being brought to the captain to be interviewed.

A tugboat came alongside with military officers and a female crew. The girls would not turn Mike and I in, [but] the Russians would not let the ship leave until someone confessed. Mike and I decided to admit it to the captain.

The Russians wanted to put us in a salt mine in Siberia, but we were away from the dock, so got away on a technicality.

As the girls started down the gangway, the first one was grabbed and thrown in the hold. The second one jumped in the sea. The Russian crew only laughed and did nothing. She was turning blue. Our bos'n [Holcomb Lammon] jumped from the ship and rescued her. She was thrown in with her sister.

About two hours later we received a signal that they had been sent to a labor camp. I think it was then I understood what Communism was all about.

Over the years the men talked about the incident, calling it the "stowaway episode." It "started innocently enough," Burbine wrote, "with a mild flirtation between one of our seamen and two sisters…. Most nights while our ship was in… Murmansk, it was the custom of the younger seamen who were off watch to walk the mile or two to the town and have a drink…before going to the local dance hall-theater…. There was absolutely no fraternization or mingling with the opposite sex, except when the music was playing; then it was back to opposite walls. This drama continued for the duration of our stay in port, with the same seaman dancing with the oldest sister most of the time. During these dances the idea of [a plan to stowaway] was formulated between this seaman and the oldest sister, now involving her younger sister….

"On the night prior to our scheduled departure," Burbine continued, "I was working in the fireroom area when [Goodrich] came through the engine room hatchway and asked me if I was going ashore this evening. Having to work, I informed him it was impossible…. He asked if he could borrow my Arctic parka for the night [since] I wouldn't be using it. Not being aware of the plan…I told him to take my parka and return it in the morning. It crossed my mind then, 'Why does he need two parkas?' But then I was thinking he would need two jackets to keep warm in the howling blizzard that was raging outside. I just dismissed the whole thing from my mind. The weather was so bad the next morning that the harbor was frozen over and our sailing time was delayed until the Russian icebreakers could clear the harbor so the ships could move....

Goodrich "dressed one of the girls in my coat," Burbine continued, "and they approached the Russian guards. The weather was so bad...snow and rain and driving winds...that the guards just waved them aboard when they showed my pass.... Everyone knew who had brought them aboard. Guess no one, myself included, ever included the names when we talked about it."

"Then all hell broke loose," when an Armed Guard gunner spotted one of the girls.

For more than half a century no one would give an opinion on who had brought them aboard. Goodrich did not relate if he and Norris ever told Captain Carini.

Later the four British destroyers arrived from Sørøya with the Norwegian refugees. The ships were promptly oiled, scrubbed out, and made ready to sail.

The SS *Henry Bacon* too was prepared for her final voyage. With a complement of forty-one seamen, twenty-eight Navy Armed Guard, and nineteen Norwegian refugees, the *Bacon* was fully-manned, fully-equipped, but somewhat crowded. Though the crew continued to be dissatisfied with the amount and type of ballast, the ship was judged to be in seaworthy condition.

CHAPTER 10

Leaving Murmansk

U nknown to those aboard the SS *Henry Bacon* and the other merchant ships in the convoy preparing to leave Russia, the Germans had moved seven or eight U-boats close to the Murmansk coast. The movement, however, was not unknown to British intelligence. On the evening before the *Bacon* and the other ships of Convoy RA64 were due to depart, Admiral McGrigor, aboard the convoy flagship ordered every available escort ship to clear the approaches to Kola Bay.

The hunt was not without reward; the British sloop *Lark* and corvette *Alnwick Castle* attacked and sank U-425, which was ten days out of Narvik. By the next morning, nonetheless, a Nazi wolf pack of about a half dozen submarines again clustered off the entrance. They did not attempt to penetrate the harbor even though the Russians did not have a protective submarine net. Knowing that U-boats would be waiting for the Allied ships, Admiral McGrigor asked the Soviets to send up aircraft to force the submarines to stay deeply submerged, but Captain Teak Allison, commanding the destroyer flotilla leader *Zambesi*, said that the Russian efforts to assist were "either negligible or useless." "The gauntlet was an unpleasant one to run," Lieutenant Gavin Hamilton, second-in-command of the *Zambesi*, said "Destroyers came out first and tried to sweep the area, attacking anything in any way suspicious. The merchant ships then were to shoot out at high speed two abreast, forming up in a convoy later."

"The departure of the convoy itself on the seventeenth of February was not well carried out due to the slowness of the various merchant vessels in taking up their convoy stations," Allison recalled. Aboard the *Henry Bacon*, Captain Carini was well aware of the delay. In fact, he wondered if somehow the authorities had forgotten about the *Bacon* which heretofore was up in the forward part of the convoy. Carini kept asking Chief Radio Officer Spud Campbell of Alabama if there was any message yet.

"No, sir."

"Gotta be a message."

"No, sir. Sorry, sir."

But finally the message did come, to the relief of the fretting captain, and the SS *Henry Bacon* moved out in one of the tail end positions in the thirty-five-ship convoy. The *Bacon* started in the "coffin corner," the last position in the convoy. "It was not a popular spot," Champlin said, "especially in thick weather. The ship tended to hang back to avoid ramming another craft." One ship, the tanker *Lucerna*, developed engine trouble and soon turned back. "It became extremely difficult to maintain an adequate anti-submarine screen round the convoy," Captain Allison explained, "and the U-boats took every advantage of our disarray."

Knowing they were surrounded by U-boats, the convoy's commander signaled to stop all engines. After a couple of hours of sounding, they dropped depth charges and, as Pozen remembered, "got one of the U-boats." "One time," Champlin recalled, "the ship's bottom seemed to scrape something and it gave us a peculiar sensation in the engine room. At this time, fireman Fergus White gave me a glance and said he thought he would go back to hacking." White was 59 years old and had driven cabs in Boston.

Spud Campbell recalled being told, "It was a well-known fact that some of the ships which always seemed to be torpedoed as the convoys left Murmansk were sunk not by the Germans but by Soviet submarines. I am still in doubt," he wrote, "of this being the case, but the records show that many ships, including some in our convoy, suffered this fate. My Latvian friend's logic was that it made little sense for the Germans to let ships enter and unload war materials in their cargo, then hit them as they left empty. Many of these ships, I know, were towed back to Murmansk and repaired to later sail under the Russian flag."

David Goodrich thought it strange, "On the way up loaded

with supplies for Russia, they sent many ships and planes to guarantee our safe arrival, but when we were empty they didn't give a damn."

When the *Bacon* was about an hour out of Murmansk, the ship made a 45-degree turn and, as Woody Pozen remembered, "as we made that turn, the Liberty ship *Thomas Scott* came into the place...the 'coffin corner'...we had just left." During the maneuver, Navy Signalman Steve Allard spotted a German submarine and blinked a warning to the *Scott*. But it was too late. A torpedo, probably aimed at the *Bacon*, missed her by about fifteen feet and struck the *Scott*, setting her afire. Engineer Champlin recalled that the *Scott* "kept her position for some time," and Pozen remembered she "foundered there awhile and listed with smoke pouring from her. She floated around for a couple of hours until she was just a speck to us.... Later I was told that a Russian cruiser came to tow in the *Scott* only to be torpedoed herself." The *Scott* sank in about eleven hours. A British sloop, the *Lark*, went to her rescue but was torpedoed as a reward. Later a Russian cruiser came out to tow the *Scott*. It too was torpedoed. The *Lark* stubbornly refused to go down and eventually was towed back into the Russian harbor. The Russians ultimately kept the *Lark* and paid the British for her in June 1945. She was formally handed over to the Russian Navy at Rosta, having previously been dismantled in accordance with Admiralty orders.

"I went off watch at twelve noon, had dinner, and went for a look on deck," Engineer Champlin reported. "Soon after, there was much escort activity—many salvos of depth charges, corvettes and destroyers running all over the pond, and alarms on the other ships could be heard besides our own. We were close together at this time." The commanding officer blinked out orders to stop all engines for a time, and for several hours they waited with bated breath as the escorts dropped a series of depth charges.

The Germans took their first bit of revenge for the loss of U-425 the night before when U-968 blasted the stern off the *Lark*, which had swept ahead of the convoy.

The *Bluebell*, a Canadian corvette, began to pick up survivors of the German craft. "I had just looked over at her," Pozen wrote, "and had turned away...when I looked again there was a great flash of fire and black smoke was billowing there." "A large dank plume of smoke" is how Goodrich described it. After he was picked up by the *Zambesi*, Pozen learned that the *Bluebell* had been torpedoed while rescuing the Germans. "Twelve men," he was told, "were rescued and of the twelve, only one lived." Goodrich learned later that the survivor had been transferred the day before "for medical reasons. I can imagine how he must feel for the rest of his life."

The authoritative British *History of the Second World War, The War at Sea,* indicated that the same U-boat that torpedoed the *Lark* also hit the *Scott*. "Her crew abandoned ship precipitately and prematurely, and she sank while being towed in." But the equally authoritative American historian, Admiral Morison, characterized the action somewhat differently in his book, *The Atlantic Battle Won.* Admiral Morison wrote that the *Scott* "was carrying a large number of Norwegian refugees, mostly women and children, as passengers; but the master effected an orderly abandonment in ten minutes, and the entire ship's company was rescued by a destroyer." The forty-one Norwegian refugees aboard the *Scott* were transferred to the destroyer HMS *Onslaught*, under the command of Captain Browning. The climax of the day's attack was yet to come.

The convoy was still steaming in an easterly direction before turning to the northwest at the end of the swept channel leading out from Murmansk. HMS *Zambesi* was moving out to port of the convoy to take up her station on the outer screen. Suddenly the corvette *Bluebell* began what appeared to be a run on another German submarine. A torpedo from Nazi U-711 struck in the ship's magazine and the *Bluebell* disappeared in a blinding flash and roar under a cloud that soared a thousand feet above the sea. The *Bluebell* was so close to the *Henry Bacon* that the crew "could plainly see the men on the deck" of the *Bluebell* just before the attack. Years after, many carried vivid impressions of the disaster.

"I started below," Engineer Champlin said. "As soon as I got past the blackout curtains in the passageway there was a violent explosion that shook the *Bacon* from stem to stern. I went out on deck and where I had seen the corvette, there was only a puff of smoke, no ship. The ship was blown to atoms...." Messman Pszybysz had just finished eating with the Norwegian refugees and noticed the *Bluebell* through the porthole as he began to get up from the table and put on his helmet. Suddenly there was smoke and a billow of flame—the shock wave hit the *Bacon* broadside and rocked her so badly "it seemed like the bottom dropped out." The Norwegians, also in the process of leaving the table, were petrified—"complete silence, not a word." Pszybysz managed what was meant to be a reassuring smile to convey "it's all right; we're still safe," and the refugees attempted to smile back to indicate they understood what he meant.

Various British officers aboard the destroyers also witnessed the *Bluebell* disaster. "She just appeared to disintegrate," according to Lieutenant Commander Bruce of the Canadian destroyer *Sioux*. Lieutenant Hamilton on the *Zambesi*, the closest ship to the *Bluebell*, told this story:

> I was looking at her when she was hit, and she quite literally went up in a cloud of smoke; when the smoke cleared there was nothing to be seen. We steamed through the area and dropped our lifeboat (one does not stop in a situation like that unless he wants to go the same way), but there were no signs of life, and later when we came back for the boat there was nobody in it.

HMS *Zest* was detailed by Captain Allison to pick up survivors. Lieutenant Commander Hicks reported that the *Zest* found only three members of the *Bluebell* crew, and only one man survived. The understatement of the day can be attributed to Allison: "These somewhat alarming events did not make for a good start for the long and arduous journey still to come."

Chapter 11

The Tempest

As the first severe Nazi attack subsided, a new enemy—capable of even greater violence—had a go at tormenting those aboard the *Henry Bacon*.

A devastating southerly gale blew up on the night of February 17–18 while the convoy was passing through the narrow strip of open sea between the north coast of Norway and the Arctic ice, in the vicinity of Bear Island. By Monday, February 19, the seaborne barometer recorded Force 10, with winds at sixty miles per hour, a full gale on the Beaufort scale. The storm reduced the running battle between the convoy and the German attackers to intermittent engagements. While individual ships became easy targets, the intensity of the storm also frustrated the stalking U-boats and torpedo bombers. "Nevertheless," *Zambesi* Captain Allison reported, "the enemy maintained their attacks both by U-boat and aircraft at irregular intervals" and "maintained constant touch with the convoy by air."

On the night of the nineteenth the gale reached its climax when seas of thirty to forty feet, driven by winds of sixty knots or more, swept across the main deck of the *Bacon*, causing her to pitch and roll in the churning Arctic Sea. The convoy was completely scattered with each ship fighting to hold itself together through the long Arctic night. Within two hours the *Henry Bacon's* flag on the aftermast was whipped to the bunting. Occasionally the distress lights of other ships became visible to the men on the *Bacon* as the ships tossed about wildly.

One of the radio officers, Bill Herrmann, was on deck after finishing his watch and described the disintegrating convoy as a "fascinating sight.... The ships looked like toys or corks bobbing around." For a period of time the *Henry Bacon* lost all contact with her companion ships when she suffered mechanical difficulties, the first in a long series of related troubles.

The storm was so strong and the *Bacon* was tossed up and down so violently that the screw frequently came out of the water and then, when the screw had no resistance, the engine sped up causing tremendous vibrations throughout the ship. The oil line from the crosshead to the low-pressure (LP) crankpin shook loose and Chief Engineer Don Haviland was called. Despite the rough weather, Haviland ordered the engine stopped so the oil line could be cut loose. Oiler Pozen explained, "There are two bearings on the crankpin and the chief told us that in order to get more oil to the after side we should put more of the forward side on the LP [low-pressure] and he said he would have to trust to centrifugal force to throw the oil to the after part of the bearing. We succeeded in repairing the oil line and got going all right."

The gale eased up somewhat by the second morning, February 20, and the escort ships worked hard to round up the convoy. The *Henry Bacon* got back to her position in the rear of the convoy during the 8 to 12 morning watch, just in time for the second large-scale Nazi attack—this one by air. Several dozen German torpedo bombers—Ju-88s—struck about 10 A.M. Despite continued heavy seas, a number of Wildcat fighter planes managed to get off the flight deck of the baby flattop *Nairana* to engage the enemy. The battle went on for three hours with blasts from the US Armed Guard on the merchantmen and the escorting warships raking the skies. Finally the attackers jettisoned their bombs and retired. Gunner's Mate Third Class Frank Reid said the *Bacon* never was in a position to fire a shot.

Later that night Bill Herrmann was on duty in the radio shack. "Several of the planes came in right between the lines of ships and low enough that they could not be shot at without endangering the neighboring vessels," he said. "I remember the escorts saying on radio-telephone, 'Stop shooting at the friendly fighters.' There was much confusion…with some possibility of effort in the defensive fire." Engineer Champlin recalled that "in their eagerness some gun crews were firing on the British planes, but I believe there were no casualties and no hits."

"That reminded me," Chief Radio Officer Spud Campbell said, "of a time earlier in the war when I was on the Liberty ship SS *Howell Jackson* in the invasion of Sicily at Gela. At that beach were many Allied Navy and merchant ships. As our American transport planes with paratroopers came over, one ship mistook these for enemy planes and opened fire. Many of the ships immediately joined the fray and, unfortunately, some of our own planes were shot down with the loss of life by many US troops. Unfortunately, 'friendly fire' is all too common in the heat of battle."

"The attacks all failed to achieve any damage," Captain Allison, the officer in charge of the convoy's outer defenses, reported. "It seems certain that the German Air Force suffered considerable losses," he added, and the official report lists three planes shot down, two more possibly downed, and four damaged by the fighter planes and the combined firepower of the warships and armed merchant ships in the convoy. This engagement was one that US Admiral Morison had in mind when he wrote that British Rear Admiral McGrigor handled the convoys "in a masterly manner, and the work of escorting, of maneuvering of merchant ships, and of shooting by (US) Naval Armed Guards was of the highest order."

German claims were incredible. While a study of official records after the war confirmed that the Allies never lost a single ship during that February 20 attack, German radio announced that it had sunk two heavy cruisers, four destroyers, and six merchant ships. Later, German U-boats were even sent in search of ships reported to have been damaged. "They seemed to get their sighting reports muddled up with their sinking reports," was the laconic explanation of *Zambesi* Lieutenant Hamilton. British assessment was that the Luftwaffe air crews made wildly extravagant claims when they made their official reports initially. These claims were enlarged upon by their superiors and then exaggerated further by the Nazi propaganda experts who prepared material for radio broadcasts.

The normal tragedies and joys of life continued aboard the ships in the convoy. A Norwegian refugee on one of the merchant ships died and was buried at sea. "It was sorrow and quiet among all the convoy during the three minutes when the body was lowered into the sea," according to refugee Richard Severin Pedersen.

"Something of happiness happened, too," he continued. "A child was born to 25-year-old Magna Gimso…a boy, the child was christened and named after the ship, *Lebaron Russell Briggs….* The birth was hailed with grenades and machine gun bullets as if it were a hailstorm.

"A report of this event was sent out over the ocean and also to the American nation by wireless. Our ship was decorated from stem to stern. From the American marine commander in chief came the order back that this ship must be particularly well guarded. The ship had to stay well within the convoy.

"We got thus both cruisers and flattops in front, after, and to our sides. It was as if a forest was planted around us.

"We had all up to this time not had a quiet sleep and rest. Often we had to sleep with life vests on in fear of U-boat attack," Pedersen recalled. "But after this happy incident we were no longer in fear of war or attack. We all knew now that in case of attack the boats in front or back of us would be attacked first."

Those aboard the SS *Henry Bacon*, Norwegians and Americans alike, were also aware that the ships in the rear were apt to be attacked first, and the *Bacon* was again back in the "coffin corner" as the convoy waited for the next foray.

At one point, Gunner's Mate Gerold said, "We were at our battle stations for almost forty-eight continuous hours. We took turns sleeping out in the weather right at our tubs."

Other difficulties continued on February 20.

"We developed steering trouble," Engineer Champlin explained. The terrifically heavy sea hitting the rudder allowed oil to escape, "causing loss of steering control between the midship wheel and the steering engine."

The telemotor system on a Liberty ship is similar to the hydraulic brake system in an automobile; for example, pressure on the brake pedal forces the brake fluid against a piston in the master cylinder which in turn presses the brake shoe against the wheel drum. If the fluid is lost, the brake pedal becomes inoperative. When the man at the wheel of a Liberty ship makes a turn, he forces fluid to a piston which ultimately pushes the steam piston of the steering-engine. This causes the rudder to turn. Again, when the fluid is lost, the wheel no longer has any control of the ship. When the tube became damaged and the fluid was lost, the *Henry Bacon* could not be steered from the wheelhouse or bridge. The only alternative was for the wheelman to move to the afterwheel, which had a direct mechanical connection with the rudder. Chief Haviland, as Pozen recalled, "worked twenty-four hours straight trying to right this." Dick Burbine recalled that one pin on the port steering engine stabilizer had sheared. "Myself and another seaman along with the engineering officer were assigned to hammer the pin back into position whenever the sea hit the rudder with sufficient force to drive the pin out. This way, we were able to maintain some headway and keep the ship headed into the gale."

"Steering from aft without the telemotor is more difficult," Champlin explained. "Therefore we were sometimes zigzagging and falling behind in the stormy sea that was getting worse.... We found ourselves out of sight of the convoy.

"The storm stayed up all night, but early next morning it calmed down and on the 8 to 12 watch we caught up and took our position again, just as an alert was received," Champlin continued. "Aircraft again."

There was a slight squabble at this point, Champlin recalls: About 1:30 A.M. the Armed Guard was dismissed—they had been at their battle stations over the dinner hour. "When they went to the messroom, everything had been cleaned up and the cooks and messmen refused to feed them unless they got overtime pay.... The skipper said he would not grant overtime, so they had to make cold sandwiches themselves out of their refrigerator." Champlin thought "This was rotten treatment of the gun crew." He then went to his room and tried to get some rest. He recalls getting settled in wearing his "stay-up-all-night" clothes when another alarm went off.

"I found out that morning that the first assistant Ed Snyder, had a severe chest cold, and he looked bad to me. On that morning the telemotor piping broke again, but it was repaired in less time than before and we held our position....

"That afternoon, on the supper relief, I saw that the oil line to the forward side of the low-pressure crank had broken off. Now the oiler would have to put more oil on the after side and hope it would run to the forward side.

"The lack of adequate ballast was causing excessive vibration in the stormy weather," Champlin explained.

The terrifically heavy seas continued to beat hard on the rudder, putting a severe continuous strain on the steering mechanism. Chief Mate Palmer and Chief Haviland and his men worked around the clock trying to solve the problem.

"There was a boy by the name of Freddie Funken from Kentucky," Oiler Pozen said, "who was the only one on the ship who knew all about this sort of thing. When the sea hit the rudder, it caused the quadrant to shake badly. Freddie made a relieving tackle which stopped the vibration, and we had no more trouble from that." The effect was to ease the pressure on the steering mechanism.

Champlin reported he was awakened from a nap because of the peculiar roll of the ship. He found that the engines again had been stopped and the *Henry Bacon* was being tossed about by the heavy waves without any power. Acting Third Mate Joe Scott told Champlin that the rudder had been "jumping up and down and also sideways."

"I went below," Champlin recalled, "and only the fireman, Herbert McIsaac, was on the watch, and he told me they were all working on the steering engine."

The steering had torn loose from the mountings and Chuck Reed said that "Big Joe" Marbach, a friendly, powerful bull of a man from Brooklyn, took two others and crawled to the steering room "to rig a manual steering affair" which could be operated on direction from the phone on the bridge.

"Evidently they did a good job to stand the storm we had later," Champlin said. "This is not everyday ship work by any means; it's a dry-dock job."

But the *Henry Bacon* fell behind again during the stop to repair the rudder, and since the weather was worsening instead of improving, the chances of catching up did not look good. Later that day, when Champlin went below for the supper relief, he found Chief Haviland himself at the throttle, replacing First Engineer Snyder who was too ill to report for duty. Ten minutes after Champlin relieved Haviland the engine started to lose vacuum and went so low that the engine almost came to a stop. "Then it would pick up again, after a minute, then go down again," Champlin said.

"I sent the oiler to get the chief because the telephone was in the room where the Norwegian couple with the baby were berthed. He came down and he thought one of the air pump valves caused it. We stopped again and changed the valve discs and checked the springs and the like."

Deck Engineer Wilmo Testerman, 24, worked with Haviland, Champlin, and Pozen for about a half hour while the *Bacon* floated without power and fell still farther behind the convoy. Pozen pounded while Haviland held a chisel to tighten the nuts on the stem of the bucket-valve. But this effort was in vain. "Evidently that was not the trouble," Champlin said, "as the condition was no different. We rolled and pitched…losing vacuum intermittently, so, of course, we were not making any headway. But no ship in the convoy could do more than maintain steerageway in the storm that came up."

The Norwegians, already frightened by the enemy attacks and the storms, were aware that things were going wrong with the ship. They concluded that the *Bacon* must be an "old ship. Anyway, the engine was old."

Zambesi Captain Allison was unaware of the mounting difficulties on the *Henry Bacon* and early on February 22 he felt the convoy was still "in good order" and "on a southerly course."

Then, when the turbulent seas began to worsen further, and the southerly wind increased instead of abated, even the ships that had been able to push ahead without difficulty were now barely able to make three knots.

CHAPTER 12

"Wind Force 12"

On February 22, 1945, the ocean storm off Norway's Lofoten Islands gradually grew and increased to what has been described as hurricane proportions, a rarity in the Arctic Ocean. Now danger engulfed the whole convoy, not just the wallowing *Henry Bacon* that had fallen so far behind. Even the British Royal Navy captains of the escorting warships, veteran seamen who had previously made many round trips to Murmansk, recall the storm with awe.

Commander R. E. D. Ryder, captain of the destroyer *Opportune*, called it "the stormiest trip of the whole war. The barograph trace was a fantastic series of steep curves and...the convoy...became hopelessly scattered." "I can remember that at about five that evening, the (barograph) pointer had gone off the bottom of the paper," Commander R. F. Jessel, commanding officer of the destroyer *Zealous*, said. "Our midshipman clambered onto the bridge and reported, 'The barometer has bust, sir.' The force of the wind was so great that it eventually knocked the waves comparatively flat, and, despite the darkness, one could see that the whole sea had gone white.

"Under those circumstances, the merchant ships were more comfortable running before the wind, which was from the northwest, and the commodore ordered a southeasterly course, which took the convoy towards Norway.

"However, in a destroyer, a following wind is far from comfortable. At about midnight the *Zealous* got thrown off her course, and I had to stop one engine and use power for 20 knots on the other to get her back on course," Commander Jessel recalled. "This frightened me, so I turned round and steamed at slow speed into the wind.

"At dawn the weather had moderated a bit. We soon sighted three or four merchant ships and two or three escorts that had also decided to heave to, and I formed them into a small convoy. During the afternoon we were found by a reconnaissance Swordfish [a british biplane reconnaissance aircraft] from our escort carrier, who told us the whereabouts of the main convoy, which we were thus able to rejoin before dark."

The HMCS *Sioux* like the other destroyers received a severe buffeting "causing damage to (life) boats and upper deck fittings and aggravating a leak in the SA (starboard after) tank and central stores," according to E. G. Boak, its commanding officer. Lieutenant Commander R. B. N. Hicks of the *Zest*, which had engaged in the Sørøya evacuation with the *Zealous*, *Sioux*, and *Zambesi*, recalled that winds exceeded eighty knots and his barometer "fell to 958 millibars, the lowest I have ever known." Lieutenant Gavin Hamilton, second in command on the *Zambesi*, agreed that Convoy RA64 "experienced the worst weather" of any of his "unpleasant journeys" to and from Murmansk. "During the night of February 22–23," he said, "we experienced a Wind Force 12," which is the highest velocity on the commonly used Beaufort scale. Force 12 indicates that winds are above seventy-five miles an hour and classified as hurricane winds. Captain "Teak" Allison of the *Zambesi* reported that his anemometer "broke after registering a gust of something over 100 knots" (120 mph) and he questioned the accuracy of his instruments.

"In *Zambesi*," Allison said, "the lowest barometer reading fell *below* twenty-eight inches. He said the contour formed on the barograph was "familiar in severe tropical storms, but I cannot recollect a similar situation in Arctic waters."

"Giant seas made ship handling very difficult and large alterations of course dangerous," he continued. "The bridge of *Zambesi* was swept continuously of huge volumes of water," and Captain Allison reported the seas were so violent that at times it was possible to see "clear under half-a-ship's length of the hulls of my consorts....

"In the van position myself, I did not see the SS *Henry Bacon* drop astern, but this she did, either through mechanical break-down or sheer inability to keep headway in these conditions."

Indeed, the faltering *Henry Bacon*, now tossed about by hurricane winds and losing vacuum intermittently, was again separated from the convoy—and for the last time. The ship's screw was thrown out of the water about half the time and the engine was cut down to 58 revolutions. Terrifying winds buffeted the ship and waves lashed the main deck, the boat deck, and even the flying bridge. The binnacle (which contained the ship's compass) was washed off the poop deck by the seas. Third Mate Joe Scott stated that "when we lost visual contact with the convoy, we received orders to change our course to 240 degrees true."

"During the storm," William Willdridge recalled, "the steering engine got out of order and [Haviland] worked on it nearly all day although he didn't have to, as it wasn't his job." Haviland wanted to complete the repair quickly so they could return to the convoy. The 27-year-veteran of the Merchant Marine who had seen war firsthand in "the war to end all wars," knew that the *Bacon* was a sitting duck if it remained outside the protection of the destroyers.

That was not the only damage to the *Bacon*. Chuck Reed recalled that "the superstructure was caved in, in one place...all but two lifeboats were carried away or damaged, liferafts were torn from their lashings, the ballast shifted and, worst of all, the main steam condenser quit, and the engines slowed to an idle. As if this were not enough," he continued, "the hydraulic lines to the steering room ruptured and we were without control. The steering engines had also torn loose from the mountings. 'Big Joe' Marbach...took two other men and crawled to the steering room to rig a manual steering affair which they operated on direction from the bridge phone."

The Norwegian refugees, merchant crew, and Navy gunners alike were being tossed about with a violence no one aboard had ever experienced. For the Norwegian landfolk the situation was utterly miserable. Most of the men were seasick, yet managed as best they could. But for the women and children it was worse. In addition to being violently seasick for so many days that they were physically weakened from lack of food, they now were being physically thrown about their quarters.

"The savage Arctic gale will live in my memory as the most terrifying experience of my life. The eventual sinking seemed an anticlimax to it," Chuck Reed said, "…The anemometer on the bridge had its bearings burned out and left the needle stuck at a reading of 112 mph. The seas grew to an estimated eighty to ninety feet. The outdoor temperature was about twenty-six degrees and the seawater about twenty-eight degrees F. We all donned life preservers and some donned the rubber Arctic suits which were designed to aid in survival in cold water, but improper use often caused the wearer to sink when it filled with water.

"We were told that we could expect to live about a minute for each degree above zero water temperature. These terrifying prospects caused one seaman to go berserk and throw himself over the side."

"You had to hang on to something to prevent being thrown across the engine room," Champlin said. "Once Woodie (Pozen) was thrown from the IP (intermediate pressure) column into the bilge gutter over the end of the floor plates. I was surprised he did not break any bones."

"Just like the movies, *Convoy to Murmansk*," Pozen cracked.

"When I finished my watch," Champlin said, "I took a look in the crew's mess and most of the crew was around there as there was no sleeping that night.

"By this time we had developed a heavy list, and it was so bad that the men sitting at one side of the mess table were nowhere near the height of the men on the other side of the table.

"I later tried lying on the deck of my room wedged between the bunks and the bulkhead, but it did not work."

Herrmann, who slept in the salon after giving up his room to a Norwegian family, recalled that "the storm forced open all my dresser drawers which were locked. I went up to get some clothing and found everything all over the room. I attempted to get some order out of the room but gave up. It was impossible to even keep from being knocked down or worse."

Captain Carini and the Navy signalmen who worked with him, Seamen Third Class Steve Allard and Johnny Fallon, did not try to sleep. With a faltering ship hopelessly separated from the convoy in enemy-infested seas now churned by hurricane winds, the captain stayed at his post on the bridge all through the night. "Without Captain Carini's courage and seamanship we were all lost," Seaman Fallon said, calling the diminutive Carini "the biggest little man that ever lived, without whom there would have been *no* survivors.... I spent the last thirty hours on the bridge with him."

A Norwegian refugee, well schooled in the ways of both war and the Arctic, pointed out that while the convoy had "kept out in open seas, close to the edge of the ice" in order to avoid being too close to the occupied Norwegian coast, "the *Henry Bacon* had been driven nearer the coast by the storm." Chuck Reed feared "that unless the storm broke and repairs were expedited, we would be within sight of the coast of Norway and the German base at Hammerfest."

Still in touch with the limited-range convoy radio, the *Bacon* received a message about 10 P.M. from the convoy commodore to change course from 210 degrees true to 165 degrees true to ride out the storm.

By midnight on February 22 the blue stern lights of some of the vessels could still be seen bobbing in the distance from the deck of the *Bacon*, but by 3:30 A.M. the next day the silhouettes of the rocking hulls and the lights were out of sight and the *Henry Bacon* had lost radio contact with the other ships. Her engines stopped once more and the ship again had to drift.

"Only Captain Carini's skill and determination—and the will of the Almighty—kept the *Henry Bacon* from being swamped and swallowed up by the Arctic Ocean," Reed said.

"While lying helpless in the towering seas, the *Henry Bacon* broached and made one roll of 57 degrees," according to Chuck Reed. "A 45-degree roll was considered critical. How she righted, only God knows."

Messman Pszybysz reported that water flooding into the *Bacon* was a foot high in the passageways and would have swamped the ship had she not been tossed upright by a following wave. Radioman Herrmann recalled "the pitch was so severe it seemed we could almost walk on the bulkheads." Incredibly, the indomitable *Henry Bacon* did right herself and once more began to move under its own power, and Captain Carini made a determined effort to locate the convoy.

About five o'clock in the morning the storm gradually began to subside. "Luck was on our side," Reed believed, "and we began to head out to sea to rejoin the convoy." After the ship had gone through a frustrating series of mechanical breakdowns, and the worst Arctic storm in the lifetime of the Arctic-bred Norwegian men, surprisingly the ship began to function reasonably well and, despite some steering difficulties, began to make significant headway.

The officers of the *Bacon* did not know that the escorting warships themselves had been scattered and were now trying to join forces and round up the merchantmen. The *Zealous*, for example, sighted four merchant ships and two or three escorts shortly after dawn and Commanding Officer Jessel formed them into a small convoy. It was not until that afternoon that the *Zealous* and her little convoy were spotted by a Swordfish reconnaissance plane from the escort carrier and guided back to the main convoy before dark.

With the *Bacon's* first engineer, Ed Snyder, still too sick to report for duty, Joseph Provencal and Lawrence Champlin were standing six-hour instead of four-hour watches. When Champlin went back on duty at 6 A.M., after a sleepless night, he and Provencal suggested to the chief engineer that the *Bacon's* engine, cut down to fifty-eight revolutions at the height of the storm, now be speeded up.

Chief Haviland consulted with Captain Carini and "soon we were turning eighty revolutions in a moderate sea and evidently making fair speed. We proceeded at this rate for about seven hours, but still did not sight the convoy."

The storm had caused external damage as well as strained almost to the breaking point the innards of the ship. One area of the superstructure of the *Bacon* had caved in and life rafts were torn loose from their lashings. At least one large raft was severely damaged.

One of the four lifeboats, number four, had been thrown from its cradle onto the deck. The forward davit had snapped off so it could not be lowered. It was not customary for merchant ships to carry extra davits and there was no way it could be repaired. One seaman observed with a shrug that not one of the four big rafts and one of the four lifeboats would be useless if the ship should have to be abandoned.

"As the late dawn arrived on the twenty-third," Campbell wrote, "we were so tired that it seemed that the improving weather was overdue. I had been on duty in the radio room more than three days and nights. This was a case where Carini insisted that I stay on duty to cover for Bill's inability to receive Morse code at the speed it was coming in. We ate snacks and sometimes dozed in our chairs. The water had been so rough, it was impossible to move around the passageways and up and down stairways. By 10 A.M. on that day we were on alert for attack but were hopeful that it would not come so that we all could get some rest."

At about 10 A.M., on the morning of February 23, the *Bacon's* radio operator received a message from one of the British destroyers that a party of German torpedo bombers was on the way out to attack the convoy. Crew members believe this was somewhere between Hammerfest, Norway, and Spitsbergen. At the time the *Bacon* was about fifty to sixty miles from the convoy. Captain Carini immediately ordered battle stations. The enemy had been spotted, Reed remembered, "apparently by a plane from our 'baby flattop.'" The *Bacon's* crew stayed at battle stations through lunch, leaving their posts by twos and threes only to go to chow. Reed said that he "had just finished my lunch and was sitting on number 4 hatch cover having a smoke when I saw someone point astern at what appeared to be a line of ducks coming low over the water.... We sat watching the approaching planes in silence—counting them over and over. There were twenty-three of them, fast two-motor torpedo bombers—H-111Ks and Ju-88s." At about 1:30 P.M., Woodie

Pozen went below to change into his heavy weather gear. "Just as I pulled on my last felt," he said, "I heard someone shout 'Here they come!'"

CHAPTER 13

"A Swarm of Bees"

Though convoy RA64's barometer readings recorded the wind at a Force 8 gale for the afternoon of February 23, the men on the *Bacon* regarded the sea as placid compared to the hurricane Force 12 velocity of the night before. The ship, despite the earlier breakdowns and lingering difficulty with the steering apparatus, was making reasonably good speed. After the hurricane winds subsided Captain Carini returned to the course set for the convoy many hours before, but he still was unable to locate any of the other ships although he had a lookout posted in the crow's nest to maintain constant watch. Unlike the commodore's ship, freighters like the *Bacon* were not equipped with radar.

Wartime regulations forbade the use of the transmitter in the radio shack, but the ship did have a Marconi receiver in the pilothouse on the bridge. The officer on watch could again receive messages from the convoy and hear the warship escorts talk among themselves.

Captain Carini, after conferring with the ship's officers, decided to turn back and retrace the *Bacon's* course on the chance that the convoy had been overtaken and passed when it was delayed to regroup following the hurricane.

About 1:30 P.M. the *Henry Bacon* made a 180-degree turn and Carini informed Third Mate Scott that he would continue the reverse course for about an hour.

"We could still hear the convoy escorts on the radio telephone," Gunner's Mate Gerold reported. Convinced he was closing in on the convoy, the captain playfully offered a five dollar bill to the first man who spotted it. Dozens of pairs of eyes peered into the distance. Some of the more fortunate had access to binoculars and gun sights. According to scuttlebutt, the ship was drawing nearer the convoy, but in reality the *Bacon* was unwittingly now heading in the wrong direction.

About 2 P.M. something began to materialize on the horizon off the starboard bow. Third powder man Gene Daniels of South Carolina on the three-inch gun spotted the forms in the east and had the hopeful notion that it was the convoy coming into sight. To young outdoorsman Chuck Reed from Michigan it looked like a line of ducks coming low over the water. Others reported they thought it might be geese. "The planes looked like a swarm of bees to me," said Pszybysz who dashed out of the shower, stopping only long enough to don his sheepskin coat and a pair of galoshes before rushing to his position on number 7 machine gun. He left his underwear and the rest of his clothes in the forecastle.

Soon it was certain that it was neither ducks nor geese, but a squadron of planes heading toward the *Bacon*. Chief Mate Lynn Palmer of New York counted twenty-three aircraft as he peered through his binoculars. As they gradually came closer, Reed and the others counted them over and over again.

Chief Donald Haviland came up from the engine room to have a look and when he came down again he told his men that the planes were approaching. Third Engineer Champlin went to his emergency station and put the engine room emergency lighting system into service. This consisted of ten kerosene lanterns which were hung in critical spots in the engine room to provide light in case the electrical power of the ship was knocked out by a hit or near miss.

Haviland ordered all watertight doors made secure.

"By dawn on the twenty-third," *Zambesi* Captain Allison said, "the weather had moderated slightly, but conditions were still very bad. As the destroyers were beginning to be low on fuel I gave orders to those on the outer screen to flood empty tanks with seawater in order to improve stability. This was done. About 10:30 all ships were alerted for an attack by...German aircraft." The alert had come from the convoy flagship, which was filled with extremely efficient early warning radar equipment, and the warning was passed along to all ships in the convoy by the limited-range, high-frequency transmitter. Alone, and perhaps fifty miles from the convoy, the *Henry Bacon* monitored the warning and Captain Carini sounded the general alarm. The planes picked up on the radar scope no doubt were from the large German air base at Bardufoss, midway between Tromso and Narvik in northern Norway, a thousand miles from the nearest British base. The distance and the impregnable coastline, with a screen of islands and thousands of fjords and sounds serving as a haven for elements of the Nazi U-boat fleet, prevented any possible British attack on Bardufoss.

Upon hearing the general alarm, the gunners and crewmen on the *Bacon* rushed to their battle stations. The refugees were herded into their cramped quarters and the ship braced for attack. The minutes passed; an hour, then several hours went by and there still was no sign of the Luftwaffe. Tension began to ease up. The gunners relaxed and the merchant seamen assisting at the gun positions drifted off in twos and threes for chow. The Navy men sat at their guns and were served in buckets. Joe Pszybysz, the messman who served on the 20mm machine gun in the stern near the big five-incher, became the butt of some good-natured kidding. This day, February 23, was Pszybysz' ninth wedding anniversary, and someone wondered out loud if the baker should take advantage of the lull and bake a cake for the occasion.

"It looks like you're going to live through it," someone told Pszybysz, who then went down to take a shower and slick up for the expected party.

Norwegian Henrik Pedersen remembers that the refugees were again "ordered to stay in a shelter under the bridge." Some men silently hoped that the planes would turn out to be Grumman Wildcat fighters from the convoy's flattop, but this dream was shattered when the planes came close enough to be identified as twin-engine bombers. Only the Germans had bombers in this corner of the world. The one lingering alternative to attack was that the twenty-three Junkers 88 torpedo bombers [Burbine believes it was Luftwaffe Group KG26, from Hammerfest], as they turned out to be, would not think enough of one old-looking, cargoless Liberty ship to bother with it when a rich prize—the whole convoy—lay somewhere nearby. Possibly even from their low altitude they would be able to see the convoy and fly on to attack the bigger game.

It did not work out that way. Perhaps the Luftwaffe pilots had not yet located the convoy, though they must have known it was close. Perhaps they did not have the stomach for a serious battle. Perhaps the Nazi squadron decided to spend only a few minutes warming up by sinking the lone Liberty ship before moving on, but the abrupt and surprising destruction of their first plane gave them pause. The pilots may have wondered briefly whether they had stumbled across a dreaded—and highly prized—Allied Q ship, a heavily armed warship camouflaged to look like a merchantman.

The bombers, equipped with two torpedoes each, worked out a pattern whereby two planes would turn in on the *Bacon* at the same time from opposite directions and both drop their torpedoes at the stern of the ship, turn, and zoom away. The fighting men on the *Bacon* knew that the die was cast. A life or death battle against impossible odds was about to begin. They were keyed to fever pitch. Captain Carini was at his post on the lower bridge barking out orders. With him were Third Mate Joe Scott and Ray Greenwell, a 37-year-old able bodied seaman from St. Louis who was serving as helmsman. An ordinary seaman was standing by as runner.

Scott said, "I remember saying to the ordinary seaman, 'Relax, man, this isn't the end.' He stood there stiff as a board. I know he was scared to death. I myself wasn't happy about it, either."

"Here they come!" a voice shouted as the Luftwaffe torpedo bomber squadron bore down on the lonely little *Henry Bacon*, still straggling more than forty miles from the protection of the convoy. Dark planes with prominent swastikas approached in a tight wing-to-wing formation, "in groups of three," Gunner Eugene Daniels remembered, about twenty-five to fifty feet above the waves and now diving in for the kill. Each bomber carried a torpedo on bomb racks fashioned on each side of the fuselage next to either engine.

Gunnery Officer Sippola acted as if ice flowed through his veins, eyewitnesses said. He ordered his men to hold their fire until the planes were at a closer range. The last few seconds seemed an eternity for the men on the guns. "We thought the order would never come," Reed recalled, "as we watched the planes break away to encircle us for the attack." Suddenly, when the planes were within perhaps a thousand yards, Sippola shouted "Fire!" Every gun on the *Bacon* roared at the same time, drowning out momentarily the roar of the planes. "The first plane," Reed wrote, "peeled off to come in on us...made his pass, dropped his torpedo, and made off unscathed."

The second was not so lucky. "The five-inch 38mm gun got one right on the nose," Pozen recalled, "and blew him to pieces." A Ju-88 exploded in midair and the flaming debris sent up a geyser of water as it spun into the ocean and disappeared. None of the German four-man crew was seen to surface. "One down, twenty-two to go," a gunner grimaced as the bombers scattered like chickens beyond the range of the Bacon's guns and began to circle the ship cautiously in a deadly game. Pozen thought they "were afraid to come in close because of the heavy barrage. They stayed out of gun range." Gunner Frank Reid recalled that, after the first kill, the German pilots "broke formation and then scattered to encircle us...to attack from all directions. They all made a run at us dropping their torpedoes, but fortunately for us, in the heavy twenty to thirty foot waves, the torpedoes went every which way."

"At this moment," Reed wrote, "the motor which powered our 5-inch gun quit and we could not restart it. Our gunner continued by hand-cranking the gun onto targets."

Captain Carini was almost delirious with joy. Like many another merchant ship master, Carini was thought to have some doubt about the ability of the Navy gunners. Suddenly the Navy boys were "my boys." The attack was not a complete surprise to the men on the *Henry Bacon* or, when they learned of it, to the officers of the convoy warships.

Chief Mate Lynn Palmer and Second Mate Fubel were on the upper bridge watching the torpedoes dropped by the attacking planes.

As the Old Man paced back and forth in the wheelhouse,

Palmer would shout down orders:

"Hard left!"

"Hard right!"

"As you are!"

The captain wanted Scott to stay with him to make sure that the helmsman would respond accurately to the orders coming down from topside. The ship began to zig and zag evasively, tugging heavily on the steering apparatus as she did so. Occasionally when the *Bacon* would slip by a torpedo, the captain would turn to the man he had selected as acting third mate and say, "You're a good officer, Mister Scott." Carini would look out the port wing of the bridge and shout, "Here they come again."

"I would get an order to 'hard to port,' then 'swing to midships,' and we'd miss another torpedo," Scott recalled.

Continuing northward at about ten knots, the *Bacon* twisted this way and that to avoid the torpedoes which bounced and turned when they hit the rough water. Some would dive below the surface and others would skip from wave to wave and explode in the water near the ship.

The Junkers made run after run and the guns on the *Bacon* blazed on. But from the beginning of the attack, the *Bacon's* damaged steering apparatus had limited her efforts to zigzag evasively. "I remember one of the planes coming very close to the ship," David Goodrich recalled. "All the guns were being reloaded. I can still see the grin on the German's face."

Down among the refugees, all was horror. Many had been seasick for days. After escaping the German evacuation in Sørøya, after surviving in the Sørøyan hills, after the hurricane, was this their final hour? The sounds of the battle above terrorized the women and little children. "It was a shock for all," Henrik Pedersen said. His wife suffered a nervous breakdown as a result of the bombing and later "was long silent and absent-minded." Young refugee August Larsen from Grunnfjord stood up to the attack bravely and helped soothe the children and women to whom the attack was a visit to hell itself.

Only the roar of the two big antiaircraft guns on the *Henry*

Bacon blurred out the sinister sounds of the torpedoes as they screamed through the air, according to Pedersen.

Traditionally the men working below the waterline in the engine room fear being trapped below should a torpedo shatter the hull above them, so the bridge kept in constant contact.

"Don't you fellows worry," Captain Carini called down. "I'll let you know when she's hit."

"How many are up there?" Fireman Herbert McIsaac asked, hoping that the early count was high.

"Twenty-three."

"Today's payday," McIsaac concluded. The other men in the engine room knew what he meant. Whenever a ship is torpedoed and the crewmen are forced to abandon ship, that is the day their pay stops. He wasn't alone in his feeling that this was the beginning of the end of the SS *Henry Bacon*. Ranking Navy noncom Jerry Gerold, in charge of the three-inch gun in the prow, said he felt that it was just a matter of time. One small, lone Liberty ship could not be expected to hold off three bombers, let alone twenty-three.

"Catch one!" Carini took time to shout to the engine room.

Later, "Catch two."

The second kill was on the starboard side and Joe Pszybysz was able to turn and see the plane hit the water and sink. Again there were no German survivors. The men on deck watched with morbid fascination as one deadly torpedo after another left a white streak in the water as it passed the ship and disappeared harmlessly in the deep.

The ship's radio officers Spud Campbell and Bill Herrmann took turns manning the radio and running up on deck. Herrmann reported that all was excitement with cannons sounding, ack-ack going off, and torpedoes missing their mark. Campbell was out on the bridge looking at the planes coming from both port and starboard. He checked with Captain Carini, who gave the order to send out the message: UNDER ATTACK BY ENEMY PLANES along with information which identified the ship and the convoy. He raced back to the radio room to send the message, but there

was no reply from the convoy escort. He did receive a signal from
a land station in Scotland, so he assumed the message was received.
All ships continuously monitored the international calling and distress band of 500 khz. He turned to Bill Herrmann and told him
he had seen torpedoes being launched and that they could expect
a hit at any moment. Since it didn't happen immediately, it was
apparent that the gun crews were doing a great job by keeping the
attacking planes at a respectable distance so the torpedoes weren't
finding their mark.

As he sat there waiting for an explosion to come, Campbell
thought about the three years in which he had been waiting, at
least subconsciously, for this moment. So many ships had been
torpedoed around his ship in convoys and hit by aircraft in ports of
North Africa, Italy, Sicily, Corsica, and southern France that he
felt that some guardian angel was looking out for him. His thoughts
flashed back to Bea in Birmingham and his family in Arley, Alabama. His Baptist faith demanded a prayer for the ship and the
crew and the Norwegian refugee passengers. He prayed that all
might be spared. He looked over at his friend Bill and saw that he
too was deep in prayer as his fingers traced his rosary beads. The
wait seemed eternal.

Seaman First Class Earl Clayton Rubley Jr., pointer on Bill
Moore's five-inch gun, was, according to Ernest Russell, "the
coolest-headed man among us." While others members of the gun
crew urged him to shoot, "he always waited the necessary extra
second to get dead on the target so as to make every shot count
deadly, and he always or nearly always hit his target."

With Captain Carini maneuvering the ship to minimize the
attacking aircrafts' target area, the attack came at the stern of the
ship. It was a major catastrophe when the motor of the five-inch
gun in the stern broke down and efforts to restart it failed. The
gunner had to crank the gun onto his target by hand. Yet the five-
incher managed to use up about twenty-three rounds of ammunition, and men like Chuck Reed remembered that they had used
up all of the ammunition from the ready box, and "we had to climb
down the elevator shaft two decks below" and carry up shell cases

and projectiles by hand. This task was performed over and over again.

Jerry Gerold's gun crew on the undamaged three-incher got off some forty rounds, and the machine guns poured out fifteen hundred rounds of 20mm shells. About fifty-eight rounds were fired every eight or nine seconds according to the official US Navy records. Guns on the *Henry Bacon* continued to blaze on as the attacking planes sped in from both sides of the ship. Number 7 machine gun heated up to the point where a shell got stuck in the breech. After Gunner Louis Walker slipped out of his harness and forced the shell partway out by recocking the gun, his loader, Joe Pszybysz, grabbed the red-hot shell with his bare hand and threw it overboard, burning himself in the process.

Walker hurried back into his harness and Pszybysz slammed home a magazine just in time for the gunner to lower his tracers and explode a torpedo skipping through the water directly towards the ship. The explosion touched off a geyser of water that sprayed the deck. "This same gunner," Reed reported, "fired until his gun barrel was red, shaking his fist at the planes and cursing at the top of his voice. His tender had left his post, and Walker changed his overheated barrel with his bare hands."

Walker scored hit after hit, and when he downed his first plane, Pszybysz licked a thumb with satisfaction and pressed it against the gun tub. "Number one for us!" he shouted.

Machine gun bullets from the Ju-88s splattered against the gun shield and, for an instant, the men were afraid that Walker was hit. Instead he reared back and shook his fist at the plane and cursed wildly at the top of his voice. As if fighting his own private war against the Nazis, Walker turned back to his gun and fired until the barrel was red. Walker marked up his second kill when he drew a bead on a torpedo before it was released from an onrushing Ju-88 about two hundred feet away; the resultant explosion blew the plane into flying debris.

A near disaster occurred in Normand Croteau's gun tub when a live shell got stuck in the hot barrel in the midst of the furious firing. The extreme heat could cause the shell to explode in the barrel at any moment. Croteau helped his loader Clyde Loar cock the gun so the shell could drop harmlessly into a canvas bag. After the hot shell was tossed over the side, Loar, who became a West Virginia minister after the war, persuaded Croteau to let him take over the firing so he could get himself a German plane. Croteau agreed to serve as loader, and Loar climbed into the gunner's harness and fired as long as the German planes remained within range. [Loar wrote, "I would say my experience on the *Henry Bacon* did figure in me being a Christian, and did have something to do with me being a minister. As ornery as I was, most of the fellows couldn't believe me as a minister. God can reach our lives."]

There was a pause in the battle. More than three dozen torpedoes had been dropped but evasive action directed from the bridge, the rough seas, and the deadly firepower from the gun tubs had combined to spoil the aim and frustrate the enemy. While from five to ten torpedoes were later classified as near misses, the *Bacon* was still unscathed. At least four planes had been downed.

Scott reported to Captain Carini that in addition to the Ju-88s shot down, three others were damaged — "they were smoking badly."

Scott called topside and asked, "How many planes are left?"

"Two!" Just two. Had Captain Carini done it again? After his incredible seamanship had saved the *Bacon* when she was foundering helplessly during the previous violent storm, had the captain and his men saved their ship from this new, this human enemy? Had they again beaten impossible odds and defied fate?

Some crewmen thought that the Luftwaffe crews had used up all their torpedoes. Or maybe they decided the SS *Henry Bacon* just wasn't worth any more losses. But on the bridge, the captain and his three top officers were less than optimistic. "After all the zigzagging," Scott said, "our helm was out of order; we were doomed for a sure kill."

Suddenly a Ju-88 that must have been piloted by a "fanatical, suicidal Nazi," as Pozen put it, raced close to the stern of the ship, banked, and dropped his torpedoes at the port side. "My heart sank when I saw the plane," Scott said. He spotted one of the torpedoes hurtling toward the ship and ordered "hard to starboard." "From the wing of the bridge," he said, "I could see the release of the torpedoes from the plane. Unknown to me was that our steering apparatus was out of order. The *Bacon* failed to respond; the faulty steering apparatus—long under strain—refused to pull the ship out of the path of the onrushing explosive. Scott noticed "the ship's tiller didn't operate." Then the torpedo hit. A terrible detonation rocked the ship as it struck number 5 hold on the port side. "Number 5 hold!" a seaman shouted. "That's where those Russian gals were hiding. I knew they'd bring us bad luck.... Hatch covers went flying in the air like toothpicks!" Scott said. "That's all I could see of them." The torpedoes actually hit between number 4 and number 5 holds, ripping the bulkhead out and blowing the debris from number 5 clear to the fo'c'sle head. There were three men in the powder magazine and, not being fools, "they scrambled out like monkeys," Pozen said.

Captain Carini gave the order to inspect the damage. Scott reported back that "the port side was split from number 5 hold to aft midship."

The Luftwaffe crew of the Ju-88 that scored the hit paid the full price immediately as the plane was caught in the crossfire between the portside machine guns manned by Mason Burr and Frank Reid. The plane went down under a rain of 20mm shells and the aircraft sank instantly, entombing its four-man crew.

The German torpedo damaged Frank Reid's gun, so he made his way to the bridge, where he stayed until orders were given to abandon ship.

When the torpedo hit the *Bacon*, Chuck Reed was belowdecks taking a projectile from the magazine. He dropped the projectile and shot up the shaft the entire distance of two decks in time to see water and debris still in the air. "The hatch cover was blown entirely off," Reed said, and he could see through the hatch opening a hole in the side of the ship with green seawater pouring in. Dozens of men were shaken and knocked sprawling. Many suffered minor cuts and bruises but, miraculously, no one was killed or critically injured by the explosion. "God was with us," Joe Scott explained.

The men on the machine guns in the stern were surprised to see the five-inch gun tub and crew intact after the smoke cleared.

The refugees were badly shaken. Pedersen reported, "The whole boat shook as if hit by an earthquake. Now we all realized that we were hit and feared we were about to sink."

Joe Pszybysz, on number 7, was thrown over his gun and dropped on the fantail and had to crawl back. Although wearing a helmet, wood from the smashed deck was driven into his ears by the explosion and had to be removed later in a hospital in Scotland. He suffered ear trouble and was subject to blackouts for several years after.

Many gunners and loaders had ignored orders to wear their battle helmets, but now they rushed to the helmet locker when the chunks of steel and wood began to rain down on them.

The mainmast came crashing down on the engine room skylight, showering the room with glass. Chief Haviland was bleeding from a cut on his forehead.

The *Bacon* quickly began to settle in the stern. Gunners stationed in that part of the ship informed Gunnery Officer Sippola that the ship appeared to be sinking and they started to leave their posts.

"Stand by your guns!" he replied sharply, and the highly disciplined men returned and continued firing at the retreating planes while the water began to rise inch by inch over their shoes. Soon the five-inch gun tub was an island in itself.

After the ship was hit, Michael Norris reported, "The Navy men did the most wonderful shooting I ever saw." The *Bacon* started to sink, "and the water was up to their knees and they were still firing." The ship began to settle almost immediately, and Carini signaled to the remaining German planes that the *Bacon* was "target destroyed."

Slowly the remaining planes of the Luftwaffe torpedo bomber squadron regrouped and abandoned any plans they might have had to attack the convoy. They headed back to their base at Bardufoss in occupied Norway. One plane was left to circle at a distance to ascertain whether the *Bacon* would in fact sink and, perhaps, to photograph her death throes. Damage was incurred all over the ship and debris from the hold was blown clear to the forecastle head. "The Germans," Reed remembered, "headed off toward their base without ever having reached the main convoy. Their price to bag one tired old Liberty ship was a high one!"

Captain Carini's two ranking officers, Palmer and Fubel, came down from topside and the three held a hurried consultation. Carini sent the men to make a personal inspection and evaluate the damage. The report came back that the side of the ship was split from the hold to midship and the *Henry Bacon* was taking water fast, though efforts were made to seal off the areas that were flooding. The deck was ripped open with huge gaps in many places. Bulkheads and seams were split and steam lines had ruptured. Thick deck planks and steel bandings were smashed and sheared.

Captain Carini, Lawrence Champlin thought, feared the *Bacon* would capsize "because of difficulties they were having with the rudder post. He ordered the sea-painters loosened on the rafts because if the boat capsized, no one would be saved if life boats and rafts were in such a position that they could not release them."

When he reached the reluctant conclusion that the *Henry Bacon* was in danger of sinking, Captain Carini, true to his word, promptly informed the men down in the engine room. Chief Don Haviland surveyed the situation briefly. With a heavy heart he brought the engine to the "stop" position. It was never to start again. He ordered Champlin to start the fire pump and Provencal secured the fuel pump. The six engine room men then on duty gathered on the throttle side of the engine and stood silently looking about for a few moments. They had worked with the engine so long that they had become attached to it—almost the way some men love a loyal woman. They did not blame the engine for the mechanical difficulties suffered by the *Henry Bacon* during the past few days. Finally Haviland broke the spell.

"Let's go," he said, and led the way up the ladder. He was followed by engineers Snyder, Champlin, and Provencal, water tender McIsaac, and oiler Ramsey. Oiler Pozen was off duty from the engine room and at his battle station on the bridge.

The dull thud and the shuddering of the *Bacon* was felt in the radio room, where Spud Campbell and Bill Herrmann waited in silence. "It finally came," Campbell said as he got up from his chair and darted toward the bridge. The captain, he recalled, was calm and very busy with orders and reports of damage. "He did pause," Campbell said, "and greet me with a grim smile, as he handed me a paper. 'My son, it has been a tough trip, but I believe it's about over.'" The captain told Campbell that the message was prewritten and contained the SOS and the ship's position. The message was to be sent out immediately. Campbell tried to express his love and admiration for the rugged old sea captain, then turned and headed back to his duty post. After the message had been sent and acknowledged—again from Scotland, the chief radio officer headed back to the bridge to report to Captain Carini for further orders. Admiral McGrigor's flagship picked up the signal, but was uncertain about the *Bacon*'s exact position and distance. Despite the rough seas, the admiral ordered out a search plane to pinpoint the location of the mortally wounded freighter.

"Over the years," Campbell reflected, "many people have asked if I was scared. I had been scared many times before during the war but, at this time, my primary feeling was one of release of tension. It also seemed I had a condition akin to getting what athletes refer to as 'a second wind' after a long run. I was no longer sleepy and dog-tired, but felt good physically. I also seemed to enter a mode of automation and did the things I was trained to do without having to concentrate. I got out the messages, put all codebooks and confidential papers and logs into a lead-weighted canvas bag, which I sealed and gave to Bill for dropping over the side into the water."

"By a feat of remarkable airmanship an aircraft succeeded in taking off," Captain Allison said. The men could only pray that the pilot would be able to land on the rocking deck of the carrier when he returned from his mission.

Captain Allison aboard the HMS *Zambesi* wrote that he had "no bearings or signals...from the survivors of the *Henry Bacon* until I actually sighted them in the exact position expected." Allison was operating on information given him by the flagship.

"We picked up the SOS of the *Henry Bacon*," Commander Ryder of the destroyer HMS *Opportune* reported. "Our telegraphist fortunately had got a snap bearing on her DF (direction finding) signal." The radiomen on the *Bacon* knew that the convoy had picked up the message because they received a faint single-dit response. The captain and his men were left to pray that help was on its way. But they all knew that there were times when a single ship must be sacrificed rather than endanger a whole convoy.

CHAPTER 14

"Abandon Ship"

"Our guns," Reed recalled, "had downed five German planes officially and, as far as we could determine, they had spent all of their torpedoes. All of the surviving crewmen that I talked to agreed that we had downed seven planes—not five."

The feats of the *Henry Bacon* were not accepted by all. Commander Ryder of the HMS *Opportune*, for example, said, "Most unlikely that a single merchant ship could shoot down this number.... With the whole convoy blazing away on previous voyages we only got one or possibly two." Yet the eyewitnesses on the *Bacon* swear they shot down five or more. Authoritative historian Samuel Eliot Morison concluded, "There is no finer instance of merchant ship defense in the history of North Russian convoys."

Captain Carini knew that if the *Bacon* actually went down, they were certainly in for trouble with one lifeboat damaged and unusable, and with nineteen extra souls to account for—most of them women and children. He did not yet know the additional handicaps that were ahead.

One of the Norwegian refugees, Henrik Pedersen, ran out on deck immediately after the torpedo hit and, without being asked, helped the captain care for those who had received minor injuries. "The German fliers were still circling over us and shooting," as he recalled. "All were shocked, but there was no panic. All was quite quiet." Now other Norwegians gathered on the boat deck and waited silently, courageously. Landsmen, who had gone through their own special torment of seasickness and fear during the earlier storms, breakdowns, and battle, appeared on deck, stoic, ready to follow orders quietly. As always, they were anxious to do whatever was asked of them.

When the time came for the order to abandon ship, Captain Carini gallantly ordered the Norwegian refugees into the first lifeboat even though it was apparent from the beginning that this decision might cost American lives, including his own. "We will use the rafts if we have to," Carini announced.

The little band of Norwegians, including sixteen women and children, could not handle the boat alone, of course, and the captain ordered a few crew members to join them. Messman Joe Pszybysz who had experience as an able-bodied seaman, was a veteran of the Normandy invasion, and possessed a highly valued lifeboat training certificate, was placed in charge of the boat by Carini. Other crewmen included Able-Bodied Seaman Donald Garatz, a capable 21-year-old six-footer from Duluth; Oiler Bill Gorman, 30, from Allison, Massachusetts; Herbert McIsaac, 42, fireman and water tender from Chelsea, Massachusetts, and First Radio Officer Spud Campbell from Alabama. Campbell was on deck when the captain wanted to launch the first lifeboat, so he was told to get in and handle the emergency radio transmitting equipment. In what might be considered a reversal of standard procedure, Captain Carini ordered Spud Campbell instead of Bill Herrmann to go with the first lifeboat in order to handle the technical chore of installing the radio transmitter and the antenna system. "Carini asked me," Campbell remembers, "if I had finished sending all distress messages and had dumped all secret and confidential documents as required by regulations. I told him that Bill and I had done so. Then the captain paused and looked me straight in the eye as he said, 'I'm putting you in the first boat along with the Norwegian refugees. I know you have the training and experience to handle the job. When this ship goes down, and it will soon, that little transmitter will be the only means of communications to the rescue ships.' He told me it was imperative that we should be found and picked up before dark, which came in midafternoon in February at that latitude. He indicated to me that it was not expected that anyone could survive until the next day. No one questioned an order from this stern, little man who was 'master of the ship,' in every way." Eugene Daniels remembered standing there "praying that we might be saved."

"I hurried back to the radio room," Campbell continued, "and told Bill what was ordered, got my papers—which were wrapped in a waterproof package, picked up the portable transmitter, said good-bye to Bill, and hurried back to the boat deck. By this time the Norwegians were in the boat and the captain was selecting some of the younger seamen who would be charged with keeping it under control in the rough seas. Captain Carini turned to me and said, 'Get on the boat and do your job and good-bye, Spud.' I still get emotional," he said, more than half a century later, "when I think of this brave hero who sacrificed himself to save the lives of so many others in the true tradition of the sea."

"Everything happened so fast,…" Goodrich remembered. "I ran across the hold to get to the boat deck. I saw a young man lying flat against the starboard side of the ship. I think he panicked. He was holding on with both hands. I tried to reach him but couldn't. He took off his glasses and put them at my feet and said he would pick them up in Scotland. I know he went down with the ship."

On his way to the boat deck, Goodrich passed the third engineer's room. "He pulled me in and told me to put on his wet suit. It covered all but my face. Thank God I did. It eventually saved my life." After Assistant Engineer Champlin left the engine room he hurried back to his own quarters for his heavy Arctic-issue coat and returned to the boat deck in time to help Assistant Engineer Provencal, Oiler Pozen, Purser Bob Hunt, and others lower the first lifeboat on the starboard side for the Norwegians. In the rough boarding one little girl suffered a broken arm, but in the excitement this went unnoticed by the crew. The other Norwegians managed well.

The first lifeboat was launched on the starboard side about twenty minutes after the torpedo hit the ship. "As the boat was lowered into the water," Campbell said, "it was released and we pushed away from the ship. The sea was relatively calm since we were on the leeward side of the *Bacon*. But as we moved away the sea became rough with thirty-foot waves tossing us."

Campbell went about the task of untying the mast sections

and erecting them vertically and fitting the mast into a clamp. Then he had to connect the antenna wire to each end of the lifeboat. The seamen on the boat were kept busy keeping the craft heading across the large waves. Otherwise, the lifeboat would have been swamped and then capsized.

One of the Norwegian women, Ane Jakobsen, 67, recalled that the boat landed bow first and "half filled with water" when it hit the waves. As Goodrich recalled, "It capsized because of the rough seas. Dick Burbine jumped in and turned it over all by himself. I don't know how he did it." To this day Burbine doesn't have the answer. For several hours Mrs. Jakobsen lay in the cold water that was trapped in the boat and she later came down with pneumonia. Later, she would complain that the boat was "half-filled with water and nothing was done to empty it." She appeared unaware that the crew had more important things on their minds at the time.

Champlin explained that he, Provencal, and Hunt on the stern could not keep up with the larger gang that lowered the bow "and that is why she hit that way." Pszybysz said the water came not so much from the launching, but from the waves that broke over the boat. Still wearing his sheepskin coat and galoshes and nothing else, Pszybysz started to row, but then switched to the bow so the waves would break against his back rather than flood into the lifeboat. "We were in danger of being swamped," he said.

"I remember one old woman [Mrs. Jakobsen] in the bottom of the boat was seasick and she looked at me with the pitiful eyes of an injured animal. She had her hand over her mouth and tears in her eyes, but didn't say a word.

"One little boy began to sit on the gunwale and I had to tell him to get off; I was afraid he'd fall over."

Inger and Sophie Pedersen, Henrik Pedersen's two- and four-year-old children, remember being wet in the lifeboat and sitting wrapped in papa's big trousers and jacket. Pedersen said that the rim of the crowded boat was "only a few centimeters over the waterline." The Norwegian men helped the crew members with the oars and, working to Pszybysz's cries of "heave-ho," they pulled away from the ship as fast as they could. "I was afraid the *Henry Bacon* would go down and we'd be caught in the suction," Pszybysz said.

As the first boat pulled away, Campbell got the battery-powered transmitter operating. He sent the information, including the ship's call letters, then put it on automatic mode. This allowed signals to be sent out for a short time, then be turned off for a time, then be sent again. In this way the small battery's power was conserved so it could be operated for a longer period of time. Campbell began putting out signals so rescuing ships from the convoy might be able to get a fix on their position should the *Bacon* go under. The captain stood on the deck and waved good-bye to the Norwegians and the handful of merchantmen.

"The Norwegian men tried to be helpful," Campbell recalled, "although the language barrier made for more confusion." He remembered being cold, then hot from exertion, then seasick from the tossing of the lifeboat.

"We all have reason to honor and praise the courageous seamen on board the *Henry Bacon* who bravely fought against an overwhelming force," Pedersen said many years later. "The seamen showed…a will to sacrifice."

With lifeboat number one launched successfully, the gang on the deck moved to lifeboat number three, the only motorized lifeboat. All the boats had been swung in during the storm, in an attempt to save them, and with continued bad weather they had not been swung out again. Boat three was particularly hard to move because it had to pass over the pudding boom which holds the boat secure. But finally the husky, sweating, heaving men, who were joined by Chief Haviland, had worked it into place. The motorized lifeboat started down in good fashion, but suddenly the after end fell free and the stern crashed against the side of the *Bacon*. The propeller of the boat was mangled and the stern caved in. The boat was smashed beyond use and left hanging over the side.

Chief Haviland, Champlin, and others hurried over to the port side to have another look at the number four boat which had suf-

fered a smashed davit during the storm the night before. The chief
thought if they could somehow work it free, it could still be used.
They cut the lines securing the boat, but by this time the boat
deck was awash and they could not push the free end off the deck.
Champlin struggled so hard that he slipped and almost fell into
the sea. Haviland was able to catch him before he went all the way
in, but Champlin got wet above the waist. Finding it impossible to
free the damaged boat, they left it hanging with one end free and
the other still attached to the davit by the falls; the block and tackle
mechanism designed to lower the boat was useless. Two lifeboats
were now unserviceable and the third had already been launched.
Only one boat was left and it could not hold more than perhaps a
third of the men left on the ship.

After the torpedo runs ceased and the ship was left sinking,
Gunnery Officer Sippola signaled his men down from their gun
posts. GM3C Bill Moore and his crew on the five-inch gun had to
wade through knee-deep water and climb over, through, and
around debris scattered near their gun tub. That area was so badly
torn up that it was difficult for the men to make their way to the
boat deck.

Certain members of the Armed Guard crew also had responsibilities for the large rafts. Ranking Gunner Jerry Gerold on the
three-incher sent his men down to the boat deck. He and his pal
Bill Brown, from Rhode Island, stayed to carry out their assignment to get the two large rafts in the prow of the ship over the side.

Gerold was assigned to the raft on the port side; Brown's assignment was on starboard. Brown managed to get his raft in the
water first and then came over to help Gerold who, meanwhile,
had almost been flattened by a swinging pelican hook that holds
the raft. Finally both rafts were in the water and they remained
attached to the *Bacon* by a rope which could be released from
aboard the raft, or from the deck of the ship. The third raft, in the
stern, was damaged by the explosion, but the men managed to
launch the fourth.

Before the rafts could be used, one of the men panicked in the
crisis and from the deck of the *Bacon* loosed the ropes holding all

three large rafts and freed the medium-sized ones as well. Presumably this was done so that the rafts would be more readily available, but the moving ship, strong winds, and eight- to ten-foot waves soon carried the rafts far from the *Henry Bacon*.

At one point Chuck Reed climbed forward to the bow, which by then was towering over the water. He saw a sailor trying to free the small two-man raft that was lashed to the three-inch gun. "When I attempted to assist him he picked up a fire ax and swung it at me, and then began to methodically chop the cork raft and throw the pieces in every direction." Panic had supplanted reason. However, one man, Seaman First Class Kermit Price, did manage to launch a one-man raft and gave the men on the ship a laugh as he paddled by jauntily smoking a cigarette and waving gaily at the crew. After the first lifeboat put over the side of the ship was away, the captain called all deck officers together to discuss the ship's condition. There was some question as to whether the ship should limp along toward the convoy. Captain Carini held out beyond the odds, and felt the ship might hold out until help arrived. This they all considered a better alternative than getting into the ice-cold sea. Spud Campbell, on the other hand, believed that the ship was a goner, but didn't want to stir the men into a panic. "He was calm and competent," he said, "but he wasn't an idiot. He knew what was happening, but couldn't show it to the crew."

The chief engineer, however, had thought differently about the situation. Chief Haviland reported he didn't think the *Bacon* would hold out because one of the compartment doors in the engine room was sprung and could not be closed tightly. "We knew if water got into the engine, that was it," the third mate said. "It wasn't long after this," Normand Croteau recalled, "the ship started to sink faster. Then a short time later the ventilator shot up from the water pressure coming up from the engine room, and the ship was tilting badly."

Scott called some of the men together and said, "Boys, we will not last long aboard ship." He urged them to put on their Arctic rubber suits. The crewmen "were afraid of the suits because some of them were too large and some too long," Scott explained. "They were afraid the suits were not watertight." Dick Burbine considered them "death traps. Once water gets into them, you'll sink like a rock to the bottom."

When Captain Carini ordered the launching of the second and only remaining lifeboat with Joe Scott in charge, he expressed optimism about the *Bacon*. "She won't sink, she won't sink," he said repeatedly. "She's a good ship." Belief again overshadowed reality. The captain believed the ship would stay afloat a long time. He thought that the British destroyers would reach them in time. What he didn't know was that the ships were about sixty miles away—about a two-hour run for a destroyer. And, by the time they arrived, the *Henry Bacon* would be gone for about an hour and forty minutes.

Even though he held out hope that the *Bacon* would not sink, when the men gathered to board the last lifeboat, Carini watched carefully to make sure that the Navy gunners who had performed so magnificently on the guns just a few minutes before would get their share of seats.

Oiler Woodie Pozen explained that at first "no one volunteered to go toward that lifeboat as they were afraid they might take someone's place. Finally some of the Navy boys got in, followed by members of the crew." Bos'n Holcomb Lammon, 23, and his brother Allan, a 19-year-old deckman, were present at the launching, and a choice befitting a biblical Solomon was made. It was decided that one brother should board the last lifeboat and the other should stay. Holcomb remembering his duties and responsibilities, decided to stay; Allan, thinking of his brother's wife and children, with great reluctance agreed to be the one to leave.

Acting Third Mate Joseph L. Scott of Norway, Maine, helped guide the boat into the water. "We were lowering our last boat," he recalled, "when someone said, 'Scotty, stand by the aft boat falls.'

"I don't know whether I was pushed or whether it was an act of God—I was in the boat waiting to unhook the boat falls aft.... I had been torpedoed in the First World War, so I knew what it was all about."

After pausing to help in the unsuccessful effort to lower the lifeboat that had been smashed by the storm, Gerold and Brown arrived on the boat deck while the last lifeboat was still being loaded and they jumped in. When Haviland and Champlin unwillingly abandoned hope of freeing the damaged lifeboat, they also walked to where number two boat was being loaded and climbed in along with a few other late arrivals.

Chief Haviland immediately set the drain, which is normally left open so an unused lifeboat will not fill with water from waves and rain. He heard Scott call out, "No more—we've got enough now."

But then Haviland, age 50, who had given his young shipmates his money, time, and goodwill throughout the voyage, found he had one more thing he could offer—his life. "Get into that goddamn boat, kid," he called out. "I've lived my life, it really doesn't matter if I don't get back." [The president of the United States awarded Donald F. Haviland the Merchant Marine Distinguished Service Medal posthumously for this action.] "None of the others had to be asked or ordered to give up his seat in the lifeboat," Herrmann recalled. "The men just waited until all nineteen refugees had found seats. The merchant seamen were also anxious to save as many of the heroic Navy gunners as possible."

Still wearing his sheepskin coat, khaki pants, and commander's hat, he climbed back on the deck of the sinking ship and joined Captain Carini on the bridge. Together the men presented a picture of two courageous leaders. Haviland made no further effort to leave the ship.

"I was the last Navy man to board the lifeboat so I feel I might be the one to have taken Donald Haviland's place," said Seaman Second Class Warren Bacheldor, the third reloader on the bow gun. "I was standing there on the deck and someone called, 'Come on, Batch,' so I jumped into the boat which was already in the water. The boat capacity was twenty and there were twenty-seven of us in it…. After staying in the lifeboat for an hour or so, six of us Navy men got onto a raft. Only two I remember were Kermit Price and William R. Brown." We pulled Price "from the water [and] that made seven on the raft. We all gave him what dry clothes we had…we were lucky so far, only wet feet. I remember giving him a sweater and rubbing his arms and legs as he almost had it…. Four months later, I received that sweater in the mail."

Someone else thought Haviland's place had been taken by a redheaded Navy boy—a description that fits Seaman First Class Cyril Patrick La Fountain, of Billerica, Massachusetts.

The 18-year-old messman, Chuck Reed, was standing nearby and said, "The chief seemed to be speaking to me. I could have taken his place, but didn't. I felt somehow that I could shift for myself." Reed added, "I think that my background of camping, boating, and general self-sufficiency gave me perfect confidence in my ability to survive." According to Goodrich, the individual who took Haviland's seat was 17-year-old Robert Tatotsky. Tatotsky, in a 1991 interview—shortly before his death—recalled he was "damn lucky to get off there myself. He remembered himself floating in the icy waters of the Barents Sea before being helped into a life raft. "Chief Haviland," he said, "volunteered to give me the last seat. Next thing I knew, we were off."

In the confusion, Champlin, though in his assigned boat, could not get to his designated spot in the midship position in the overcrowded craft where he was to release the falls by pulling the lever in the bottom of the boat. As a result, when the boat was waterborne it was nearly smashed against the side of the *Bacon*, but the men were able to fend it off until someone could get at the lever. Finally the boat was free in the water.

Forty-three-year-old Scott, who had experienced such a calamity before, was the ranking man in the boat and took charge. "I gave orders oars up and out," Scott said, "so we went hunting for the rafts." His plan was to find the floating rafts and load them with men from his overcrowded lifeboat. When he was leaving the side of the *Bacon* he called back to the men still aboard that, if he was lucky, he would return for another load. Scott waved and the men on deck waved back.

The seas were running high and the wind was strong, but within a short while they spotted one of the large rafts and approached cautiously. "I didn't want to put a hole in the lifeboat," Scott explained, "and I didn't want to lose anyone."

Navy gunners Gerold and Brown, though among the last to enter the lifeboat, were among the first to relieve the overcrowded conditions by scrambling aboard the very raft they themselves had released. But it was no longer attached to the ship; rather it was floating free. Bill Moore, who had been in charge of the five-inch gun, climbed aboard with Gerold and Brown. Others were Elias Banian, a quiet Armenian boy; Warren Bacheldor, a crusty, good-hearted lad from Maine, and John Ramsey, the tallest man on the *Bacon*.

Gerold and Moore had equal rank, gunner's mate third class, but Gerold outranked Moore by date of service and according to military protocol was nominally in charge of the raft. However, he immediately secured Moore's agreement that they would make all decisions together. "I couldn't get all the boys on that raft," Scott recalled. "Some were seasick and cold and froze to their seats and couldn't move. So I still had quite a boatful left." Champlin, one of the older, more experienced men, related that the lifeboat was easier to handle after the handful of men had switched to the raft. "Some of the younger men did not realize the danger they were in," Champlin said. "They did not seem to think it was important to keep the boat out of the trough and head out on to the sea. Some of them were trained only for gunnery, and Scott kept telling them we had to control the boat or be swamped."

At least one Navy man, Warren Bacheldor from Scott's native state of Maine, recognized Scott's seamanship. "Thanks to Scott...for the safe handling of that boat; it was a fine job in very, very rough seas."

Scott's lifeboat continued its search. "I sighted another raft so we went for it, only to find it was badly damaged and I was afraid to get too close to it, as the sea was getting worse, and it began to snow a little...." That raft probably was the portside raft damaged by the explosion. Scott was afraid to take the lifeboat too close since the sea was getting worse, so he let the raft float away. Howard Gray, a 17-year old Merchant Marine wiper, recalled, "The sea was so rough it was impossible to maneuver the boat back to pick up anybody. It was all we could do to keep from being swamped." Scott said, "My heart sank very low when we were on the crest of a high wave and I could see the bow of the *Henry Bacon* going down. The next time we rode high, the *Henry Bacon* had sunk; how many went down with her I didn't know....Oh, how I wish I could have saved more lives."

In a deposition made by Joe Scott on March 23, 1945, he indicated the following casualties:

Captain Alfred Carini, Chief Engineer Donald F. Haviland, Lynn R. Palmer, "he was with the captain on the bridge just before the ship sank and probably went down with the ship,..." Carl D. H. Fubel, "...just as the boilers blew up shortly before the vessel sank. Walker said that the ventilator blew up and parts of it smashed in Fubel's head. He believes that Mr. Fubel was killed instantly,..." Robert J. Hunt, "...had been feeling very sick for some days before we were torpedoed. He jumped over the side just before the *Henry Bacon* went down. Before leaving the ship, he had rendered first aid to one of the gun crew,..." Holcomb Lammon, "...was last seen on the main deck forward, endeavoring to improvise a life raft. He jumped over the side just before the vessel sank,..." Robert Cramer, was last "...seen jumping over the side of the ship,..." Frederick C. Funken, "...was seen jumping over the side of the ship,..." Donald P. Schiesher, "...some of the crew informed me that this man froze to death and his body slipped off [the improvised raft] into the water,..." Edgar B. Snyder, "...suffered from a cold for about a week [before the *Bacon* sank]. He jumped over the side of the ship just before she sank,..." Joseph E. Provencal, "...while [he] was being lifted out of the water by one of the destroyers, he lost his grip and drifted into the screws of the propeller,..." John W. Mastracci, "...died of exposure [on an improvised raft], Cornelius Kearns, "...he was standing [on the starboard side of number 3 hatch] just before the ship upturned and sank...," George W. Shipka, "...froze to death on the improvised raft,..." and James Martin, "...the captain of the destroyer *Opportune* informed me that this man was last seen in the water alongside the destroyer. They could not reach him as his body drifted away."

Jerome Gerold stated in an official report that "four Navy men were lost while being hoisted aboard the destroyer *Opportune* by hooks. They had on kapok life jackets which seemed to be entirely inadequate for any strain by these hooks, as a result of which these life jackets ripped and the four men were lost."

In the same document, Gerold said he saw Sippola "in the water hanging to a piece of wood. When the destroyer came alongside they threw him a line. He let go of the piece of wood to grab the line but failed.... He went down and was not seen after that." He attested that four members of the gun crew, Armstrong, McQuistion, Lomelino, and Frank Reid, were also witnesses.

In a document from the Office of the Chief of Naval Personnel, the list of Armed Guard grew to include: Sippola, Allard, Burr, Harlacher, Mayden, Potvin, and Rubley. "The date of such determination [of death] be fixed as of 15 May 1945, the date on which information conclusively established their deaths...." Normand Croteau was also listed as missing in action, but that error was later corrected.

When he was deposed, night cook and baker George Bartin remembered: "Aside from Lynn R. Palmer, whom I saw dead in the water [He recalled that Palmer's body "was motionless, his head hung forward and foam was coming from his mouth.... I understand that the doctor on the British destroyer informed the crew not to pick up anyone in the water who was foaming at the mouth."], I know of three others in the crew who died in the water before I was rescued. They were:

Purser Robert J. Hunt, "about twenty minutes after I was in the water, I saw this man let go of a piece of timber to which he was clinging...he drifted away from me...; Able-bodied Seaman

Frederick C. Funken, "about one hour after I saw Mr. Hunt, I saw this man motionless in the water. He was foaming at the mouth...his body drifted away from me...; Bos'n Holcomb Lammon, "was clinging to the same timber that I was...because of the excitement of seeing the rescue ship, he let go of the timber and as soon as he did so, his body submerged and never came to the surface again. He had discarded his life preserver some time before....

CHAPTER 15

Take to the Water

Official reports stated that there were more than thirty men stranded aboard the *Henry Bacon* without lifeboats or rafts. Goodrich puts the number at "about twelve." All crewmen had been warned that no human could survive in the Arctic Ocean in the winter for more than a short time, about five minutes when the water was 38 degrees Fahrenheit.

Two of the more ingenious men—Bos'n Holcomb Lammon and Gunner's Mate Frank Reid—began making rafts even before the last lifeboat was launched. They used the heavy 12-by-12 inch beams left on the deck of the *Bacon*, previously used to cradle the locomotives that they had carried to Murmansk, Clyde Loar remembered. The lumber was located in the chain room.

"We figured that the men would need something to climb on when the *Bacon* went under," Reid explained. Working independently but assisted by other crew members, each man formed a rectangle with four beams and lashed the ends together with rope. Heavy planks from the hatches and deck were tied on for a covering. It was a herculean task considering how little time they had. After completing their rafts, both Lammon and Reid turned them over to others.

Lammon, a veteran of the SS *Azalea City* and the SS *Jerome K. Jones*, made his way to the main deck forward and, giving no thought to saving himself, concentrated on assisting other members of the crew to get clear of the ship. "His endeavors in the short time between our torpedoing and the time he jumped over the side no doubt saved many lives," Third Mate Scott stated in his official report to the US Navy.

Reid climbed to the boat deck where the second lifeboat was

still being launched; Reid was assigned to this boat. At this point Lieutenant Sippola called out, "I'd like some men to volunteer to stay on the machine guns on the bridge in case the Germans come back to strafe." "I'll go up," Reid said immediately. "After all," he recalled later, "I was the petty officer in charge of the 20 mm machine guns." "I'll go with you," volunteered Mason Kirby Burr. "I'll go, too," said Reid's buddy Steve Allard. Reid added, "Maybe there were others who I didn't see."

"The three of us went back up on the bridge from the boat deck together to man the 20s. There was too much milling about to know who took our seats in the lifeboat which was getting ready to be lowered.

"When I reached the bridge I checked the clip on the forward gun portside and put in a full magazine—60 rounds. Burr went to the aft gun tub on portside and loaded that one.

"There was still this one lone German plane watching us. I guess he wanted to see if we were really going down.

"The plane was too far away to hit, but I thought I'd let the Krauts know that the *Bacon*'s guns were still operating, so I fired one burst.

"The burst also gave me a chance to see that the gun was still working." Raymond Franklin Reid contends he was the last man to leave the *Bacon*.

Chuck Reed, 18, one of the ship's messmen who served on Bill Moore's five-inch gun crew, left his companions and went to his cabin on the starboard side a little forward of the galley to get his Testament and other valuable papers. As he let himself down the companionway past the galley, he noticed the lights were still on so he stopped at the water fountain for a drink.

"I seemed to be as one in a dream suspended—extraordinarily calm and calculating," he recalled. "A sailor rushed frantically past me, but stopped short to see me at such an everyday act, and asked why I didn't get off the ship as she was sinking.

"I explained that we might be without water for a long time, and why didn't he, too, get a drink? I held the fountain while he drank, and then we both went topside."

They reached the boat deck just in time to see Haviland give up his seat for a younger man. "I didn't know his name, but his courage I'll never forget."

After the men had tied some of the lumber and threw the crude rafts over the side, the men started jumping in. "I froze," Goodrich recalled. "Sitting on the gunwale, it looked like a hundred feet to the water. Thank God the steward [Clayton Ingram] was still aboard as he pushed me off. I hit the water [and] went down deep because of the weight of the rubber suit."

After avoiding the attack of the berserk sailor who destroyed at least one of the cork rafts with an ax, Reed decided to fend for himself and walked down the deck to the port side until he found a spot not too high from the water. "I took off my Arctic boots, helmet, and mittens, checked my life vest, and jumped over. As soon as I surfaced and got my breath, I began to swim away from the ship.

"After swimming for what seemed like hours," he continued "I found a large timber floating which had previously supported the rail equipment on the deck. I climbed out of the water onto the timber and sat there looking at the ship, wondering whether I was far enough away from it to avoid the suction when she went down.

"Once I saw Captain Carini come out on the bridge wing to look. I was perhaps seven hundred yards from the *Bacon*," Reed said, "and could see her each time I would bob up on a wave. Her lights were still burning, even as her bow approached the perpendicular. As she almost reach a perpendicular position, I heard the whistle blow a long salute, then a boiler erupted with…a whoosh….

"She slid quietly under. All that remained now was the cold wind, a little snow, and bits of debris here and there. I was shaking so badly that I could barely stay on my timber. The waves were still quite high, and the only time I could see about was when I came up on the crest of a wave.

"I spotted a sailor in a life jacket two or three crests away from me, but could get no response from him. After an hour or so, I spotted a six-man raft. I called and blew my whistle (each life vest had a police-type whistle and light) and for awhile they seemed to come nearer. I found that I could paddle the timber slowly, and after some time I worked near enough to shout to them.

"They refused to take me aboard at first, saying that they didn't have supplies enough. I pleaded, and finally left the timber and swam to them. I recognized one fellow who had been very nice to me, so I concentrated my pleas on him. It may have been Warren Bacheldor who was kind enough to convince the others I could come aboard. He finally helped me aboard and gave me a cigarette"—a bit of solace in the days prior to the surgeon general's warnings. Someone also gave Reed a turtleneck sweater which he later traded for a pair of English seaboots and a Camel.

"I told them about the fellow floating in the life jacket a short distance away," continued Reed, "and finally talked them into paddling over to look for him. We found him unconscious and hauled him aboard the raft. He was 'Big Joe' Marbach." In addition to saving Reed and Marbach, the men on the raft had rescued Kermit Price, who had amused the crew earlier bouncing by in his one-man raft.

Bacheldor recalled, "We all gave him what dry clothes we had; we were lucky so far, only wet feet. I remember giving him a sweater and rubbing his arms and legs as he almost had it. Four months later I received that same sweater in the mail." After picking up the three men from the Arctic waters, Bacheldor said, "We sat staring at each other hoping and praying to be rescued before we drifted to the German-occupied coast of Norway."

Gerold reported that the men "took oil and rubbed it all over our exposed skin and rowed to keep our circulation."

Steward Clayton Ingram, 29, said he was standing near the rail of the *Bacon* with Deck Engineer Wilmo Testerman, 24, and suggested they both jump in. "But I can't swim!" Testerman protested. Ingram pointed out that he couldn't sink with his life jacket and added, "Just do what I do." The men leaped into the water together and, after paddling a short distance from the ship, Ingram turned to see how Testerman was coming along. Perplexed when he couldn't see him, he heard a cry from the opposite direction, "Hey, Stew, come on!" Looking about, he saw Testerman way ahead of him. An adrenaline rush appeared to be a great swimming instructor.

Dick Burbine (an 18-year-old wiper) remembers being ordered to a lifeboat by Chief Engineer Haviland "with a fire axe to cut the lashing lines on the bow of the boat. The freezing water and ice rendered the boat's falls useless. While doing this, the lifeboat was hit by a rolling swell. It lifted the boat and me into the sea. I was hit on the head by the lifeboat, which knocked me unconscious for a while. I came to under the overturned craft, in an air space. My feet were tangled in some lines and other flotsam. I was able to pull off my boots and surface. I found a one-man life ring floating nearby and latched onto it. Due to the wind and current I was swiftly swept away from the ship. While floating about,... darkness fell and I could hear yelling and screaming from the surviving crew members foundering around the freezing sea. Due to the motion of the sea the life ring was like a cork; one minute on top of a long roller, the next in the bottom of a deep trough. On one of these movements I was able to swim and reach Woodrow Wilson Pozen, a fellow black gang member."

Oiler Woodie Pozen was one of those left aboard the *Henry Bacon* after helping lower the two boats that got away safely. "I saw no boat for myself," he said, "except the one that was fouled up on the deck, so Dick Burbine and I and some of the others pushed it over the side. Dick Burbine was in it (as were David Goodrich and Michael Norris).

"The undertow from the sinking ship had a tendency to draw the boat into this whirlpool. Burbine had hold of the side of the boat and was trying to pull himself up on it. I saw he couldn't make it, so I went down the mainline to get into the boat and help him drag it forward, and just as my foot touched the gunwale of the lifeboat, it capsized. I had just let go of the mainline.

"I went right down the side of the ship—the suction from the sinking ship pulled me down three times. I was beginning to lose my head.

"Finally, when I came up the boys in number two lifeboat were cheering me on. I saw Burbine on a lifeboat which was approximately two hundred feet away. I don't know how I got there, but I did. Burbine pulled me into the float.

"At this time a Navy boy, Silas Doe (seaman first class from Connecticut) jumped into the water. He kept yelling to us that he couldn't make it and calling for us to help him. To leave our places on the raft and jump into the water would have been suicide, so we kept cheering him on and telling him he could make it.

"Finally he got to the raft. We pulled him aboard. He had no shoes or stockings on so I opened my sheepskin coat and let him put both his feet under my armpits.

"At that time a big wave came along. We were sitting on the end of the float and it knocked the Navy boy and me into the water again. I became frightened and was clinging to the side of the raft. Dick pulled us both on again.... The Navy boy began complaining about his feet again and I told him I didn't care whether his feet were freezing or not. I told him my feet were frozen and so were Dick's, and to stop beefing. After I talked gruff to him, he stopped complaining and kept quiet.

"The high waves seemed to carry us from the ship, but we could still see it and could see figures on it and we were closer to it than the lifeboats. At that moment there was an explosion and when I looked again there was no more ship."

"When the water reached the deck of the bridge," Reid wrote, "we three [Steve Allard, Mason Burr, and himself] jumped in and started to swim away...the ship in sinking loomed over us and things were falling off the decks, such as ventilators, etc.... One piece of falling debris struck Mason and killed him...and broke Steve's arm. Steve and I checked Mason and there was nothing we could do, as he was already dead."

Staunch Captain Carini announced calmly that he intended to stay aboard and go down with his ship, and Chief Engineer Haviland, who gave up his seat in the last lifeboat, indicated he would do the same.

"If I can't bring all my boys back, I'm not going back either," the captain said at one point. "I do not want to go back without a full crew." Except for those who had volunteered to remain aboard to the last to fight off any possible strafing attack, the rest were left to make their own decision as to when and how to leave the ship. Captain Carini, following his concept of the tradition of the sea, went to his cabin and opened the safe which held the valued possessions that crew members had turned over to him for safekeeping, and the ship's funds as well—some $75,000 according to scuttlebutt, but probably less than $1,000 according to the *Bacon's* former master. Few if any survivors were present when the captain opened the safe and handed out the money, obviously hoping that some of them would survive. Normand Croteau, loader of one of the 20 mm guns on the bridge, entered the captain's quarters when the safe was open but empty. The captain, Lieutenant Sippola, and Signalman Steve Allard were there when he arrived. Croteau recalled that the captain broke open a bottle and gallantly proposed a toast to glory. He passed it around to keep the men warm. "I don't recall how many of us had a sip, but I'm sure most of us did. He said if we did have to get off, we were going to be cold because we would have to get into the water. All the lifeboats and rafts were gone."

Lieutenant Sippola offered Croteau a .45-caliber pistol, but Croteau said he'd rather not take it in case he had to abandon ship. He did accept a pair of powerful binoculars which he later lost in the water. Radioman Bill Herrmann came to join the men when they were coming out of the captain's quarters, but Carini told him to stay at the radio. After Croteau left, the captain told the men to help themselves to his liquor supply. Signalman Steve Allard took two bottles—one for himself and one for Frank Reid who had remained at his gun station on the bridge. Croteau later saw that Allard was carrying something, and although Allard told him it was whiskey, Croteau thought he was just joking. "I didn't really know what he was carrying," Croteau observed, "but I remembered he had a beautiful Bible on board which belonged to him; he once took it out when someone quoted a saying wrong from the Bible."

Radioman Herrmann could have left the ship in the first lifeboat with the Norwegian refugees but was still on duty at his post in the radio shack because Spud Campbell, the other "Sparks," happened to be on deck when the captain wanted to launch lifeboat number one. After hearing the order to abandon ship, Herrmann put all the codebooks in a weighted bag and threw it overboard. Both he and Campbell had broken radio silence to send out SOS calls to convoy RA64 when they were under attack by the enemy planes.

As a final act before abandoning ship, Campbell locked the key down with a hook to send out a continuous signal and give a direction-finding bearing to the convoy. "This actually saved our lives," Herrmann said, "because they got a perfect fix on our position. When I last left the radio shack, I put the key down again and put the transmitter on battery operation.

"The direction-finding beam that was sent out when we locked the transmitter key down so as to give a continuous signal was in violation of FCC (Federal Communications Commission) regulations, because we were jamming the distress frequency of 500 kilocycles." Later, Herrmann was told by the British that the signal lasted about an hour before it was silenced with the sinking of the ship. Toward the end Herrmann was offered a bottle of vodka by the chief mate and a bottle of scotch by his friend, Purser Bob Hunt, but he declined "with some regret." Hunt teased Herrmann, "You sure picked the right trip for your first voyage." When he was ready to leave the ship, the only thing the former Ben Bernie musician took with him was the mouthpiece from his clarinet.

"While still on deck we discussed how high the water would come before we would step out," Herrmann recalled. Finally the time came and "all we did was walk down to the water line, about midship, and step into the water." When Herrmann reached the water he thought, "Boy, this is *really* cold." His feet became numb immediately and he kicked off his boots. "We had our life jackets on so we just started swimming around in the water and tried to cheer each other up."

Herrmann felt all along that he would be saved, but nevertheless he wondered if this was the time to say his prayers. "But then I felt that possibly I would have had to have them said before that to do any good."

Herrmann recalled that he was in the water at some distance from the ship when the seawater apparently reached the hot boiler and exploded through the stack. "The ship reared up with its bow in the air and went down. Debris from the deck was scattered and that's how I got a twelve-by-twelve beam that I used for a perch."

Purser Robert Hunt had been sick for some days before the torpedoing, but instead of leaving the sinking ship early, he stayed aboard to render first aid to one of the gunners. This act earned him the Mariner's Medal. George Bartin, night cook and baker, saw Hunt shortly after Bartin jumped over the side of the vessel. Hunt had also jumped over.

"About twenty minutes after I was in the water, I saw this man let go of a piece of timber to which he was clinging," Bartin said. "I should judge he was about thirty-five feet from me at the time. He drifted away from me; I believe he had died at that time."

"Hunt was frothing at the mouth when I last observed him in the water," Herrmann said, "and I presumed he was dead of exposure."

Like Bob Hunt, Assistant Engineer Edgar Snyder had been ill for several days before the final attack and he also died in the water near the *Bacon*. He had jumped over the side, and Herrmann, then riding two beams, thought he heard him say good-bye to those near him just before he drowned. Others said he sank without saying a word, being dragged under by his rubber suit.

Joe Pszybysz, in the first lifeboat with the Norwegians, spotted a fellow messman, George Shipka, 20, of Elizabeth, New Jersey, clinging to a large beam. Riding high waves, he saw Shipka signal when the boat was on a crest, but when the boat reached the peak of the next wave, Pszybysz could again see the beam, but Shipka was gone.

There were fewer and fewer men left aboard the *Bacon* and there was still doubt in the minds of many of the remaining men whether it was wiser to jump into the freezing waters or take their chances that the *Bacon* would stay afloat until help arrived. "Maybe she'll float," Carini said optimistically. "Don't you leave until you have to. Maybe she'll stay afloat."

Little groups were scattered here and there and Lieutenant Sippola stopped to talk with Reid, Burr, and Allard just before he decided to abandon ship. Finally, the tilt of the ship in the water caused Sippola to announce that those who wanted to take their chances on the makeshift rafts should jump in and climb aboard. Seamen Eugene Daniels of South Carolina and Charles Harlacher went over the side of the ship together. "The water was so cold I felt I could hardly make it," Daniels said. "We swam as fast as we could to get to the rafts so that we could keep together if we were rescued. We also had to get far enough from the ship so that the suction when the ship sank would not take us down.

"We straddled the raft boards and held on with our hands…. Again I prayed—this time aloud—as the men had asked me to do so. If ever there was a time and a need for prayer we felt this was it."

With men acting independently and jumping into the water at different points, no one can be absolutely sure who was the last man to leave the SS *Henry Bacon*. But certainly Normand Croteau was one of the last.

Croteau reported that he, Donald Mayden, Elmer Potvin, and Earl Rubley had returned to their 20mm machine guns. "When the planes left, we got off of our guns," Croteau said. "We stayed behind the smokestacks on the bridge. We were just talking, and some were saying what would have happened to the Russian girls, because the torpedo hit just where the girls were hiding. Croteau and others returned to the deck after leaving the captain's quarters which was one level lower than the wing of the bridge. Chief Haviland commented that he did not think the ship would hold out because one of the compartment doors in the engine room did not close and the water would flood that area. "I don't remember what Potvin, Mayden or Rubley said or did at the last," Croteau said, "maybe because most of the talking was done by the captain, chief engineer, and Steve (Allard). As for these three gunners, anyone will tell you that they were of the quiet type. And being of the quiet type it would be just like them to stand and listen to conversation.

"If they got off before me, or stayed on the *Henry Bacon*, I don't remember," Croteau said. "I don't remember anything else about them, except that they stood at their 20mm to prevent the German planes from strafing. All three—Potvin, Mayden, and Rubley—were lost.

By now the last Luftwaffe bomber had disappeared, but a new plane gradually appeared on the horizon and approached the *Bacon*. Alert gunner Frank Reid trained his machine gun on it and he and the men still on the ship were relieved when it turned out to be an F4F Grumman Wildcat from the small British aircraft carrier that accompanied the convoy. With the sea as rough as it was and getting worse, it was surprising to the men that a plane would dare leave its ship—in this ungodly weather.

The captain told Signalman Steve Allard to flash an SOS to the plane with his battery-operated light from the bridge. The plane responded by blinking that help was on the way. Allard repeated the blinker messages out loud for the men standing by as the exchange was flashed back and forth between the fighter plane and the sinking Liberty ship. They now knew that help was on the way, but would it arrive in time?

Men had gathered on the starboard side of the ship when suddenly the water pressure blew a heavy wind ventilator off its 20-inch sleeve and shot it into the air. The ventilator was so large that no man could wrap his arms around it.

Second Mate Carl Fubel was standing on the upper deck starboard side amidships. Gunner Louis Walker, who had so distinguished himself during the attack, saw the ventilator smash Fubel in the head, killing him instantly. "It seemed to me," Croteau said, "that the captain was just staring at the water shooting out of the vent-chute" as he let a life jacket he was holding slip to the deck. "Perhaps five or six men had handed life jackets to the captain; I think Steve Allard was the last one to offer him one." One of the crew members pointed out to the captain that he was the only one without a life jacket—that he really should have one on. But the captain did not respond. As each life jacket was offered him, Carini let it slide to the floor, as several crew members recalled.

When the water began shooting out of the vent-chute, men started down the stairs on the starboard side, but with the heavy starboard list of the *Bacon* they switched and hurried over to the port side. The current was moving from starboard to port and Croteau said that, while no one mentioned it, he thought all of them feared the suction of the sinking vessel would be greater on starboard because of the list.

One of the makeshift rafts was still nearby in the water when Croteau reached the edge of the bridge and jumped into the water "which was about five to eight feet from the handrail."

He was surprised to find that Allard was not right behind him. Shortly after he was in the water the ship exploded. Ballast showered him like a sandstorm and he was struck in the back, near the spine, apparently by a jagged piece of metal. Spotting an empty five-gallon can from the ship, Croteau clung to it for a short while. "It took about five minutes to get my breath," he said. "The water was so cold that it seemed I couldn't get any air into my lungs, but as I adjusted to the water temperature I began to breathe easy again."

The top of the wheelhouse blew off in the explosion and Gunner Louis Walker, who was in the water at this time, climbed up on it and then helped young Croteau crawl aboard. They later rescued James Martin, the youthful seaman who, like Walker, had joined the ship in Scotland.

While Croteau thought Allard was joking about the package containing whiskey, Gunner's Mate Frank Reid knew otherwise — he had received one of the bottles and they each had a drink. Burr, who was with them, declined. Reid and Allard then put the caps back on and, in jest, threw the bottles into the water. "We'll be right with you," Allard called out. "There was one thing that Allard carried inside his coat," Reid said. "It was a large picture, about 12 by 18; it was a photo of his wife."

After the ventilator shot off and water poured through the vents, the ship began to sink faster. Obviously there was little time left. Allard, Reid, and Mason Burr gathered together with Captain Carini and Chief Haviland on the bridge for a final farewell. As far as Reid could tell, there was no one else left aboard the ship.

Reid believed that both Captain Carini, 62, and Chief Haviland, just 50, felt they were too old to stand the rigors of the cold water and the Arctic air.

The three gunners preparing to leave were all husky young men in their early 20s. The veteran seamen wished the youngsters good luck and the men shook hands solemnly as they separated. As the gunners turned to leave, the captain and the chief walked slowly back into the bridge house. They were never seen again.

The *Henry Bacon* was poised at what Reid described as a 45-degree angle, and the water was almost to the edge of the bridge. He, Allard, and Burr stepped into the Arctic from the aft end of the bridge—less than two feet above the water level. All were wearing life jackets.

"I was the last man off the ship alive," Reid swore.

As soon as they were in the water, perhaps thirty yards from the ship, the SS *Henry Bacon* reared up on her prow and towered above them. As they were looking straight up at the ship, the *Bacon* was rocked by an explosion—a piercing hissing sound as air rushed out of the bowels of the ship. A hailstorm of debris came tumbling off the decks and landed in the water around the young bluejackets. A heavy object, possibly a ventilator that had been forced free, fell from a deck looming over the trio and crashed down on two of them—Steve Allard and Mason Burr. Allard cried out that his arm had been hurt, but there was no sound from Burr. Reid and Allard swam to his side and found his head bloodied.

"Steve and I checked Mason," Reid said, "and there was nothing we could do, as he was already dead." Mason Kirby Burr's body floated off in the heavy seas, borne afloat by his life jacket. Croteau, who knew Burr well, saw his body a few minutes later. "I told Walker I saw Burr and I thought he was all done because he looked battered. Walker said, 'Let's not talk about it.'" "After we left Mason's body," Reid continued, "Steve Allard and I didn't see anyone for five or ten minutes."

Allard told Reid that his arm was broken and that he could not use it. A strong swimmer, Reid managed to find some large planks, about twenty feet long, and he brought one to Allard. They were almost totally submerged in the Arctic waters—"just our arms were over the planks. We just used them for buoyancy."

Reid lost his knee boots and socks when he walked into the water from the bridge and he attempted to warm his feet by putting them into a brown canvas bag designed to hold first aid equipment. Bags of this type were kept at the gun tubs and some were now floating in the debris.

The waves were increasing and had reached some twenty to thirty feet. Reid and Allard were tossed about in the debris which had fallen from the ship and they struggled to make their way toward the other men who were visible from the peaks of the waves. Reid said that he did not think of possible suction when the ship was going down and added that they were "very lucky in that detail as...all the water came in the air vents and out through the forward ventilator holes, hatches, and such, so she sank with what you might say was no suction...."

"Just before she went down the last of the air was released from her with a loud sound."

Woodie Pozen was close enough to the *Henry Bacon* so he "could see figures on it"—probably Captain Carini and Chief Haviland. "At that moment there was an explosion and when I looked again there was no more ship." The *Henry Bacon* was gone forever. She was the last Liberty ship to be sunk by the German Luftwaffe in World War II, only four months before the war in Europe came to an end!

Captain Carini was awarded the Mariner's Medal posthumously. The presentation was made to his wife, Mrs. Josephine Carini of Long Island City, Queens. Witnessed by some ten thousand persons, the presentation was made in a public ceremony on the steps of the Sub-Treasury Building on Wall Street and Nassau Street, New York City, on October 3, 1945, by Captain Hewlitt R. Bishop, Atlantic Coast Director of the War Shipping Administration. Mrs. Carini later returned to Genoa, Italy.

CHAPTER 16

Rescue

When the SS *Henry Bacon* slid under the waves to the ocean floor, it left a huge emptiness in the Arctic for the survivors who had been clustered about her. A casual observer on a high-flying plane would have seen nothing but a moderately rough ocean below. But a closer observer hovering low over the scene would have distinguished two lifeboats, one large Navy raft, two makeshift rafts, and pieces of debris bearing frightened and freezing survivors. Adrift in the huge empty ocean, the group felt very alone. Many of them had already seen death. Perhaps a dozen men had died by the time the *Henry Bacon* reached the bottom.

Captain Alfred Carini and Chief Haviland went down with the ship. Young Second Mate Carl Fubel was killed outright by the explosion just before the sinking. Gunner Mason Burr was killed when a ventilator slid off the deck and struck him in the head. Three other gunners, Donald Mayden, Elmer Potvin, and Earl Rubley, were not seen after the *Bacon* went under. Purser Robert Hunt found a piece of timber after he jumped into the ocean, but he lost his grip and died of exposure. First Assistant Engineer Edgar Snyder had been ill and perished in the water. Messman George Shipka slipped from a large beam and was lost. Second Cook Cornelius Kearns was last seen by the steward, Clayton Ingram, on the starboard side of number 3 hatch. Presumably he died with the ship or shortly before.

Though no one at that time could know the full extent of casualties, they all were aware that death was in the air. Yet the sailors found grim humor. At least at first. "Hold on, fellows," someone shouted, "We're only a mile from land. Straight down." Those who had jumped into the Arctic Ocean suffered more severely than those able to keep somewhat dry in the lifeboats and on the rafts. About an hour after he witnessed the death of Bob Hunt, George Bartin saw Able-bodied Seaman Frederick Funken, floating motionless, foaming at the mouth, and carried away by a life preserver. Extreme sleepiness and occasional frothing at the mouth were observed as symptoms of freezing to death.

"Such men probably never knew what happened," Herrmann said. "I would think death was peaceful and a relief from the fight for survival." Later, Seaman Donald Schiesher, 23, of Chicago Heights, Illinois, froze to death and his body slipped off a raft and was lost. Chief Cook John W. Mastracci, 40, of Revere, Massachusetts, also died on a raft. A former contractor and a ten-year veteran of the Merchant Marine, Mastracci had survived two earlier wartime sinkings—in 1941 while returning from Egypt, and later coming home from Oran. He had the end of his elbow shot off in the latter engagement and had shipped out on the *Bacon* after convalescing at home since August.

Mastracci, according to Goodrich, "started us singing 'I've got a lovely bunch of coconuts; there they are a standing in a row,' popularized both by Freddy Martin and His Orchestra and game-show impresario Merv Griffin, and then we sang 'Roll Out the Barrel'…. It was getting dark," he recalled, when "finally John said 'Well, boys. I think it is time to pray,' and led us in the 'Lord's Prayer.'"

"All was quiet for awhile, and then some of the men started to drift from the raft. I remember George Shipka from Elizabeth, New Jersey. He was sitting across from me. His big brown eyes were staring at me and he was smiling. In the distance we saw a masthead light. I yelled at George, 'Hold on. I can see the light; it's coming closer,' but I was talking to a dead man."

Shipka, a messman who had survived a torpedoing in the Mediterranean the year before, would have been 22 years old in March 1945. He had joined the Merchant Marine in 1943. His former ship was split in half, but the crew was able to keep it together with cables while it drifted to the Italian shore. He left a wife and a 2-year-old daughter. His uncles, Private First Class Bartholomew

Delasey and Sergeant Frank Delasey, were both killed the year before in France. In addition to the immediate danger of freezing to death and dying of exposure, some of the survivors had a gnawing fear that they would not be found before darkness, which comes early on winter nights in the Arctic. Ernest Russell recalled "at the sinking time we had about three hours' daylight left of the day." Even those who had escaped getting drenched in the ocean did not imagine they could survive the night. Others feared the possibility of drifting to the Norwegian coast and being captured by the Germans.

After Signalman Steve Allard and his buddy Frank Reid had made their way through the heavy seas to the group of men floating on pieces of debris, they told about the messages they had received from the plane before the *Bacon* went under. "We told the men to hang on, that the plane said that help was on the way," Reid reported. But the very sight of the plane had already brought that message to the men in the water. Oiler Woodie Pozen, on a three-man raft with Dick Burbine and Navy man Silas Doe of Cheshire, Connecticut, had a typical reaction: "A Grumman Wildcat from the aircraft carrier came over and dipped his wings, which I suppose was his way of telling us not to give up hope."

The men actually in the water, clinging to beams, planks, and the like, tried to group together to bolster each other's morale. There was less likelihood, they felt, that anyone would be overlooked when the destroyers arrived. Gunner Reid recalled that he tried to get everyone to talk or sing, "But I guess mostly we all prayed. I remember asking Daniels to say a prayer." Daniels recalls that the men asked him to pray aloud: "Dear God, please help us. I know you will, as you have helped us before. And if it's Thy will, may we be rescued. Amen."

Even those out of water began to freeze. "Oh, it was getting cold," Joe Scott, commanding lifeboat number two, said. "I began to sing to keep warm, as I knew we had so little time left. So I prayed to God in my own way for help soon, or we would not live the night through." But after three hours in an open boat "we had it. I had seen so many go down; I was sick that I couldn't help them." Almost as an omen, "From out of nowhere came a flock of seagulls over our heads, as if to shield us. I could almost reach up and touch them.... I looked up and said, 'Thank you dear God in heaven, I know you have sent your angel to guide us and watch over us.'"

While the seagulls were an answer to a prayer for Scott, Frank Reid had a different reaction. "I remember seagulls flying very low over us like vultures, and how they would cock their heads to one side to watch us."

When he hit the water, Croteau wrote, he saw a five-gallon can "near me...it was empty and I hung onto this a few minutes until Walker picked me up onto the wheelhouse top. It was when I swam over to get the five-gallon can is when I thought I saw Burr." Russell believed he saw Burr's "skull bursted by a vent which had been propelled by the...boiler of the ship." Croteau continued relating what happened after the explosion. "I was already hit in the back by some heavy object." The five-gallon can fell near me from the explosions...many things were falling and I thought I would surely get hit from more objects than I did."

Walker, Croteau, and Martin were able to cling to the roof of the wheelhouse, but the weight of three men caused it to ride below the surface of the water. When the men squatted on their knees, the water was waist-deep. "We took turns standing up and rubbing our legs to start the blood circulating," Croteau said. Martin gradually began to get very glassy-eyed and Walker and Croteau tried unsuccessfully to keep him conscious. "I started to mumble something," he wrote, "he looked at me and said, 'What's the matter.'" Croteau told him "I was saying a prayer so things would take a turn for the better. It was starting to get dark and the men knew if they weren't picked up before dark, they would have a small chance for survival." "With this thought in mind," Croteau continued, "he [Martin] looked at the men and said, 'I never prayed before. Please, pray out loud so I can pray with you,' and I did.... "When we thought he died," Croteau continued, "I guess we just didn't want to believe it because we hung onto him as if he were alive. I guess we were telling ourselves he might still have a chance."

According to official British Admiralty records, the convoy received the message that the *Henry Bacon* was torpedoed at 2:26 P.M. By 3 P.M. a bearing had been obtained which established the position of the *Bacon* at about forty-seven miles astern of the convoy and heading in the wrong direction.

"It will be appreciated that in operations of this kind," Captain "Teak" Allison of the *Zambesi* said, "relative positions are all-important. The geographical position of the convoy flagship, and indeed *Zambesi*, was fairly accurately known, within three or four miles, by means of special radio devices, and it is certain that the *Henry Bacon* without such aids could well have been considerably in error in her position."

While the *Bacon* sent out a direction-finding beam, the commanders of the convoy felt it necessary to risk sending a plane off the deck of the carrier in the turbulent seas. In 1945 direction-finding techniques were not considered reliable by everyone and, of course, did not establish the distance. Spud Campbell, on the other hand, believed that "direction finders at the time were sufficiently accurate to 'home in on a transmission' and would become more accurate as the rescue vessel approached the lifeboat. It would not establish the distance but if the destroyer continued in the direction indicated by the beam, it would eventually find the lifeboat." The carrier plane, as it hovered over the survivors, reported the position of the sinking ship and her estimated distance from the convoy. At the same time the convoy was able to obtain a direct radar fix on the aircraft. While shipborne radar in 1945 might not have been able to pick up another surface vessel fifty miles away, "it will be appreciated," Captain Allison explained, "that an aircraft at two thousand feet would be visible on the radar screen at sixty-five nautical miles. In addition, the radio signal from the aircraft would be D/F'ed by the carrier. The rescue force was then given the bearing and distance of the survivors."

Just like the roles they played during the evacuation mission at Sørøya, Captain Allison and the HMS *Zambesi* were named to lead the small flotilla, which included two other destroyers—the *Zest*, which had also been to Sørøya, and the *Opportune*, com-

manded by Robert Edward Dudley Ryder, a very tough, power-
fully-built officer who had seen service with a naval unit on the
Antarctic continent. Early in World War II he won the Victoria
Cross, the most highly coveted decoration of the British military,
for bravery in the face of the enemy during a commando raid at
St. Nazaire. His citation read, in part: "For great gallantry.... He
commanded a force of small unprotected ships in an attack on a
heavily defended port and led HMS *Cambeltown* in under intense
fire from short range weapons at point blank range. Though the
main object of the expedition had been accomplished in the beach-
ing of *Cambeltown*, he remained on the spot conducting operations, evacuating men from *Cambeltown* and dealing with strong
points and close range weapons while exposed to heavy fire for
one hour and sixteen minutes, and did not withdraw till it was
certain that his ship could be of no use in rescuing any of the
Commando Troops who were still ashore. That his motor gun-
boat, now full of dead and wounded, should have survived and
should have been able to withdraw through an intense barrage of
close range fire was almost a miracle." Worn before all other decorations, the Victoria Cross all too often must be awarded posthumously.
After the war, Ryder became a member of the British Parliament.

"We were given no position," Ryder said, "and simply ran back
on the bearing we had taken ourselves." Commanding Officer
Allison explained that after he received information and instructions from the flagship, he divided his squadron accordingly. "I
disposed the vessels in line abreast about visibility distance (perhaps two miles) apart, and steered north at the maximum safe speed.
With the wind astern, we were able to make about twenty knots
without suffering structural damage.... "No bearings or signals were
received by me from the survivors of the *Henry Bacon* until I actually sighted them in the exact position expected." It was about a
two-hour run for the destroyers.

The survivors in the lifeboats and rafts and on debris in the
water sighted the approaching ships and began to send up flares—
using their Very pistols—just before darkness would have closed
in. Spotting the flares, Captain Allison ordered the *Opportune* "to

deal with the boats, while *Zambesi* endeavored to rescue the men floating in the water. [The] *Zest* was ordered to carry out a circular antisubmarine patrol around the area to guard the slow-moving ships from attack." Commander Hicks of the *Zest* pointed out that "by astonishing good luck the sinking coincided with an afternoon of relative calm, so that the rescue was not the impossibility it would been on almost any other day."

The Norwegians, who had been in the open boat the longest, had, like the others, seen the English reconnaissance plane long before. "We all knew they had discovered us, but hours had elapsed and the darkness was slowly approaching," Henrik Pedersen of Sørøya recalled. "The weather also had started to increase. All aboard started to fear that if help did not arrive we might go under. The boat was small and the sea large, many thought. The American seamen aboard were silent...and all were serious."

Pszybysz remembered wondering if the Grumman fighter from the carrier could possibly have been the one he had worked on when he was employed by Grumman in Long Island some years before. "An angel out of the sky!"

A little girl of three years asked, "Papa, won't we see land soon?" She thought the men had rowed so long without reaching shore. "No land yet...but soon help will come." Time passed.

A seaman mumbled something but the Norwegians did not understand. He then pointed to what appeared to be a dark spot and soon it was recognizable as a ship. "It was the English destroyer *Zambesi*," Pedersen recalled. "The same which had fetched us from Sørøya." It was, however, the HMS *Opportune* which was assigned to rescue those in the lifeboats.

"It meant a lot to me as I had been in a similar plight once myself," reported Ryder of the *Opportune*. "The first three men picked up were from a Carley float," Ryder reported to the Admiralty. "As the ship approached them they appeared in good spirits and good health but it was soon found that they were almost completely numb with cold. The second raft they approached had another three men on board, and finally they found a large but hastily constructed and rapidly disintegrating raft from which six men were rescued. During this time the bodies of five others were observed in the vicinity."

"We got two boatloads and some of the rafts.... They were pulled over the side without ceremony as we were expecting to be attacked." As Captain Allison recalls the story, Ryder was in command of a decoy ship early in the war. The decoys were known as "Q" ships in the First World War. "This type of antisubmarine warfare," Allison continued, "proved a failure in World War II and was fairly soon discontinued. Ryder's ship was sunk by a U-boat in midocean (Atlantic) and, as far as I can gather, he was picked up by a friendly vessel after more than *twenty-four hours* in the water, hanging on to a piece of wreckage. The strength of his constitution may be judged by the fact that he was the only survivor." Captain Allison did, however, add that "this story is secondhand and cannot therefore be relied upon. Ryder himself never mentioned this experience to me." Ryder did in fact attest to his experiences.

The refugee lifeboat was drawn to the side of the destroyer by a line thrown from the warship. Pszybysz remembers the lifeboat rubbing up and down against the side. "As a wave came," he said, "we would hand up a woman or a child to the British sailors." Then the rest climbed aboard—the Norwegian men and mariners Campbell, Garatz, McIsaac, Gorman, and Pszybysz. "I was going to untie the boat," Pszybysz said, "but someone on the destroyer yelled 'Don't bother,' and simply cut the rope after we were all aboard." Pszybysz remembered many hands grabbing him and his sheepskin coat, and the good feeling he had when he felt something solid on the rescuing ship. As he started below, one of the British sailors handed him a lit cigarette.

Third Mate Joe Scott said there was a "cry of joy" from the men in his lifeboat when they sighted the *Opportune*. "We knew we were saved," Scott said. "We wouldn't have lasted another hour if help didn't get to us." Among those rescued with Scott were Engineer Lawrence Champlin, Wiper William Gray, Deckman Allan Lammon, Fire Tender William Willdridge, and Fireman Fergus White. Champlin reported that the *Opportune* found the boats "in the nick of time."

After the *Opportune* spotted the survivors, "she came up to us," Reed recalled, "and got us on the lee side. The seas were still heaving, and boarding her via the rope boarding net was no small trick. The boarding net was woven like a large fishnet, with squares about 12 inches by 12 inches, the entire net being about twenty feet wide, hanging from the rail down into the water.

"We were told that a Navy man who had been on the bridge of the *Henry Bacon* during the final minutes was floating on the roof of the pilot house, and the *Opportune* had attempted to rescue him before us. He had an arm missing, was semiconscious, and couldn't get hold of the net. He slipped into the water and was last seen washing under the stern of the *Opportune*. I heard also that another destroyer—probably the HMS *Zealous*—had picked up one of the German pilots, questioned him briefly, and had him thrown back into the sea…. The British greeted us with cups of hot beef broth laced with rum—nothing could have tasted better!"

"The refugees were picked up first and then we went up the net one at a time, leaving the two boats adrift," he said. "I thought I was in good shape when I was in the boat, but when I got on the deck of the *Opportune* my legs buckled under me and two seamen carried me to the captain's tub where they gave me a hot bath. The circulation came back in a short time and I was all right." Scott said that after he was taken aboard the *Opportune*, he went down to check on the condition of the Norwegian refugees. "When they saw me, they hugged me and kissed me, and cried. I didn't know what they were saying, but I know they thanked us all and God for being so good to them as their troubles were over. Ryder called him to his cabin and thanked me for a job well done. 'Scotty,' he said, 'we have thirteen breaks on deck and if the sides hold we will make it.'" Scott was greatly concerned over the heavy losses: "Oh, how I wish I could have saved more lives." But he also was extremely grateful to the British rescue party. "I thanked the boys and the captain for us all, and asked God to watch over those boys in the British Navy." David Goodrich believes he owed his life to a British sailor by the name of John Scott, who jumped overboard to save him.

Commander Ryder also went down to see the Norwegians in the wardroom. "They were a pathetic sight—suffering fearfully both from their experiences and from seasickness. He was taken by a young boy (apparently August Larsen) "who was as bright as anything—the only one conscious—and he was pretty well in charge—a most impressive effort."

After rescuing those in the lifeboats, the *Opportune* moved on to save those who had managed to climb aboard the only large raft that was serviceable. Most of these men had been transferred to the raft from Joe Scott's overcrowded lifeboat shortly after leaving the side of the *Henry Bacon*; three others had been pulled out of the water—Chuck Reid, Joe Marbach, and Kermit Price. Normand Croteau remembered Price as getting off on the starboard side "on what we call a one-man raft. It was very small and he came floating by the bridge in this small life raft smoking a cigarette and waving at us in a jolly mood. This always stuck in my mind because it was an example of the good spirits of the crew."

The ranking Navy man on the raft, Jerry Gerold, recalled that the destroyers arrived shortly before it began to get dark, and just when the waves were getting bigger. "We kept watch but couldn't even see any other rafts or survivors around…. All at once someone said he saw a mast. We all stood up and looked, but we were in the hollow of a wave. As we rose to the top, we saw a destroyer and I was so happy I cried.

"Elias Banian, an Armenian boy who was very shy and never had anything to say, almost had a fit when he saw the destroyer. He fired the Very signal pistol. I fired the Very pistol, everyone wanted to shoot the red flares to let the destroyer know where we were.

"'Maybe they didn't see us,' someone would say. 'Shoot another one.'" The destroyer was then maybe a mile away and was blinking signals to the merchantmen. As Chuck Reid recalled, the men "fired the flares with recklessness."

"What a sight to see!" Reed added. "A British destroyer was named HMS *Opportune*—and *how* opportune!

Warren Bacheldor told of the rough seas: "When the raft would go up, they'd grab a man, and so on until the last one, which was me."

Gerold agreed in thinking "it was a tough job getting aboard the ship. My hands were so stiff, and my legs didn't work so well either....

"I couldn't walk good when I got aboard so two of the fellows took me below and took off all my clothes and gave me a nice warm blanket. Then came some of that famous British rum with hot soup.... I'll never forget how swell they treated us..." Reed reported that the crew of the *Opportune* "were a rugged lot, and very generous with their meager fare.... One Limey gave me his huge leather seaboots and another loaned me his hammock. I finally gave up the hammock, as the combination of it and a turtle-neck sweater seemed to attract the lice which the poor Norwegians were still infested with. I found the bare deck less attractive to both me and the lice." Gerold and the other Navy noncoms were put forward in the British petty officers' mess.

Normand Croteau and Louis Walker were still floating atop the roof of the wheelhouse of the *Henry Bacon* with young Martin, who was unconscious and glassy-eyed, before the *Opportune* came into view. Croteau said he and Walker really thought Martin was dead, but "I guess we didn't want to believe it and we hung onto him as if he were alive. I guess we were telling ourselves he might still have a chance....

"The *Opportune* swung its stern towards the raft and hit kind of hard, so Walker and myself grabbed onto the net that hung over the side and we couldn't notice what was going on because some sailors from the *Opportune* came over the side to get us." He didn't realize what was going on "because I was put onto a stretcher and carried to sick bay. I was told on board that the sailors couldn't recover Martin's body." Walker's legs were badly frostbitten. After he was hospitalized there was some talk of amputation but, fortunately, this was not necessary. Walker was treated aboard ship, then spent thirty days in a US Navy hospital at Roseneath, Scotland.

Croteau was placed in the sick bay aboard the *Opportune* where the doctor worked on his back to find the piece of metal that struck him when the *Henry Bacon* blew up. "They had to put tongue depressors across my mouth to bite into because they had no anesthesia," Croteau said. "They couldn't work on me for long because the wound was very close to the spine." Croteau was later dropped off at the Faeroe Islands for x-rays and he stayed in a small English Army hospital in the Faeroes for more than a month before being shipped back to the United States where he was examined further. "The piece of metal everyone thought I had in my back was never there," Croteau concluded.

Inasmuch as the men on the *Opportune* first attended those in the lifeboats and on the rafts, they were the ones who picked up the great bulk of the survivors—56 of the 64 who were saved.

Captain Allison left the toughest job for himself—to locate and rescue the men on small rafts and those clinging to debris in the water.

"The task of picking up the men floating in their life jackets was very difficult," he explained, "because although the weather had moderated considerably, there was still a heavy sea running. The men in the water were quite unable to move to help themselves climb on board, as their limbs were paralyzed by the cold. It was quite impossible to tell whether a man was dead or alive before bringing a ship 360 feet alongside—the ship's vertical motion might be ten or twenty feet and rolling up to fifteen degrees. It was thus necessary to send men from the ship on lines into the water in order to grasp each man as he floated in his life jacket and drop him up a jumping ladder on board.

"In many cases the operation was fruitless as the man was already dead.... The first three men we picked up were from a Carley float. As the ship approached them they appeared in good spirits and good health. But it was soon found that they were almost completely numb with cold." Oiler Woodie Pozen remembered the incident well. He had already begun to drift off into a probable final sleep when his young friend, Dick Burbine, yelled at him and said he could see a destroyer. "I told him I thought he was seeing things," Pozen said. "Then I looked up and saw the crosstrees of the destroyer. I waved my arms like the devil. With wonderful maneuvering the captain of the destroyer, which I later found was HMS *Zambesi*, got to us." Burbine disagreed with the hand-waving. "We were unable to stand up when they set us on the deck [of the *Zambesi*]. Our clothes were frozen to our bodies, and had to be cut off. We were so frozen, we couldn't use our hands to reach for the ropes."

"Burbine and the Navy man (Silas Doe) were able with the aid of a few sailors from the destroyer to get aboard," Pozen continued. "I had hold of the heaving line which they had thrown to me. They told me to tie it around myself, but my hands were so numb and I was so exhausted that I called to them and told them I couldn't make it." But, they would not let him perish. "They yelled down to me, 'Hold that line; don't let go!'" One of the destroyer's crew members, whose name Pozen would never know "came down a Jacob's ladder onto the raft and tied the line around me. I weighed so much with all my wet gear on that it took fifteen or twenty men to pull me aboard.

"Four men grabbed me, one by each arm and one by each leg and carried me facedown into the shower room. Then they took off all my clothes, put blankets on me and took me, to a bench and made a bed for me. Later the doctor came in and asked me how I felt, but I was too dazed to know.

"Then they brought in George Bartin, night cook and baker. They sat him on the table. He was frothing at the mouth and had a vacant stare in his eyes. I called his name, but he didn't answer. Finally they put him into bed and that was the last I saw of him until the next day."

Bartin had had a rough time of it. He and Bosun Holcomb Lammon were submerged in the Arctic for several hours and shortly before the destroyers appeared they were clinging to the same piece of timber. "Because of the excitement of seeing the rescue ship," Bartin related years later, "he (Lammon) let go the timber and as soon as he did so his body submerged and never came to the surface again. He had discarded his life preserver some time before."

The Meritorious Service Citation attached to Holcomb Lammon's official record states, "He worked indefatigably until the last moment and then jumped over the side. He was not among those rescued. His courage, skill and determination to save lives, without thought to his own safety, will be a lasting inspiration to all seamen of the United States Merchant Marine." Lammon was awarded the Mariner's Medal posthumously.

Bartin also reported seeing the body of First Mate Lynn R. Palmer, less than 75 feet from him, a few minutes before Bartin was picked up by the *Zambesi*. "He still had on his life preserver," Bartin said of Palmer. "His body was motionless, his head hung forward, and foam was coming from his mouth. The destroyer did not pick him up after I had been taken aboard. I understand that the doctor of the British destroyer instructed the crew not to pick up anyone in the water who was foaming at the mouth.... When I got aboard the destroyer I saw Palmer's body still floating in the water. There is no doubt in my mind that he was dead." Gunner Frank Reid, who ended up with only a timber for himself although he had built a raft for others, was trying to hold an unconscious shipmate afloat when the rescuers approached. It was a shipmate he did not know. "The destroyer pulled up as close as possible," he recalled, "to block the wind and make for a calmer sea." He climbed partway up "as the ship rolled and when she rolled again I got farther up and locked my arm in a life ring that had a rope at-tached—supplied by a British sailor, who jumped into the water. The *Zambesi* crewman asked if he was all right, and I said, 'Yeah.'

"'Hold on to the ring and they'll pull you aboard,' the voice said. 'I'll take care of this other fellow.'" But the other merchant mariner was dead and they abandoned his body. The last Reid remembered before passing out was a voice saying, "We've got you now." When he came to he was tied in a bunk so he wouldn't fall out, and his clothes had to be cut away because they were frozen to his body. The British sailors rubbed him with a Turkish towel and when the blood started to circulate, Reid, a two-hundred-pounder, leaped to his feet in his delirium and started swinging his big fists at his benefactors. When they had calmed him down, they gave him a shot of rum, hot broth, and the "ever-present British tea." Reid's buddy, popular Steve Allard, was less fortunate.

Despite his broken arm, Allard managed to survive until the *Zambesi* arrived. He was unable to hang on to the steel ring he was offered, and a daring British sailor climbed down into the water and tied a line to his life jacket. The men on the *Zambesi* began to pull him to safety, but when he was about halfway up his jacket ripped off and he fell back into the Arctic. Allard—the man who was always so cocky, so willing, so able to take care of himself— was lost. His death was particularly difficult for his mates to comprehend and acknowledge.

The third powder man on the *Bacon's* five-inch gun, Eugene Daniels of South Carolina, was one of those rescued by the *Zambesi*. He stated that it had already started to snow before the destroyers arrived. "It was a beautiful sight as the British destroyer came into view," he recalled. "As it came close enough, I grabbed one of the ropes hanging over the side. As I bounced up and down in the rough water I was almost on deck one time." He spotted a Jacob's ladder over the side of the ship and put his arm through it and hung on. "The British sailors tied ropes to me and pulled me aboard…. I passed out then. When I came to, I asked them to put me in a warm place. They told me I was in the warmest place on the ship and had six blankets and a hot water bottle. The cramps were so bad that the doctors and sailors massaged me.

"There was a strange rattle in my chest. I had heard of the 'death rattle' and wondered if I was thawing out or dying." Daniels said that he and Charles Harlacher had "stayed close together until the rescue ship came…Harlacher seemed to be alive at that time," Daniels said. "I was surprised to learn that he had not been saved."

Second Assistant Engineer Joseph Provencal, age 41, was perhaps the only man over 35 years of age who had been immersed in the Arctic and was still alive when the destroyers arrived. He was within minutes of being saved. He caught the line that was thrown to him, but fatigue and numb hands caused him to lose his grip when he was more than halfway up. He fell back into the icy ocean and was slammed against the side of the ship by a big wave. Witnesses saw him drift under the ship's propeller. "There is no doubt that he was killed instantly," Third Mate Scott reported later.

Navy Lieutenant Sippola, who had directed the amazing defense of the SS *Henry Bacon* before she succumbed to overwhelming odds, approached the *Zambesi* clinging to a rapidly disintegrating makeshift raft with six of his Navy gun crew. The sea was so rough at that point that the only possible rescue was by throwing lines to the men. Sippola, whose first child was born back in the States during this voyage, assisted the men by securing lines to their bodies and waited until they were hauled aboard the *Zambesi*. The lieutenant refused to be rescued himself until the last man on his raft was safe. But then the line thrown to him fell just beyond his reach. He abandoned the life raft to grab the rope but, due to exposure and exhaustion, was unable to keep afloat. Lieutenant Sippola sank and did not reappear. The Navy Silver Star was awarded him posthumously for "unfaltering leadership, valiant fortitude and self-sacrificing devotion to duty in the face of extreme peril." The Navy listed six members of his gun crew as eyewitnesses.

"By 1800 (6 P.M.) It was rapidly getting dark," Captain Allison, commanding officer of the rescuing destroyer force, said, "and the weather was worsening, so that [the] *Zest* was ordered to assist."

By this time only a few survivors were left in the water and the *Zest* retrieved the pair that had swum from the ship together— Deck Engineer Wilmo Testerman and Clayton Ingram, the steward who had cared for the Norwegians on the *Bacon*. While securing a life preserver from a raft, Ingram was hit by a violent wave and suffered a leg injury; he was later hospitalized in Glasgow.

According to the notes he made at the time, *Zest* Commander Hicks said he "learned of Captain's (Carini's) madness in turning back (in the wrong direction) and then his heroism in giving up his place in the boat to his Norwegian passengers." Second radioman Bill Herrmann was the only officer rescued by the *Zambesi*. The 32-year-old professional musician had managed to secure two of the large beams used to hold the locomotives and he kept most of his body out of the water during the hours he was bobbing about in the Arctic Ocean before the destroyers arrived. Still adrift, he remembered having heard that if a man has the will to live he would have a better chance to survive. "So," he said, "I tried to get into that frame of mind." After the *Zambesi* drew along-side, he said, "I remember seeing people throw grappling hooks on lines down to us in the water." Like some others, Herrmann lost consciousness just at the point of rescue—his grappling hook parted from his coat and he was saved by a *Zambesi* officer who went over the side of the vessel on the nets. "It was by the grace of God I survived," Herrmann said later. "I believe the reason was because of the daily rosary which I said morning and night through-out the trip.... The chap who saved me," he reported, "was a young subaltern from Australia."

Several men from the *Zambesi*—including Lieutenant G. A. Hamilton and Lieutenant Rodney Bowden—repeatedly climbed down into the violent and icy sea to rescue men from the *Henry Bacon* who did not have strength to climb aboard. "As second in command of the ship," Lieutenant Hamilton said, "it was my re-sponsibility to get the men out of the water as quickly as possible. They were too far gone to do anything for themselves, and I had absolutely no alternative but to go into the water and put ropes around them to haul them up.

"Under the circumstances you will realize that this is not an order that one can give anyone else, and I had no choice in the matter.... Far more credit really is due the other officer, Lieuten-ant Bowden, and one rating (enlisted man)...who *volunteered* to continue this chilly task after I had been hauled out."

"Darkness fell sometime before 1800," Allison recalled, "and it was no longer possible or even likely that we could find further survivors. In this circumstance, I ordered the four destroyers to follow *Zambesi* in company to rejoin the convoy."

The *Zambesi* heroes were decorated for their part in the res-cue upon the recommendation of their commanding officer, Cap-tain Allison. "It should be noted," Allison remarked, "that these men were continually at hazard of being crushed by the ship her-self, despite the great care that was taken in handling her." Captain Allison also laid particular stress "on the self-sacrifice of the crew of the *Henry Bacon* who faced almost certain death to give safety to the Norwegians in the boats....I need hardly add that every effort was made to make the Norwegians and US sailors as comfortable as possible on the last lap of the journey to Scapa Flow."

In retrospect, Commander Jessel said, "Had I known, at the time, of the extent of the risks involved, I am sure I would have been much more frightened than I actually was."

British Lieutenant Hamilton, who had himself gone into the Arctic waters many times to rescue survivors, turned over his cabin to an American. "I do not even know if he was officer or rating. He got the cabin because, having swallowed a lot of fuel oil, he was worse off than the others, most of whom recovered in 24 hours," he said.

Bacheldor recalls that "all the ships left their extra food in Murmansk, so we didn't have much to eat for a couple of days. I remember once they threw a loaf of bread down the hold and we fought for a piece." Again, Dick Burbine took exception: "The crew of the *Zambesi* treated us as long-lost mates, with cigarettes, rum, scrambled eggs, and friendship befitting royalty. They shared what small luxuries they had with us. The food wasn't the best in the world, but it was the best they had. We ate the same food as the British sailors."

The *Bacon* had been sunk, but it took its toll on the Germans. The Germans, however, did not see it that way. As Commander Hamilton wrote: "It was not always easy to appreciate what went on in the Germans' minds. We would witness an attack and, later the same evening, hear the German radio report of the incident bearing not the faintest resemblance to the facts. Now who told the lies?" After having served five years in this war, Hamilton had his own opinion, "and it was at this state of the war, that there was a bit of each. First the pilots, sent out on a task with dire threats of failure, came back with some possible claims. These would be magnified by the commanding officer of the base as a matter of principle, and by the time it was processed by the propaganda ministry, it had become fantastic…"

To illustrate his point, Hamilton cited two signals received on the outward run from Scapa—the *Bacon* was not in this group:

"To all escorts, from the Admiral commanding first cruiser squadron. I congratulate the escorts and convoy on so decisively defeating this forenoon's torpedo attacks. Preliminary assessments show two certain, one probably by fighters, and four certain, five probably by gunfire of escorts. Next time single-engine aircraft must not be fired at, we lost one fighter, and had three damaged, but both pilots are safe."

The signal left doubt in Hamilton's mind "whether our losses were all due to our own action…but that evening, as we ploughed smugly along," he received another message from the admiral:

"According to Hee Haw, all ships in company had been sunk."

Hamilton agreed "they had to make that claim, although no ships had been sunk…they were pretty desperate [at that juncture of the war]. How much better to get a straggler and sink him, than have an abortive attack on a well-defended convoy? You may even get home with a picture of a ship sinking, and you don't have to admit you never made contact with the main force. *Henry Bacon* may well have unwittingly drawn the enemy's fire; there can be little doubt that they knew the convoy was not far away, and that they could have found the main body had they had the stomach for a fight."

CHAPTER 17

The Way Home

"No Arctic convoy ever suffered a more severe buffeting" than RA64 carrying the Norwegian refugees to Scotland in February 1945, according to the official British history of the war. Yet only three ships were lost—the corvette *Bluebell* and the SS *Horace Gray*, both just outside Murmansk, and, some days later, the SS *Henry Bacon* off from Norway's Lofoten Islands. The last voyage of the *Henry Bacon* ended at 67 degrees north, 07 degrees east—just north of the Arctic Circle. The time—1520 (3:20 P.M.).

Of the ship's total complement of eighty-six: forty-one merchant seamen, twenty-six Navy Armed Guard, and nineteen Norwegian refugees—more than a quarter were lost, fifteen seamen and seven Navy gunners. Among those who died were the highest ranking men on the ship—the captain, the first mate, the second mate, the chief engineer, and the first and second assistant engineers, and the lone Navy officer in charge of the Armed Guard gun crew.

In his report on the event, British Captain Allison, who headed the rescue, said, "In these waters the chances of survival are very much greater if the men can be kept from being totally immersed. This was well understood by the crew of the *Henry Bacon*. Nevertheless, all the billets in the boats were given to their passengers, the Norwegian refugees, and thus all were saved at the sacrifice of many who subsequently died of exposure in the water before help could reach them."

The sacrifice of the Americans was also recognized by the Norwegians both officially and unofficially. One humble Norwegian refugee showed his friendliness in self-conscious fashion by showing his beautifully carved meerschaum pipe to Chuck Reed.

"He tried to explain to me that in Norwegian it was called a 'peepa'," Reed said. "He was pleased when I complimented him on it (I, too, am a pipe-lover) and it appeared that the pipe was his only remaining possession. All of the Norwegians conducted themselves discreetly and unobtrusively, and clung only to themselves."

Norwegian Colonel Gunnar Johnson, who risked his own life countless times for his people, was aboard the *Zambesi* and contacted many of the American survivors, as did the Norwegian communications officer Sublieutenant A. S. Andrassen. As a gesture of gratitude, Colonel Johnson insisted on giving his stateroom, which was the captain's day cabin, to Radioman Bill Herrmann. Johnson's only expressed regret in leaving the fine cabin was that during the trip back from Murmansk he had found it quite impossible to read the only nonofficial book in the cabin, *The Life of Lord Fisher*, more than twice. "While pleased with the idea of living in the captain's cabin," Herrmann said, "I tried to turn down the offer because I was perfectly happy on the bridge."

One of the *Bacon*'s oilers, Woodie Pozen, reported: "While I was sitting on a bench on the destroyer, a Norwegian colonel, who I later learned was responsible for the evacuation of the refugees from Norway, said to me, 'The Norwegian Government and the Norwegian people will never forget what the American seamen have done for them.'" He was right. The Norwegian high command in London commended the "spirit, loyalty, and ability of the officers and crew of the vessel *Henry Bacon* of the United States commercial fleet." The commander in chief of the Norwegian forces, Crown Prince Olaf of Norway (later King Olaf), said in a message to Vice Admiral E. S. Land, administrator of the United States War Shipping Administration: "On receipt of this heroic tale, I find it incumbent upon me to express to you, Sir, my appreciation and admiration of the outstanding discipline and self-sacrifice displayed by the *Henry Bacon*, in pace with the finest traditions of American sailors." Land responded by saying, "As you may know, this letter and the rescue of these Norwegian subjects were the basis of a press release recently published by the War Shipping Administration."

King Haakon of Norway presented the Norwegian War Medal to all crewmen, surviving or deceased. The Norwegian king also honored Captain Allison, who headed the British destroyer expedition that first evacuated the Norwegian refugees from Sørøya and then saved nineteen of them, along with the Americans, after the sinking of the *Henry Bacon*. He was made a commander of the Order of St. Olaf. Later, Captain Carini's widow was presented with the Mariner's Medal [the equivalent of the armed services Purple Heart] by Vice Admiral E. S. Land. It read in part:

> ...He was one of those men upon whom the Nation depended to keep our ships afloat under the perilous seas, to transport our troops across those seas, and to carry to them the vitally needed material to keep them fighting until victory is certain and liberty secure.

> ...Let me, in this expression of the country's deep sympathy, also express to you its gratitude for his devotion and sacrifice.

Regardless of the words of praise for the captain, the South Atlantic Steamship Line and the War Shipping Administration were not through with him. Mrs. Josephine Carini petitioned for his back pay. "It appears," J. M. Quinn, comptroller for the War Shipping Administration, wrote on November 6, 1945, "that the estate of Captain Carini has requested payment of the balance of the wages due the Master at the time the subject vessel was sunk. However, the Agent indicates that the balance of the Master's account according to their records is $665.65 due from the Master, after taking into consideration all the known transactions. It is admitted that if there was any cash on board at the time of sinking it was lost with the vessel."

South Atlantic replied, November 26: "We have attached to these statements photostatic copies of receipts covering cash drawn, copies of advance sheets covering New York and Greenock advances, copies of vouchers covering two men paid off at Greenock, copies of receipt for cash drawn at Greenock and copy of Master's wage voucher.

"In reference to the items of $42.13 and $43.92 due to the Master for errors and discrepancies in slop chest accounts of *Rob-*

ert Toombs Voyage No. 1 and No. 2, we attach statements showing how we arrived at these figures. Also, we attach a statement showing a credit to Captain Carini of $8.88 for errors made in his slop account while Master of *John Gorrie* Voyage No. 4.

"It had been our intention to handle with Captain Carini upon his return to the United States, as Master of the *Henry Bacon*, the slop chest discrepancies from previous voyages but unfortunately he was lost with his vessel.

"We might advise that Mrs. Carini has been pressing us for a settlement of the wages of $801.10 and we have informed her we were unable to pay this amount unless we receive the authority of the War Shipping Administration in view of the fact that Captain Carini's account reflects a balance due of $604.64 taking into consideration the wages due. There is a slight difference in the final figure of $604.64 against the figure given in our letter of October 29th which difference was accounted for due to changes made to us in crediting the Master with slop chest sales on *Robert Toombs* Voyage No. 2.

"As both Captain Carini and his Purser were lost with the vessel, we do not know whether there was any actual cash in the safe at the time of sinking." The records do not reflect if the matter was ever settled.

The Merchant Marine Distinguished Service Medal was presented, posthumously, to Chief Engineer Donald F. Haviland. That citation read:

> In February 1945, SS *Henry Bacon*, an American Liberty Ship, in which Chief Engineer Haviland was serving, departed from Murmansk, North Russia, carrying Norwegian war refugees. A few days later during a heavy gale, the vessel was forced to drop out of Convoy RA-64 to effect repairs to her steering gear. The ship was then attacked by twenty-three German planes. The *Henry Bacon* shot down several planes and damaged others, but received one hit which caused her to founder. The lifeboats were filled with all of the Norwegians and some of the crew members, but could not accommodate all remaining personnel. When this situation became known to Chief Engineer Haviland, he insisted on climbing back on board ship giving his place in the lifeboat to a younger man. Shortly thereafter, he went down with the ship.

His unselfish action in sacrificing his life to save a shipmate constitutes a degree of heroism in keeping with the highest traditions of the United States Merchant Marine.

Boatswain Holcomb Lammon Jr. also received a Meritorious Service Commendation for his actions that February day....

One lifeboat had been smashed in the storm and another capsized in lowering. Three of four life rafts had been released prematurely and drifted away. The two remaining lifeboats were filled to capacity with all of the passengers and some members of the crew, but could not accommodate all remaining personnel. Realizing this situation, Lammon immediately undertook the task of improvising additional life rafts in the hope that he might thereby save more of his shipmates. He worked indefatigably until the last moment and then jumped over the side. He was not among those rescued. His courage, skill and determination to save lives, without thought to his own safety will be a lasting inspiration to all seamen of the United States Merchant Marine.

Following notification of her husband's death, Mrs. Lammon requested a verification of the amount of overtime wages due her husband, and she enlisted the aid of Congressman Frank Boykin. S. D. Schell, executive deputy administrator of the War Shipping Administration, advised that "it is therefore impossible to credit Mr. Lammon with any amount other than the thirty-one hours overtime which are of record prior to the loss of the vessel."

Lieutenant Junior Grade John Carl Sippola was presented the Silver Star posthumously. His citation read in part:

[He] coolly directed a steady barrage of gunfire against the savagely striking aircraft and, fighting off the furious attack for approximately twenty minutes, succeeded in damaging three and in destroying five others before a German torpedo struck with deadly accuracy in the No. 5 hatch, sinking the ship and forcing the survivors into the icy, heavily rolling seas. Adrift and clinging to a life raft with six of his crew when a British rescue vessel subsequently came alongside...Sippola steadfastly refused to accept aid for himself until lines were secured to each man and were taken safe aboard the rescue ship. Weakened by exposure to the icy waters and by the strenuous physical effort expended in saving his men, he was unable to remain afloat long enough to reach the lines thrown to himself and sank, overcome by exhaustion. [His] unfaltering leadership, valiant fortitude and self-sacrificing devotion to duty in the face of extreme peril upheld the highest traditions of the United States Naval Service. He gallantly gave his life in the service of his country.

Raymond Franklin Reid received a letter from the Navy Department, Bureau of Naval Personnel, on December 12, 1945, which stated in part:

> Courageously remaining at battle stations, the Armed Guard Crew poured a steady stream of fire into the enemy planes, shooting down five and damaging three, until the vessel suffered a direct hit and the order was given to abandon ship.

Almost four years later [July 5, 1949], Reid received a Navy Unit Commendation Ribbon "for outstanding heroism in action against enemy forces en route Murmansk to the United Kingdom...." To his neighbors, Reid was "definitely not the extrovert type," and they never heard a word about his service during the war. "He simply never talks about it," they wrote, "and [he's] surely not the type to brag about his heroism."

Joseph Scott received the Norwegian War Medal, and also a letter from Raymond D. Sullivan, operating manager of the South Atlantic Steamship Co., dated April 17, 1945, which read in part:

> ...I desire to take this opportunity to congratulate you on the excellent work you did aboard the *Henry Bacon*...I think that for you to have been away from the sea as long as you have been and to have felt the urge to do your part in the best way that you could serve by going back to the sea at your age was extremely fine and patriotic....

For their part in the war, members of the Armed Guard were awarded 8,055 decorations or commendations for the period ending in August 1946. These included: 6 Navy Crosses, 2 Legions of Merit, 75 Silver Stars, 54 Bronze Stars, 24 Navy and Marine Corps medals, 563 Commendations by the Secretary of the Navy, 2,778 Commendations by the Bureau of Naval Personnel, and 4,553 entries into their service records.

For the British fleet, the *Zambesi* was scrapped in 1959; the *Zealous* was sold to Israel in 1955 as the *Eluth*, and sunk by Egyptian missile boats on October 21, 1967.

The quick recovery of the survivors, the fine treatment received by the Americans and Norwegians aboard the British destroyers, and the rough return trip were, of course, anticlimactic. Twelve of the sixteen destroyers that took part in convoy RA64 had to be docked for hull repairs because of the battering they had taken in the heavy seas.

Sublieutenant Ian Rodney Bowden, the officer who jumped overboard and tied a line to Dick Burbine and helped rescue Pozen and Bacheldor, received a commendation from Sir Henry Ruthven Moore for his gallantry "in going over the side of HMS *Zambesi* on a bowline in a heavy sea in northern waters to rescue survivors from a merchant ship, despite great risk of frost-bite and bodily injury." Bowden remained in the Royal Navy and retired as the captain of the royal yacht, HMS *Brittania*.

Ships from the sorely tried convoy stopped at the Faeroe Islands for fuel; fueling at sea would have been impossible. They arrived within a day or two of the sinking of the *Bacon*. Persons needing hospital treatment were put ashore, and survivors on the HMS *Opportune* were transferred to the HMS *Zealous,* which proceeded through the Minches to Greenock, Scotland, where Crown Prince Olaf met the Sørøyan refugees when they landed on March 1. Commander Jessel did not believe it true that the prince *met* the survivors on landing. "I am sure," he wrote, "I should have been informed if royalty had been present." The prince, he said, "may have done so later." Dick Burbine disagrees.

He recalled that when the survivors of the *Henry Bacon* arrived at Scapa Flow, they were mustered on the main deck forward and presented to the crown prince. He, in turn, trooped the line and took time to shake hands and speak with each man. He made a point to thank each of them for saving the lives of the Norwegian civilians at a great cost of lives to our crew. He then dressed front and center and again thanked and saluted the survivors. "I find it difficult," Burbine said, "to explain the feeling of joy and pride I felt shaking hands with the future king of Norway. To us he represented all the things that I valued in mankind, strength, honesty, courage, and a fierce devotion and dedication to his people and his homeland."

The Sørøya folk were taken to a camp outside Glasgow that had been built as an evacuation site for local people in case of an air raid. Here they met with fellow refugees who had traveled on other ships in the convoy and there were many joyous reunions. The contrast between living in the Sørøyan caves and living in camp near the city of Glasgow was described as "dizzying." The Sørøyans were sought out and interviewed by newspaper reporters and some told of their experiences on the radio. They developed their own society and soon young women were taking defense jobs and men were entering the armed services. Only children and old folks were left in camp. At the end of the war, some months later, the group returned to rebuild Sørøya.

The HMS *Zest*, with Steward Ingram and Deck Engineer Testerman aboard, had arrived in Scapa Flow two days earlier, on February 27. Those pulled out of the water by HMS *Zambesi* were also landed at Scapa. According to Pozen, all the men rescued from the sea landed at Scapa Flow. They were put aboard a train at Thurso, Scotland, and they were taken to Perth. At Perth they changed trains for Glasgow. In Glasgow they were met by a representative of the War Shipping Administration, Owen P. Maier. "We went through the usual procedure of questioning by the Coast Guard," he said. The survivors, as Frank Reid wrote, "were put up at a Seabees base at Roseneath," until they could get passage home. Chuck Reed was put in the US Army 316th State Hospital outside Glasgow. When a crew member visited him and told him they were heading for Liverpool, Reed asked permission to leave. "The Army doctor wouldn't let me out, so when the war was quieted down, I broke open a locker in the back, got my clothes on, and hitchhiked back to the hotel" where other members of the crew were staying. They rode the train from Glasgow to Liverpool, where they picked up the SS *Wakefield*. "Among my mementos of the episode of the SS *Henry Bacon*," Reed wrote, "I still have the seaboots the Limey gave me, a picture of the HMS *Opportune* from the same sailor, my water-soaked seaman's papers, and an abiding faith in God by whose grace I still live."

Another souvenir Reed brought home was discussed in correspondence he had with Dick Burbine: "Someone remembered that I was a Michigan deer hunter and asked me if I'd like to try getting a Remington 03-A3 rifle home. This gun was thrown in the lifeboat with the Norwegians and taken aboard the *Opportune*. I stripped it, put it under my clothing and, believe it or not, got it home! It has bagged a lot of game over the years!"

When they got to Scotland, Bacheldor recalled, "all we had in charge was a third class gunners mate…they didn't know who we were or where we came from…so for a couple of days we couldn't get a change of clothes…we needed them as we had been eight days and nights in them."

"As the only officer rescued by *Zambesi*," Herrmann said, "I was sort of in charge of the men from the British point of view. As we were about to leave the ship by tender to go ashore, we discovered that the Navy men were nowhere about, so I went searching and found them below, lost in red tape. I arranged for them to get British petty officer uniforms so they could go ashore.

"When we got ashore, the US Navy had not yet had anyone there to meet them so we arranged their passage on the train. The merchantmen who had been met by War Shipping Administration representatives and given an advance in pay offered to chip in for the fares for the Navy men, but when the conductor heard this he gave them free passage."

There was no hero's welcome for the Navy gunners when they reached their first naval station in Glasgow. "You're not in the lifeboats now," they were told, and set to work sorting twelve by twelve timbers. As Jerry Gerold recalled it: "No one there seemed to care if we were taken care of or not. They finally gave us clothes to wear and, instead of leaving us rest like we needed, they made us work each day until we left. Some of the men had been in the water two-and-a-half hours and suffered from exposure, but it didn't mean anything to anybody in the camp."

Without an officer to plead their case, members of the Navy Armed Guard, who had lost all their possessions when the *Henry*

Bacon went down, were not issued clothing, although individual Seabees gave them their extra shirts, pants, and coats. The merchant mariners, who were not obligated to wear specific uniforms, received clothing from a Canadian Red Cross unit stationed in Scotland. They all remembered that their pay ended when the *Bacon* went down.

While Able-bodied Seaman Raymond Greenwell and Oiler Pozen joined the Merchant Marine pool in Glasgow, waiting to ship out again, the other twenty-four surviving crewmen sailed for the States on the USS *Wakefield* on March 12. The Navy gunners were assigned duties aboard the same ship.

Some of the men, including David Goodrich, waited a few weeks before being sent to Liverpool, England, to board a troopship bound for the United States. "The Statue of Liberty," he recalled, "never looked so good." He later joined the Army and served in World War II and Korea.

The survivors were met, upon their arrival in the continental United States, by agents from the Federal Bureau of Investigation [FBI] and Naval Intelligence. "They gave us a Travel Control Landing Card," Dick Burbine recalled, "and without as much as a thank you, were free to go home. That was the extent of our government's gratitude." Forty-seven years after the *Bacon* went to her watery grave, Burbine received the Mariner's Medal from the US Maritime Administration. A year before, he received—finally—the Norwegian War Medal awarded to Burbine and the rest of the crew in 1945. He was at sea when the medal was awarded and, apparently, mailed to his home in Massachusetts...but it never arrived. Contacts with representatives of the Norwegian government brought the replacement. He also noted that he had received ribbons to accompany three theater medals, Atlantic, Pacific, and Mediterranean, but that "the medals themselves have not even been manufactured..." In the 1980s, Burbine noted, he received his medal. He had to purchase it through the mail.

Burbine remained in the Merchant Marine until 1950, when he joined the US Marine Corps. Eight years later he left the Corps and rejoined the Merchant Marine service. He finally retired in

1966...and joined the police force at the University of California, Berkeley, where he helped quell the student riots there.

After landing in Newport News, Virginia, on March 20, the men entrained for New York and arrived March 21. One of the saddest events for the men from the *Bacon* was the arrival of mail for the mates who were lost. Eugene Daniels recalled that the "ship sank on the 23rd of February 1945; 23 planes came and 23 men lost their lives. In a month's time we were back in the States, and my leave started on the 23rd of the month. And very fitting and comforting through it all, the 23rd Psalm."

Second Radio Operator Bill Herrmann went back to Sheeps-head Bay Training Station, Brooklyn. One of the casualties of the *Bacon* was Herrmann's clarinet, one which he used so well with big bands. Before being reassigned he found a brand-new clarinet in his seabag. He was then invited to "It's Maritime," a radio program presented by the Columbia Broadcasting System in cooperation with the War Shipping Administration. On that show, the Sheepshead Bay Orchestra played his arrangement of "Bell Bottom Trousers," and the cast dramatized the story of the gallant men of the SS *Henry Bacon*. Herrmann went back to a ship after he brushed up on radio code. "I haven't practiced," he said, "since I gave the distress signal on the *Bacon*."

Robert Tatotsky suffered stress and frostbite and was hospitalized for several weeks before returning to sea duty. After a few more ocean trips, the young man realized he had suffered hearing loss from his experience with the *Bacon*. Like Burbine, he joined the US Marine Corps, serving for the remainder of World War II and two months of the Korean War. "I was willing [to stay], but they said, 'Go home, daddy.' They thought I had enough." He was denied disability pay because the government had determined his hearing impairment was not "service related." In an attempt to reverse the decision, Tatotsky wrote President George Bush, but never received a response. To add insult to injury, he said he had been waiting forty-five years to receive a three-hundred-dollar stipend promised by the Russian government to all personnel involved in the Murmansk run. "They haven't done one blessed thing for me," he said. "I just want what's coming to me. I just want what's rightfully mine." He also waited for the Russian War Medal. "They can't even pay their debts from World War II," he complained, "but they want us to feed them. It just makes me bitter. I haven't received a thing and it's not right. I mean, why play games? Either give it to me or don't."

There was a long-delayed postscript involving one of the youngest fatalities—Mason Kirby Burr, seaman first class, from Lansdowne, Pennsylvania, who joined the Navy in January 1943, as soon as he became seventeen years of age. Young Burr performed magnificently on his machine gun during the blazing battle of February 23 and later was killed as he sought to leave the ship. Frank Reid and Normand Croteau were among those who saw his body carried away by the waves.

More than four and a half years later [October 1949], his body, encased in a block of ice and in a remarkably good state of preservation, was washed ashore on the Norwegian coast far north of the Arctic Circle. It is likely the body had been tossed across an ice floe by the high waves and gradually covered with ice as it floated northward. Returned by Arctic currents, it was found by Norwegian sailors in October 1949, and buried in an isolated grave at Kvalsund, plot 1, row 3, grave 3. Oddly enough, Kvalsund is near Sørøya and just a few miles from Hammerfest, the northernmost town in the world—some five hundred miles northeast of the spot where the *Henry Bacon* was sunk.

When American authorities were notified, the body was transferred to the United States Military Cemetery at Neuville-en-Condroz, Belgium, where it was examined by a special, scientifically trained unit of the American Graves Registration Service. The identification of Mason Kirby Burr was accomplished by a comparison with the dental record and physical characteristics of young Burr.

The United States Navy notified his father, Major Harry S. Burr, an active veterans organization official in Philadelphia, and offered to send Mason's body to the United States. With Major Burr's assent, the body was returned to Lansdowne, Pennsylvania, where funeral services were held on March 12, 1950, exactly five years to the day after Burr's surviving shipmates set sail for the United States from Scotland. Major Burr declined an official offer to open the coffin.

The body of Mason Burr was shipped to Washington, DC, on March 13, 1950, and when it was lowered to its final resting place in Arlington National Cemetery mourners could see the dome of the Capitol of the United States from the grave site. Haunting strains of taps were heard across the Potomac River by those traveling on Henry Bacon Drive to Memorial Bridge. This honor may be regarded as symbolic for all who lost their lives on the last voyage of the SS *Henry Bacon*.

In 1962, Major Burr wrote that he had visited with the secretary of the navy and talked about these men and "at that time he said he was sure they all would be honored by their government but to date nothing has been done while, during all this time, lots of persons that never were in any danger or fought for this country have been honored with our top honors. This is something that has hurt me a lot, for surely if anyone should be honored, these few men that fought against such great odds should be honored with more than just a plain service medal."

On October 7, 1992, then-Russian ambassador Vladimir Lukin presented bronze medals to nearly two hundred Liberty ship crews, Merchant Marine sailors, and Navy Armed Guard gunners. "You are the true heroes," the ambassador said, and added that his country should have honored US seamen "years ago. You can blame the Cold War, insufficient communication, or state bureaucracy." None of those reasons, he said, "justifies the delay." A spokesman for the ambassador said that about 50 medals were awarded at a 1991 ceremony in Washington, and about 230 others were mailed out. As far as anyone knows, Dick Burbine was the only member of the SS *Henry Bacon* to receive such a medal. His was one of the 230.

To date, no singular recognition by the United States government has been made to the valiant men of the *Henry Bacon*. The closest to national acclaim came on February 23, 1992, when

Massachusetts Governor William F. Weld proclaimed that date as "SS *Henry Bacon* Day," and urged the citizens of the common-wealth to celebrate the event and participate fittingly in its obser-vance. As part of his proclamation, Weld said: "The Merchant Mariners and the Navy Armed Guard aboard the SS *Henry Bacon* realized the highest standards of courage under fire and compas-sion in the face of total sacrifice."

Spud Campbell married his sweetheart Bea a month after the *Bacon* sank. "Life's too short, we thought at the time." As of this writing the Campbells have been married over 56 years! After a brief honeymoon in Florida, the couple returned to the bride's hometown of Birmingham. There they were met by Bob Hunt's mother, who had traveled down from North Carolina. She had received a telegram from Washington that merely said that Bob was "missing in action." "That was the hardest thing," he recalled, "I ever had to tell someone, that Bob was dead in that frozen north, and to try to explain to her that there was no space in the lifeboat for Bob."

In another ironic twist, as Gerard O. Haviland, nephew of the chief engineer, wrote in the *Weymouth News*, February 23, 1994: "Several days after my father's funeral, my mother received a tele-phone call from a man who identified himself as Robert Tatotsky. He told her that he had been a member of the *Henry Bacon* crew on its last voyage in 1945, and asked if he could speak to my father.

"Suspicious because of the unusual timing of the call," the widow told him she'd have another member of the family return his call. Several days passed, then Gerard made the call, and heard "an incredible story" of that "frightful ocean voyage." Tatotsky told him he had joined the Merchant Marine service at 15 and served as a cabin boy on coastal colliers. In October 1944 he joined the *Bacon* as a messman. After the *Bacon* was torpedoed, Tatotsky re-alized there were not enough spaces in the life boats for everyone on board.

"Frightened and shivering violently," the account continued, "Tatotsky watched from the deck as the final lifeboat was lowered in the freezing ocean. He knew then that he had only moments to live and began to wonder what his life would have been like had he been given a little longer time on earth.

"Suddenly the lowering of the last lifeboat stopped, an older man climbed from the boat, grabbed Tatotsky by the arms and pushed him into the lifeboat shouting 'get into that goddamn boat, kid.'" According to Tatotsky, the older man then said, "I've lived my life. It doesn't really matter if I don't get back."

"The older man," Gerard Haviland wrote, "was my Uncle Donald." While they talked, the nephew learned that the man whose life his uncle saved had been trying to locate the chief's brother, so he could thank him for what his brother had done. When he was told that the brother had died recently, Tatotsky said, "Well, I'll just have to wait until I get to heaven then." Bob Tatotsky died in late 1993.

In December 1993, Gerard Haviland received a package from the Russian embassy in Washington. In it was a letter from the Russian ambassador, explaining that, on behalf of President Boris Yeltsin, a posthumous award of the Russian Medal of the Great Patriotic War was being conferred on Chief Haviland, "in recognition of the bravery and sacrifice…in helping the Russian people to survive World War II."

Perhaps this book will be a fitting tribute to their actions above and beyond the call of duty.

CHAPTER 18

After Action Report

In a Navy Department confidential—later declassified—memorandum: "Survivors believed that the ship would have floated longer if the hatches amidship had been dogged down. The fact that they were not dogged down was discovered too late.... Survivors stated that one life raft was very rusty and some of the life rings failed to float. The painters on the raft were untied."

In all military actions, the command structure wants to know exactly what happened—and why. The questions of who, what, where, why, when, and how are asked. Eyewitnesses and experts are called upon for accounts and opinions. The validity of the "after action" reports vary. In the inquiry into the sinking of the *Henry Bacon*, several survivors also had questions about what went wrong. Some had answers, based on what they had seen firsthand and their experience as seamen.

Herbert McIsaac wrote about the mistakes made. He believed that Captain Carini made a single mistake, but that mistake was compounded by the action of others. Carini's mistake was "he didn't believe in securing the painters on the life rafts that were a war measure. They were secured on the stays and could be released by flipping a goose-neck contraption...which caused the rafts to slide overboard."

The painter was used to keep the rafts in range of a ship in times of trouble, "especially when the vessel had headway. This wouldn't have been noticed had the able-bodied seaman, who released them, waited until the vessel had slowed to a stop." Survivors of other Liberty ship sinkings alerted other ships going into Murmansk to watch out for this and ensure that *all* painters were secured. This warning, McIsaac believed, was ignored on the *Bacon*.

The second mistake, in McIsaac's view—and one which he heard but didn't see—"We lost the use of number 4 lifeboat" which had to be secured because the davit had snapped, "leaving no way to launch it. That left us three." After Burbine launched number 1 life boat, with the refugees and crew members with the emergency SOS kit, "the next to go over the side [number 3] jammed her forward falls. Now anyone knows [that] the fall must be chopped or cut, but never a forward one. It's always the after one, so that the vessels headway doesn't swamp the boat...."

"It was the same able-bodied seaman who made this mistake, thereby losing another means of escape. Number 2 was [sent] overboard without any incidents, and when the water reached number 4. She got buoyancy and with a little push she was able to get floated...."

"Now this discrepancy left a lot of men who had to go overboard, and to this day I can't see how they ever survived in those cold waters."

He continued in debunking a CBS radio account, which stated that the cooks were serving sandwiches. "Well, this I know. Mastracci was passing ammo in the after locker when the ship was hit. He couldn't swim when he hit the water, but when he got the outboard motor, he sure could a minute later..."

"Now, as for Captain Carini going the wrong way: who knows?...The *Henry Bacon* was sucker bait and her purpose was to draw the enemy out or why should she have passed so close to Hammerfest when we were going by there? Close enough that you could see the buildings, but not define what they were.... My contention is that any man who went to sea as long as Captain Carini would know what course he was on without a compass. Admiralty gave him credit for saving the convoy, and I'll always believe that."

Some countered that there was no way one could foresee the steering problems Carini faced. The steering problems on the *Bacon*, however, did not begin on that final run from Murmansk. Ben Kuta, the captain whom Carini succeeded, had had trouble with the steering on the *Bacon* earlier and contended that he had "more trouble with steering [on the *Bacon*] than on any other ship [he had sailed]." But still others questioned the captain's judgment. They were not alone.

Commander Hamilton, second in command of the *Zambesi* wrote: The "*Henry Bacon* refused to cooperate, maintaining that our position was wrong and hers correct. We returned to her (if I remember rightly) twice, after first giving her instructions, and finally returned to the convoy....

"Communication with stragglers was by loud-hailing equipment pointed at her bridge. Most ships had similar equipment for reply; if not, one passed instructions and finished by saying 'wave your hand if you have got it.' As far as I remember the straggler in question had hailing equipment, as I can remember an argument in which he was both adamant and, alas, wrong.

"It was a tragic and unnecessary waste of life, and one which will always typify for me personally the best and the hardest-to-get-on-with of the American personality. They were sunk because they refused to admit they were wrong, and insisted on going away from the convoy. Yet when the ship went down, their Norwegian passengers were put into the only surviving lifeboat, and the crew took to the water which, in those regions, was as good as suicide."

Captain Allison concurred in the mistaken location of the *Bacon*: "Survivors informed me that previous to the attack by the German Air Force, the *Henry Bacon* was steaming north under the mistaken impression that she would have achieved a position ahead of the convoy, which was on a southerly course. The result of this action was to place *Henry Bacon* about forty miles astern and north of the convoy at the time of the attack on her."

Allison also added that "It will be appreciated in operations of this kind that relative positions are all-important. The geographical position of the flagship and indeed [the] *Zambesi* was fairly accurately known, within three or four miles, by means of special radio devices, and it is certain that the *Henry Bacon*, without such aids, could well have been considerably in error in her position....

"Radio signals concerning the attack were received in the flagship of R. A. McGrigor, but no certainty of position could be obtained. In this circumstance, despite the weather, the admiral decided to fly off a search aircraft to locate and report the exact relative location of the *Henry Bacon*. By a feat of remarkable airmanship, an aircraft succeeded in taking off and reporting accordingly."

Lieutenant Commander Hicks, commanding the *Zest*, wrote in his notes of February 23, "learnt after of Captain's madness in turning back and then his heroism in giving up his place in the boat to his Norwegian passengers..."

Members of the *Bacon*'s crew decided to seek damages from the government, based on their contention that the ship was not seaworthy and that command did not follow proper procedures to safeguard their lives and property.

Following depositions and testimony, the Maritime Administration, US Department of Commerce, made its findings:

> The vessel [SS *Henry Bacon*] sailed from Boston on November 17, 1944 for New York via the Cape Cod Canal, Long Island Sound and the East River. It carried 280 tons of permanent rock ballast and made the voyage in good weather and without incident. The vessel arrived in New York on November 19, 1944, at Pier 60, North River, and during its stay in New York certain minor repairs were effected under the personal supervision of the government's representative and the ship's chief engineer.

> At the Port of New York, on November 21, 1944, shipping articles were signed.

> When the SS *Henry Bacon* departed from the Port of New York on December 4, 1944, she was in A-1 seaworthy condition, laden with war cargo, and fully equipped and supplied for a trans-Atlantic voyage. The vessel sailed in convoy bound for the United Kingdom on orders. The weather was fair and the seas were moderate. The lifeboats were rigged outboard, and fire and boat drills were conducted weekly after putting to sea.

> The vessel arrived in the United Kingdom on December 18, 1944, and after calls at several intermediate ports for naval orders and routing instructions, the vessel departed from Scotland in convoy for Murmansk, Russia. The voyage was made under fair weather conditions and the SS *Henry Bacon* arrived at Murmansk (Kola Bay) on January 17, 1945, where her cargo was discharged.

While at the Port of Murmansk, 2,000 tons of sand ballast were placed in the Nos. 2, 3, 4 and 5 holds of the *Bacon*. At the request of British and American military authorities, 19 Norwegian refugees were placed aboard the *Bacon* for transportation to the United Kingdom.

The *Bacon* departed from Murmansk on February 17, 1945 with a draft of 14 feet forward and 18 feet aft, in a convoy of about 40 ships. The vessel was fully manned with a crew of approximately 41 seamen and a Naval armed guard complement of about 28 enlisted sailors. On the day of departure, the *Bacon's* steering apparatus was tested and found in good working order and she was fully equipped, manned and in A-1 seaworthy condition.

Two days out the *Bacon* ran into heavy weather which culminated in a severe storm during the night of February 19th. Seas of thirty to forty feet, driven by forty-five mile an hour winds, swept across her main deck, causing the ship to pitch and roll. Other vessels were separated from the convoy and displayed distress signals which were visible aboard the *Bacon*. The *Bacon* herself temporarily lost contact with her companion ships when she suffered engine difficulties, but retained her position and continued voyage with the convoy.

More inclement weather was encountered on the 21st, and by the night of the 22nd the *Bacon* was in the midst of a severe Arctic storm. Winds of seventy-five miles per hour buffeted the ship and waves as high as forty feet lashed the main deck, the boat deck, and even the flying bridge. The binnacle was washed off the poop deck by the seas; lifeboat No. 4 was thrown from its cradle into the deck with its bow stove in and its forward davit damaged.

A breakdown in her telemotor system forced the *Bacon* to separate from the convoy during the course of the storm on the night of the 22nd. Repairs were effected in the rolling sea within two hours and an attempt was made to overtake the convoy which, by midnight of February 22nd, was still in sight not more than a quarter of a mile off, as the blue stern light of one of the vessels could be discerned from the *Bacon's* decks. But by three-thirty of the morning of the 23rd, the faint silhouette of the rocking hulls of the convoy were observed for the last time as the *Bacon* lost contact with the other ships when her motors stopped and she started to drift.

When the *Bacon* again got under way, she pursued the course set for the convoy but by early afternoon of the 23rd as yet no sign of other vessels had been observed although a lookout had been posted in the crow's nest to maintain constant and vigilant watch. Wartime regulations forbade the use of radio communication and the Captain, after conferring with the ship's officers, determined to retrace the *Bacon's* course for an hour on the chance that the convoy had been overtaken and passed during the calm weather which followed in the wake of the storm. Shortly thereafter, at about three-fifteen in the afternoon, the *Bacon* was attacked by 23 JU 88 German torpedo bombers.

After a valiant but futile fight in which three enemy planes were shot down by her armed guard, the *Bacon* succumbed to an aerial torpedo which struck her port side aft near No. 5 hold. Her side was opened to the seas by the explosion and ten minutes later orders were given to abandon ship.

Lifeboat No. 1, containing the Norwegian refugees and several of the crew, and lifeboat No. 2, fully loaded with members of the crew, were successfully launched. Lifeboat No. 4, incapacitated from the storm of the previous day, was unfit for use. An attempt to launch lifeboat No. 3 ended in failure when one of the men on the forward bitt let go, the fall causing the boat to capsize. Two life rafts had been destroyed by the explosion of the torpedo, but two other life rafts and a donut raft were sent afloat.

Approximately 45 minutes after she was abandoned, the SS *Henry Bacon*, her captain still aboard, went down by the stern. Survivors were picked up two hours later by three British destroyers responding to an SOS wired from the *Bacon* before she sank.

It is claimed by libelants that the *Bacon* was unseaworthy because the breakdown of the telemotor system caused her to leave the protection of the convoy and subjected her to enemy attack. Sufficient evidence is lacking, however, to support this contention. The evidence is that the Coast Guard certificate issued to the *Bacon* after her annual inspection in November of 1944 indicated that the ship was in seaworthy condition. While not conclusive, the approval by the Coast Guard of the equipment aboard a vessel is entitled to considerable weight (*Tatem v. Southern Transp. Co.*, 72F. Suff 44, 46, aff'd 166 F. 2d 1020).

Nor was the *Bacon* unseaworthy or her masters negligent in failing to provide sufficient ballast for the voyage from Murmansk. Captain Mirteenes, an employee of the War Shipping Administration, testified that 2,000 tons of temporary ballast was the Government requirement for Liberty ships in trans-Atlantic crossing during the winter of 1945. He stated that, in his opinion, ballast of 2,000 tons would render a vessel of the *Henry Bacon* type seaworthy to negotiate the treacherous seas around Murmansk.

The testimony of Kapanaux, assistant marine superintendent for the South Atlantic Steamship Line, which acted with respect to the *Bacon* under a General Agency Service Agreement, indicated that a mean draft of 10 feet would render a Liberty ship reasonably safe to make a trans-Atlantic voyage. Captain Mirteenes stated that a ship with a mean draft of 16 feet would be a seaworthy vessel, when Captain Sheridan declared that a draft of 14 feet forward and 18 feet aft of the *Bacon* was proper for the trip from Murmansk to the United Kingdom. Libelants' own expert witness, Captain McDonagh, testified that the *Bacon* could not have covered the distance from Murmansk to the place of torpedoing, a distance of 800 miles, at an average speed of seven or eight knots per hour, had her propeller been out of the water because of a low draft and insufficient ballast.

The evidence compels the conclusion that the *Bacon*'s telemotor system was in seaworthy condition and that sufficient ballast had been placed aboard at Murmansk to negotiate the anticipated voyage with safety, in the absence of extraordinary circumstances. Although evidence indicate that rolling in heavy seas would not of itself normally cause a telemotor system to get out of order, the testimony on cross-examination of Captain Sheridan, the expert witness of respondent, supports the conclusion that the severe storms encountered by the *Bacon* on her voyage caused the damage to the telemotor system.

Libelants claim that the master of the ship was negligent in failing to keep the *Bacon* in convoy position when the telemotor system broke down. There was clearly no negligence here, for the master promptly switched to the manual steering apparatus when the telemotor became damaged. However, because the binnacle had been swept from the poop deck by the seas during the storm, it was impossible to steer by compass, and the *Bacon* was forced to leave the convoy to head into the wind and seas where she could be guided by the stars.

The evidence is insufficient to find that the *Bacon* had a list caused by leaks in her hold or was in any other way unseaworthy.

Libelants assert that the Master of the *Bacon* erred in retracing his course in an endeavor to come upon the convoy during the afternoon of the 23rd. It is difficult to see, however, how the *Bacon* would have escaped destruction by the enemy had she adhered to the original course or gone to the straggler's position. Furthermore, the decision of the Master in reversing his course was done in his own discretion after discussion with the officers of the vessel and, however unfortunate it may appear when viewed after the event, cannot be declared negligent at this time unless arbitrary or unreasonable (*Roberts v. United Fisheries Vessels Co.*, 141 F. 2d 288 cert. Den. 323 US 743; *Johnson v. United States*, 74 F. 2d 703), which it was not.

The final claim that liability rests upon the respondent is based upon the negligent maintenance and unseaworthiness of the life-saving equipment aboard the *Bacon*. There is no more proof to sustain these contentions, however, than those already discussed. The Coast Guard inspection in November, 1944 included a close examination of all life-saving equipment. Nor were the lifeboats negligently maintained by being rigged inboard in their cradles instead of outboard ready to be lowered. The manner of carrying lifeboats rests in the master's discretion after consideration for the safety of the boat and the crew. Not only did the rough seas around Murmansk amply justify the master's decision to keep the lifeboats inboard but, despite this precautionary measure, lifeboat No. 4 suffered severe damage from the seas. Finally, it has not been shown how the rigging of the lifeboats inboard was in any way causally related to the injuries complained of.

It was no act of negligence for the Captain not to repair the damaged lifeboat immediately for it was clear that the trouble to the steering apparatus warranted his immediate attention. The fact that lifeboat No. 4 was never repaired sufficiently to be launched was explained by the libelant, Champlin, who stated in his deposition that the davit remained damaged because there was no replacement, as merchant vessels did not customarily carry extra davits aboard.

The lifesaving equipment under normal circumstances was sufficient for the crew, the armed guard and the nineteen refugees who boarded the *Bacon* at Murmansk.

For whatever reason the forward bitt of lifeboat No. 3 was dropped during its launching, insufficient evidence is presented to show that it was caused by negligence or unseaworthiness.

9. On the day the ship left Murmansk, her steering apparatus was tested and it was in good working order. [Note: The typescript did not list other numbers.]

11. The SS *Henry Bacon* was equipped with four lifeboats, with a capacity of 118; four life rafts, with a capacity of 76; and two smaller rafts, with a capacity of 30.

The facts as determined by that inquiry ignore the realities under which the *Bacon* lived and died. Early in the ship's life, Josephine Carini, wife of the captain, was forced to go to Washington and plead the case for the *Bacon* so the ship could obtain needed equipment. Tools which Chief Engineer Haviland repeatedly requested, tools which were essential to the maintenance of the ship, never were obtained. In one instance the crew was forced to use a chisel to tighten nuts on the bucket-valve. No proper wrench was available. Another eyewitness said they had to make do with a simple monkey wrench to make other repairs, though the chief engineer had repeatedly ordered proper tools.

The government's contention that two thousand tons of sand ballast were placed in four holds is debated by several survivors. The ballast loaded at Murmansk was inadequate—to say the least. Chunks of concrete from bombed-out buildings were unstable in the hold, as were the boulders of frozen sand. When the ballast shifted, the ship listed badly. At one point it experienced a roll of 57 degrees; 45 degrees is considered critical. To this day Dick Burbine believes the ballast was adequate. "The ship righted herself," he said. "If the ballast wasn't right, the *Bacon* would have tipped over…which she didn't." The *Bacon's* steering problems, however, that led to a "manual steering affair," did not begin on her last voyage. It was an ongoing problem, one that even Captain Kuta experienced.

The government gave short shrift to the repairs made by the chief engineer and members of the crew under desperate conditions. The government assertion that repairs were completed "within two hours" is open to question. Eyewitnesses, including those who worked on the repairs, reported that Chief Haviland worked around the clock to effect the repairs.

Some may say that it was an act of God, the storm, or fate, but when the storm caused the screw to be thrown out of the water half the time, the screws were not standard operating screws. The screws that propelled the *Bacon* had been shortened by the Russians when they made repairs in December 1944. Dick Burbine, however, disagreed, saying that a new propeller was installed either in Boston or New York before they went to Italy. No one could have anticipated the loss of the binnacle that contained the ship's compass. The storm washed it off the poop deck, leaving the captain to navigate by a more primitive method. Could anyone have anticipated the failure of the motor on the 5-inch gun?

Was it human error? Did Captain Carini make a fatal mistake

in making a 180-degree turn and go in the opposite direction of the convoy? The government's assertion that the *Bacon* could have survived "in the absence of extraordinary circumstances" denied the fact that the ship *was* operating under extraordinary circumstances.

Not all the survivors were aware of the inquiry, even to this day. If the government had tried to get all the survivors' testimonies, it would have been an impossible task. Merchant mariners, unlike members of the US Navy, are not easily tracked. Following the sinking of the *Bacon*, many of the survivors looked to ship out on another merchant ship. They scattered to the four winds. Their home addresses changed as they moved from place to place. More than half a century later it is virtually impossible to point a finger and say what—or who—was to blame. In August 2000, when records were declassified, no evidence of the inquiry surfaced, even though several depositions by crew members...copies the authors already had in their possession...appeared in the mass of papers. One interesting note found was a bill for $570.99, covering supplies to the *Bacon*, dated June and July 1945—months after the ship had sunk. The War Shipping Administration believed it must have been another ship. In fact, an Army transport. Perhaps that friend of the junior Bacon's wife was correct. Perhaps another *Henry Bacon*, one the history books don't list, was at the Normandy invasion after all.

On April 10, 1945, the War Shipping Administration recommended "that an expenditure of $116,669.02 be authorized to cover the work...on the SS *Henry Bacon* with the understanding that all work was performed under the provisions of the Warshiprep contracts, and that the Maintenance and Repair Organization will make the necessary apportionment of the cost involved." The recommendation was approved April 21, 1945.

In interviews and correspondence with almost all the survivors, one element remains constant. The *Bacon* encountered major problems, problems outside the expertise and training of its crew, but still its skipper coped. Captain Carini was the biggest little man who ever walked a ship's deck, and his crew was one of the most valiant in the history of the US Merchant Marine service.

Selected Bibliography

American Merchant Marine Veterans, *Juan de Fuca* Chapter, Carlsboro, Washington; www.tenforward.com/bud

"Base Grad and New Clarinet to Ship Again." *Heaving Line*, Vol. 10, No. 7 [June 2, 1945].

Before We Go Back, A Pictorial Record of Norway's Fight Against Nazism. London: Published by His Majesty's Stationery Office on behalf of the Royal Norwegian Government Information Office, 1944.

britannica.com. Electronic version of the *Encyclopedia Britannica*.

Browning, Robert M. Jr. *U.S. Merchant Vessel War Casualties of World War II.* Annapolis, Maryland: Naval Institute Press, 1996.

Buchheim, Lothar-Gunther. *U-Boat War.* Translated from the German by Gudie Lawaetz. New York: Bantam Books, 1979.

Bunker, John. *Heroes in Dungarees: The Story of the U.S. Merchant Marine in World War II.* Annapolis, Maryland, 1995.

_____. *Liberty Ships: The Ugly Ducklings of World War II.* Annapolis, Maryland: Naval Institute Press, 1972.

Conversations/Correspondence/Interviews with:

[Norwegian survivors and relatives] Richard Severin Pedersen, Henrik Pedersen, Ellen Pedersen, Ane Jakobsen, Inger Pedersen, Sophie Pedersen; Mrs. Rovor Floer; Sverdrup Dagavold, Henry Johnsen.

[*Bacon* survivors] Warren M. Bacheldor, George Bartin, Dick Burbine, Spud Campbell, Lawrence E. Champlin, Normand Croteau, Eugene Daniels, Clayton Ingram, Donald H. Garatz, Jerome F. Gerold, John E. Fallon, David Goodrich, William M. Gray, William H. Herrmann, the Rev. Clyde Loar, Joseph Marbach, Herbert McIsaac, Michael Norris, Woodrow Pozen, Joseph S. Pszybysz, Raymond Frank Reid, Ernest C. Russell, Joseph L. Scott, Chuck Reed, William Wildridge.

[Family/Friends of *Bacon* Casualties] Flora Haviland McGrath, Marie Provencal, Olga Seppola, classmate of John Sippola's sister; Alice M. S. Lammon; Major Harry S. Burr; Mr. & Mrs. Frank Schiesher; Helen [Sippola] Balbovsky, Lt. Edward Yerow, USNR.

[Foreign sources] H. F. Langley, Historical Section, Admiralty; Lieutenant Commander R. C. Whiting, Joint Warfare Staff; Commander Gavin Hamilton; Captain A. O. Solomon, Naval Secretary, Royal Canadian Navy; Lieutenant Commander Eric E. G. Boak, Commanding Officer, HMCS *Sioux*; Dr. Tessin, counsel in the archives, Bundesarchiv, Militararchiv; Yuri I.

Bobrakov, Press Department, Embassy of the Union of Soviet Socialist Republics; Dr. Stahl, Militargeschichtliches Forschungsamt; Mr. Frieseke, Junkers Flugzeug-und Motorenwerke; Anders Buraes, European Free Trade Association; Rolf Jerving, Norwegian Embassy, Information Division; Carl Semb, professor, Uileval Hospital, Dept. III; Alexander Draper, the Secretary of the Admiralty; Thor Heyerdahl; Captain R. B. N. Hicks, D.S.C., R.N. [Ret.], commander of the *Zest*; Commander R. F. Jessel, D.S.O., D.S.C., R.N., commander of the *Zealous*.

[American sources] Commander Hugh Howell Jr., Naval Reserve Association; Senator Richard B. Russell, U.S. Senate, chair, Committee on Armed Services; Local 88, Masters, Mates and Pilots; James H. McKoy; Dr. Maurer, U.S. Air Force Historical Division; Hugh H. Howell Jr., Judge Advocate, Old Guard of the Gate, City Guard of Atlanta.

[American shipbuilders] E. H. Wilson, Strachan Shipping Company; J. B. Abbott, Maritime North Carolina Shipyard; Bart G. McGarry, Maritime Administration, Atlantic Coast District; K. F. Sutherland, Marine Superintendent, United States Lines.

"Convoy to Russia Beats Gale, Planes, U-boats." *Sunday* [British] *Empire News*, April 1, 1945.

Cook, Alistair. *Alistair Cook's America*. New York: Alfred A. Knopf, 1973.

Cooper, Sherod. *Liberty Ship: The Voyages of the* John W. Brown, 1942–1946. Annapolis, Maryland: Naval Institute Press, 1997.

Correspondence/Memoranda/Files from the US War Shipping Administration, supplied by the US Maritime Administration, Department of Transportation.

Gleichauf, Justin. *Unsung Sailors: The Naval Armed Guard in World War II*. Annapolis, Maryland, 1990.

Gorlaski, Robert. *World War II Almanac, 1941–1945*. New York: Perigree Books/ G. P. Putnam's Sons, 1981.

govspot.com

Hart, B. H. Liddell. *History of the Second World War*. New York: G. P. Putnam's Sons, 1970.

"Heroism on the High Seas." *International Musician*, XLIV, no. 3 [September 1945]

Hoehling, Adolph A. *The Fighting Liberty Ships*. Kent, Ohio: Kent State University Press, 1990.

Hughes, Terry, and John Costello. *The Battle of the Atlantic*. New York: Dial Press/James Wade, 1977.

Johnson, Amanda. *Norway: Her Invasion and Occupation*. Decatur, Georgia: Bowen Press, 1948.

Larsen, Karen. *A History of Norway*. Princeton: Princeton University Press for the American Scandinavian Foundation, 1948.

Love, Robert W. Jr. *History of the US Navy*. Volume 2: 1942-1991. Harrisburg, Pennsylvania, 1992.

Lund, Robert. "The Bloody Road to Murmansk." *Saga: True Adventures of Men*, July 1956.

Mason, David. *Who's Who in World War II*. Boston/Toronto: Little, Brown and Company, 1978.

Moore, Captain Arthur R. *A Careless Word—A Needless Sinking: A History of the Staggering Losses Suffered by the U.S. Merchant Marine, both in Ships and Personnel, during World War II*. Kings Point, New York: American Merchant Marine Museum, U.S. Merchant Marine Academy, Kings Point, New York, 1990.

Morison, Samuel Eliot. *The Atlantic Battle Won, May 1943–May 1945*. In *History of the U.S. Naval Operations in World War II*. vol. X: "The Atlantic Battle Won—May 1943–May 1945." Boston: Little, Brown & Co., 1956.

Oxford Companion to World War II. J. C. B. Dear, general editor; M. R. D. Foot, consultant editor. Oxford/New York: Oxford University Press, 1995.

"Preliminary Report on Germany's Crimes Against Norway." Oslo, 1945, for use of Allied International Military Tribunal.

Riesenberg, Felix. *Sea War: The Story of the US Merchant Marine in World War II*. New York: Rinehart, 1956.

Roskill, S. W. *The War at Sea*. Vols. 4 and 5. London: Her Majesty's Stationery Office, 1960.

Ruegg, Bob, and Arnold Hague. *Convoys to Russia, 1941–1945*. Kendal, England: World Ship Society, 1992.

Sawyer, L. A., and W. H. Mitchell. *Liberty Ships*. London: David & Charles, 1970.

————. *Victory Ships and Tankers*. Cambridge, Maryland: Cornell Maritime Press, 1974.

Schofield, B. B., and L. F. Martyn. *The Russian Convoys*. London: Blackwood, 1964.

Stokesbury, James L. *A Short History of World War II*. New York: Quill/William Morrow and Company, 1980.

"Summary of Merchant Marine Casualties of World War II." Washington, DC: US Treasury Department, US Coast Guard, 1950.

"Tatotsky remembers the Murmansk Run." by Rich DeMarco, *Chelsea Record*, November 29, 1991.

The Seafarers Log, vol. VII, no. 13. New York: Seafarers' International Union, March 30, 1945, May 6, 1945, May 14, 1945.

The Second Great War. Sir John Hammerton, ed. London: Amalgamated Press, 1939.

The SIU at War: True Experiences in the War at Sea of Members of the Seafarers International Union. Booklet published by the union, August 1944.

The US Merchant Marine at War, 1775–1945. Felkner, B. L., ed. Annapolis, Maryland: Naval Institute Press, 1999.

US Maritime Commission. "US Merchant Marine at War, Report to the President." Typescript: Washington, DC, 1946.

US Merchant Marine in World War II, including "Men and Ships in World War II, including Armed Guard," "Merchant Marine Organizations," "US Maritime Service Veterans," "Chronology of US Merchant Marine in Peace and War Since 1775." www.usmm.org

"The U. S. Merchant Marine Struggle for Justice and Recognition: A Chronology," American Merchant Marine Veterans [AMMV]; www.ifu.net/ ~halladay/mmv1.htm

USN Armed Guard. www.armed-guard.com

The United States Navy in World War II. S. E. Smith, ed. New York: Quill/ William Morrow, 1966.

Valentine, Paul W. "From Russia With Thanks; Liberty Ship Mates Honored for Action in North Atlantic." *Washington Post*, October 8, 1992.

Young, Brigadier Peter. *The World Almanac Book of World War II*. New York: World Almanac Publications, 1981.

Photo Gallery

1. Henry Bacon Sr., noted maritime engineer and donor of the name of the SS Henry Bacon. [family photograph]

2. Katherine Bacon McKoy, daughter of Henry Bacon, in a formal pose. Photo was taken in the library of her home in Wilmington, North Carolina, on Easter Sunday, 1941, by her brother Carl. [family photograph]

3. Members of Henry Bacon's family at the launching of his namesake ship. Jimmy McKoy is second from the left in the front row, still wearing his brand-new suit. Katherine Bacon McKoy is in the center rear. [family photograph]

4. The Henry Bacon *sets sail. [US Maritime Administration]*

5. Henry J. Kaiser shaking hands with workers from his Liberty ship yard. [US Department of Labor]

6. Captain Alfred Carini. [sketched by Lawrence C. Champlin]

7. *The last party. Members of the Navy Armed Guard, their wives, and dates enjoy themselves at the Broadway Brewery, New York, before shipping out. [left to right: Lucille and Normand Croteau, unknown, Alice and Bill Brown; Howard "Porky" McQuistion; Bill Moore and his wife; and Rosabel (Roby) and Warren Bacheldor.]*

8. *Gunnery Mate Third Class Raymond Frank Reid, standing at attention. This particular photo was made into a postcard, which the sailors could send out without an envelope.*

9. Hiding in Sørøya. [Norwegian publication, undated]

10. Sørøya children and adults, awaiting rescue. [Norwegian publication, undated]

11. Sørøya. [Norwegian publication, undated]

12. English transport Norwegian refugees from Sørøya. [Norwegian publication]

13. Dr. Henrik Pedersen. [identification photo]

14. Navy Guard about to board the Bacon. Mason Burr is at far left. [Burr family collection]

15. Chuck Reed, aboard the Henry Bacon, New York, December 1944. [Chuck Reed]

16. Dick Burbine in 1945.
[Dick Burbine]

17. Robert Tatotsky, in his
uniform as a member of the First
Marine Division. [Dick Burbine]

18. Chief Radio Officer Earnal S. "Spud"
Campbell in 1945. [Spud Campbell]

19. Members of the Bacon's crew; Frank Reid and Bill Moore are first row center and
right.

20. *Members of the crew in Italy; front row, Clyde W. Loar, Charles Haviland; back row, Normand Crouteau, Bill Moore.* [Normand Croteau]

21. *The Navy Armed Guard enjoying some vino in Bari, Italy. Lieutenant Sippola is wearing his service cap, and seated in the right foreground.* [Normand Croteau]

22. *Members of the Navy Armed Guard taking in the sights at Bari, Italy. [Normand Croteau]*

24. *The crew enjoys some fishing. Cyril Patrick La Fountain, lost on the Bacon, is seen standing in white T-shirt. Eugene Daniels is in the lower right.*

23. *Eugene Daniels [left] and Elias Banian holding the results of a day's fishing.*

25. Jerry Gerold pigging out on watermelon. [Jerry Gerold]

26. Herbert McQuistion doing what many mariners do in their spare time: enjoy the local attractions. [Jerry Gerold]

27. Normand Croteau. [vending machine photo]

28. Shipmates, Eugene Daniels, Ernest Russell. [Eugene Daniels]

29. *Herbert McIsaac. [Herbert McIsaac]*

30. *Normand Croteau at his antiaircraft gun on the SS* Henry Bacon. *[Normand Croteau]*

31. *Navy Armed Guard, manning the 5-inch gun on the* Henry Bacon. *[Jerome Gerold]*

33. HMS Zambesi. *[Official Admiralty photo]*

32. *The* SS Henry Bacon *awash in high seas. [Normand Croteau]*

34. HMS Zephyr *sailing into convoy. [Allison collection]*

35. HMS Zest. *[Official Admiralty photo]*

36. HMS Opportune. *[Allison collection]*

37. HMS Onslaught. *[Official Admiralty photo]*

38. HMCS Sioux. [Official Admiralty photo]

39. Commanding officers of the Second Destroyer Flotilla, 1946; front row, Jessel, Allison, Jenke; back row, Pearce, Beattie, Palmer, Laron. In typical British fashion, Allison wore a beard during Pacific operations, but shaved it off while in the Arctic zones. [Allison collection]

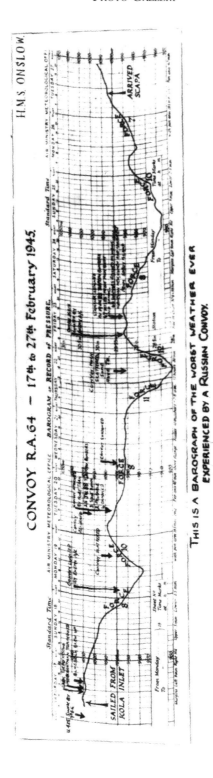

40. Barograph chart of RA64, 17th–27th February 1945, taken from the HMS Onslow. [Allison collection]

41. *Junker Ju-88 in flight.* [US Air Force]

42. *Junker Ju-88 after being hit by gunfire from a Navy ship–not the* Henry Bacon. [US Air Force]

43. A Norwegian girl from Sørøya, with both arms broken, is carried to a waiting ambulance by a British sailor. [Official Admiralty photo]

REP/GEC

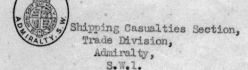

Shipping Casualties Section,
Trade Division,
Admiralty,
S.W.1.

11th June, 1945

Harry S. Burr, Esq.,
  812, Rader Avenue,
   Yeadon, Pa.

Dear Sir,

     In answer to your letter of the 23rd May, I regret to
inform you that the vessel on which your son was serving was
sunk as a result of aircraft attack on 23rd February 1945,
whilst homeward bound from Russia.

     At the time of the attack the vessel was a straggler
from the convoy, owing to a bad storm. The survivors from the
vessel were picked up from lifeboats and rafts several hours
after the casualty occurred by escort vessels, and were later
brought into the United Kingdom. It is with extreme regret I
have to inform you that your son's name does not appear on the
list of known survivors, and that in the circumstances I am
afraid there is very little hope of his survival.

     I would take this opportunity of offering you my
deepest sympathy in your anxiety.

     Yours faithfully,

      E.A. Burrows.
   Commander (S) R.N.R.

44. *Letter from the British Admiralty, informing Mason Burr's father of his son's death.*

45. *Rear Admiral Edwin P. Foster, USN, presents Norway's War Medal posthumously to Seaman Burr's sister.*

46. *Two young women from Sørøya, their lives were saved by the sacrifice of the men of the* SS Henry Bacon.

47. Three survivors of ship sinkings, included [center] Robert "Chuck" Reed. Others were [left] George B. Ziegman, and [right] William H. Dyer. Neither Ziegman nor Dyer served on the Bacon. [Public Relations Division, US Coast Guard]

48. Five survivors of torpedo attack and sinking pose aboard a Coast Guard-manned troop transport. Bill Herrmann, second radio officer of the Bacon, and Wilmo Testerman are second and first on the right. Others did not serve on the Bacon. Pictured [from left to right] are Michael Do Valan, Charles W. Spapak, Marion F. Clay, Herrmann and Testerman. [Public Relations Division, US Coast Guard]

49. *Warren Bacheldor and his wife, Robie, getting some much needed rest in May 1945. [Jerry Gerold]*

50. *Getting some sun! [from left:] Herbert, nicknamed "Porky" McIsaac, Warren Bacheldor, Clyde Loar, and Jerry Gerold. The photo was taken at Silver Springs, Florida, May 1945.*

51. *Survivors of the* Henry Bacon, *Deland, Florida, May 1945.*

52. *Spud Campbell with Lebaron Russell Briggs, born in 1945 on the ship that bore his name. [Spud Campbell]*

53. *Spud Campbell [right] with Norwegian naval officer Per Danielsen, as they were interviewed for a Norwegian Broadcasting Corp. documentary in 1999 at the point of rescue from Søyøra in 1945. [Spud Campbell]*

Members of the Crew of the SS *Henry Bacon*

Name	Age*	Rank	Job	Fate	
Allard, Steve		Seaman 3rd Class	signalman	lost	
Armstrong, Warren		Seaman 1st Class	navy gunner	survivor	
Bacheldor, Warren		Seaman 2nd Class		survivor	
Banian, Elias		Seaman 1st Class	navy gunner	survivor	
Bartin, George	25		night cook and baker	survivor	b: 8/4/19; d: 12/75 Oreg.
Brown, Bill		Seaman 1st Class	navy gunner	survivor	
Burbine, Dick	18		wiper	survivor	
Burr, Mason Kirby		Seaman 1st Class	navy gunner	lost	
Campbell, Earnal "Spud"	22		first radio officer	survivor	
Carini, Alfred	62	Captain	commanding officer	lost	
Champlin, Lawrence E.	40		3rd assistant engineer	survivor	
Clay, Marion Franklin	17		mess-/utility man	survivor	
Colchester, Cecil Percy	62		2nd mate	survivor	
Cramer, Robert Lorenzo	18	Able-bodied Seaman		lost	
Croteau, Normand			coxswain	survivor	b: 2/1/25 d: 1/83 R. I.
Daniels, Eugene		Seaman 1st Class		survivor	
Doe, Silas	19	Seaman 1st Class		survivor	b: 1/1/25; d: 3/1/85
Doe, John	39			survivor	b: 4/6/06; d: 12/55 Mass.
Dysinger, Carl	30	Seaman 1st Class	navy gunner	survivor	b: 3/25l5; d: 12/83
Fallon, John		Seaman 3rd Class		survivor	
Fubel, Carl Daniel Henry	22	3rd, then 2nd Mate		lost	

Name	Age*	Rank	Job	Fate	
Funken, Frederick Charles	24	Able-bodied Seaman		lost	
Garatz, Donald Hilary	21	Able-bodied Seaman		survivor	
Gerold, Jerome "Jerry"		Gunnery Mate 3rd Class		survivor	
Goodrich, David S.	17		utility man	survivor	d: 7/24/00
Gorman, William "Bill" Peter	30		oiler	survivor	
Gray, William Moffett	17		wiper	survivor	
Greenwell, Raymond "Ray" Ernest	37	Able-bodied Seaman		survivor	
Harlacher, Charles		Seaman 1st Class	navy gunner	lost	
Haviland, Donald Francis	49	Chief Engineer		lost	
Herrmann, William "Bill" Adolf	32	2nd Radio operator		survivor	
Hunt, Robert "Bob" Judson Jr.	20		asst. purser	lost	
Ingram, Clayton	29		steward	survivor	
Kearns, Cornelius Aloysius	39		2nd cook	lost	
La Fountain, Cyril Patrick		Seaman 1st Class		lost	
Lammon, Allan McKee	19		deck man	survivor	
Lammon, Holcomb Jr.	23	Bosun		lost	
Loar, Clyde		Seaman 1st Class	navy gunner	survivor	
Lomelino, George Arrel		Seaman 1st Class	navy gunner	survivor	
Marbach, Joseph "Big Joe"	32	Able-bodied Seaman		survivor	
Martin, James Dick Jr.		Able-bodied Seaman		lost	
Mastracci, John W.	40		chief cook	lost	
Mayden, Donald		Seaman 1st class	navy gunner	lost	
McClelland, Harold		Seaman 1st Class	navy gunner	survivor	
McIsaac, Herbert	42		fire and water tender	survivor	b: 9/2/02; d: 2/76 Mass.
McQuistion, Howard		Seaman 1st Class	navy gunner	survivor	
Moore, William M. "Bill"		Gunnery Mate 3rd Class		lost	

Name	Age*	Rank	Job	Fate
Norris, Michael Frank	22	Utility		survivor
Palmer, Lynn Ranson	37	2nd mate, later 1st mate		lost
Potvin, Elmer		Seaman 1st Class	navy gunner	lost
Pozen, Woodrow "Woodie" Wilson	29		oiler	survivor
Price, Kermit		Seaman 1st Class	navy gunner	lost
Provencal, Joseph Ephram	41	3rd, then 2nd assistant	engineer	lost
Pszybysz, Joseph Stanislav	32		mess-/utility man	survivor
Ramsey, John Charles	34		oiler	survivor
Reed, Robert "Chuck" Collins	18		mess-/utility man	survivor
Reid, Raymond Frank		Gunnery Mate 3rd Class		lost
Rogers, John Francis	16	Ordinary seaman		lost
Rubley, Earl		Seaman 1st Class	navy gunner	lost
Russell, Ernest		Seaman 1st Class	navy gunner	survivor
Schiesher, Donald Peter	23	Ordinary seaman		lost
Scott, Joseph Lories	43	Able-bodied Seaman	acting 3rd mate	survivor
Shipka, George William	20		messman	lost
Sippola, John		Lieutenant (JG)	navy gunner	lost
Snyder, Edgar Burton	37	2nd, then 1st assistant		lost
Tatotsky, Robert	17		engineer	survivor b: 2/16/27; d: 6/93
Testerman, Wilmo M.	24		messman	survivor
Walker, Louis	30		deck engineer	navy gunner lost
White, Fergus Edward	57		Seaman 1st Class	survivor
Willdridge, William	29		fire and water tender	survivor b: 1/15/15; d: 10/67 Mass.
Williams, Marion Montague	25	Ordinary seaman	fire and water tender	survivor

*Crewman's age in 1945

Officers of the British Recovery Vessels

Admiral Roderick R. McGrigor
Commander of the convoy

Commander R. E. D. Ryder

Lieutenant Commander R. B. N. Hicks
commanding HMS *Zest*

Captain J. H. Allison
commanding HMS *Zambesi*

Commander R. F. Jessel
commanding HMS *Zealous*

Lieutenant Commander E. E. G. Boak
commanding HMCS *Sioux*

Commander Gavin Hamilton

North Russian Convoy RA 64

Left Kola Inlet, February 17, 1945; arrived Loch Ewe, February 28, 1945

Escorts on Duty

Cruiser   HMS *Belona*

Escort Carriers
HMS *Nairana*
HMS *Campania*

Destroyers HMS *Onslow*; transferred to Pakistan
HMS *Onslaught*; transferred to Pakistan
HMS *Offa*; transferred to Pakistan
HMS *Orwell*
HMS *Opportune*
HMS *Zambesi*
HMS *Zealous*; transferred to Israel
HMS *Zest*
HMCS *Sioux*
HMS *Whitehall*

Sloops   HMS *Lark*; torpedoed by U-boat February 17, 1945,
salvaged by Russia and renamed *Neptun*
HMS *Bluebell*; torpedoed and sunk by U-711 in
the Barents Sea, February 17, 1945
HMS *Lapwing*; sunk by U-boat March 20, 1945
HMS *Alnwick Castle*
HMS *Bamborough Castle*
HMS *Rhododendron*

Destroyers (Escort reinforced February 20, 1945) by:
HMS *Savage*
HMS *Scourge*
HMS *Zebra*

Destroyers (Fresh destroyers arrive from Scapa Flow, February 23, 1945)
HMS *Minge*; transferred to Egypt, 1955; sunk by Israeli
aircraft at Berencia, May 16, 1970
HMS *Scorpion*; transferred to Netherlands Navy
HMS *Cavalier*; preserved as a museum ship, 1974

American Cargo Ships
>   SS *Allenson B. Houghton*
>   SS *George H. Pendleton*
>   SS *Joshua W. Alexandra*
>   SS *John Le Farge*
>   SS *Silas Weir Mitchell*
>   SS *J. D. Yeager*
>   SS *Bernard N. Baker*
>   SS *Thomas Scott*; torpedoed February 17, 1945
>   SS *R. Ney McNeely*
>   SS *James Kerney*
>   SS *Benjamin H. Hill*
>   SS *Charles M. Schwab*
>   SS *Francis C. Harrington*
>   SS *Charles Scribner*
>   SS *John Ireland*
>   SS *Caesar Rodney*
>   SS *Warren Delano*; straggler at Faeroes, arrived United Kingdom,
>   March 4, 1945
>   SS *Philip F. Thomas*
>   SS *Jose Marti*
>   SS *Henry Bacon*; torpedoed and sunk by German aircraft,
>   February 23, 1945
>   SS *John A. Quitman*
>   SS *Crosby S. Noyes*
>   SS *Henry Villard*
>   SS *Edmund Fanning*
>   SS *Lebaron Russell Briggs*; baby born on board
>   SS *Henry Winkoop*; Norwegian civilian died aboard, and buried
>   at sea

United States Tanker
>   *Paul H. Harwood*

British Cargo Ships
>   *Samaritan*
>   *Empire Celia*; straggler at Faeroes, arrived March 4, 1945
>   *Empire Archer*

British Tankers
>   *Nacelia*
>   *British Promise*
>   *Black Ranger*

Norwegian Cargo Ship
>   *Idefjord*

Norwegian Survivors

Henrik Pedersen and
Ellen Pedersen, parents of
Sophie, 2
Inger, 4
Johan Pedersen and
Emilie Pedersen (with child), parents of
Elbjorg, 6
Modrat, 7
Ragna Pedersen, 40
Aasel Pedersen
Karen Pedersen
Ane Jakobsen, 67, Henrik's aunt
August Larsen, 16
Simon Mortensen and
Berit Mortensen, parents of
Bjarne, 4
Eldor, 6
Sigvart, 7
Nils, 8

Index

Y

Yalta Conference, 2-3
Yeltsin, Boris, 209

Z

Zambesi, 1, 71, 73, 75, 76, 77, 79-85,
    87, 109, 112, 113, 117, 121, 124,
    132, 179, 181, 187, 188-191, 192,
    196, 200, 201, 202, 203, 213, 236,
    250, 251
Zealous, 75, 77, 79, 82, 123, 124, 128,
    182, 200, 201, 250, 251
Zebra, 251
Zephyr, 73, 236
Zest, xvii, 75, 76, 77, 81, 82, 113, 124,
    179, 181, 190, 202, 214, 236, 250,
    251
Ziegman, George B., 244
Zito, Frank J., 33